APR 2 8 1994	NOV 2 5 1995
MAY 2 4 1994	FEB 1 0 1996
JUN 1 7 1994	MAR 1 3 1996
JUL 2 1 1994	MAY 2 4 1996
AUG 2 0 1994	FEB 1 1 1997
JAN 2 0 1995	
MAR 1 8 1995	MAY 5 1997
AUG 2 1 1995	MAR 6 1999

POISONED DREAMS

Also by A. W. Gray

Bino
Size
In Defense of Judges
The Man Offside
Prime Suspect
Killings

A. W. GRAY

POISONED DREAMS

A TRUE STORY OF MURDER, MONEY, AND FAMILY SECRETS

A DUTTON BOOK

DUTTON
Published by the Penguin Group
Penguin Books USA Inc., 375 Hudson Street,
New York, New York 10014, U.S.A.
Penguin Books Ltd, 27 Wrights Lane,
London W8 5TZ, England
Penguin Books Australia Ltd, Ringwood,
Victoria, Australia
Penguin Books Canada Ltd, 10 Alcorn Avenue,
Toronto, Ontario, Canada M4V 3B2
Penguin Books (N.Z.) Ltd, 182–190 Wairau Road,
Auckland 10, New Zealand

Penguin Books Ltd, Registered Offices:
Harmondsworth, Middlesex, England

First published by Dutton, an imprint of Dutton Signet, a division of Penguin Books USA
Inc.
Distributed in Canada by McClelland & Stewart Inc.

First Printing, November, 1993
10 9 8 7 6 5 4 3 2 1

 REGISTERED TRADEMARK—MARCA REGISTRADA

LIBRARY OF CONGRESS CATALOGING-IN-PUBLICATION DATA:
Gray, A. W. (Albert William)
  Poisoned dreams : a true story of murder, money, and family secrets / A.W. Gray.
    p. cm.
  ISBN 0-525-93710-2
  1. Trials (Murder)—Texas—Fort Worth.—2. Poisoners—Texas—Fort Worth. 3.
Marriage—Texas—Fort Worth. 4. Fort Worth (Tex.). I. Title.
PS3557.R2914P6 1993
813′.54—dc20   93-30617
                                                                            CIP

Printed in the United States of America
Set in Plantin
Designed by Leonard Telesca

For Terry and Nancy Murphy,
Their daughters, Colleen and Alison,
Major sleuth lover Dr. Joseph Link, Jr.,
and the children at Notre Dame Special School of Dallas.

She cried with thirst at midnight,
And (Oh mercy on my soul!)
I drew clear water from the nearby brook
and added Nightshade to the bowl.

—from "The Poisoning of
Alicia" by William Trent
Holmes (1783–1854)

What man did poison the fruit? 'Tis verily
a question.

—Widmark, the Court Jester,
from "Autumn Midnight," a
play by Robert Wilkes

When someone gunned down J.R., and viewers endured a summer of rabid debate before finding out that the shooter was the unassuming little Crosby girl, America had a long and scenic look at the grounds surrounding Dallas' Presbyterian Hospital. With J.R. in intensive care and Sue Ellen charged (wrongfully, just as your mother knew all along) and in the sheriff's custody, Bobby and Pam and Cliff and the gang strolled, frowned, and exchanged suspicion-casting glances on Presbyterian's sunlit lawns. Always in the background, visible between the trunks of stately elms and sycamores, the tall sandy brick building and its white-pillared porch were burned indelibly into the nation's consciousness. Come September, J.R. recovered from his coma to (rather grudgingly) clear Sue Ellen, and to emerge, evil leer intact, through Presbyterian's portals, ready to gyp and plunder for yet another season.

The TV show's producers had done their homework. Presbyterian in fact lies a stone's throw east of Central Expressway on Walnut Hill Lane, a lovely tree-lined boulevard, and is the most picturesquely accessible medical facility to the Ewing offices, the site of J.R.'s attempted assassination. The hospital's manicured lawns, sculpted shrubs, and electronically monitored parking areas cover a full half mile of frontage along Walnut Hill, and the curving drive that leads from the street and separates into forks—in one direction the main entrance and in the other the emergency room—winds among the same lawns and beneath the same trees where Pam and Bobby plotted and strolled.

Just a few miles south of Presbyterian is wealthy Park Cities, and the hospital by right of location is the receiving and recuperation point for the gallbladder surgeries, ulcer treatments, and sedately proper heart attacks had by Dallas' super-rich. A full third of Presbyterian's rooms are private; by contrast, Parkland, the county facility on Harry Hines Boulevard, has practically no private rooms at all. If one can afford to be sick in Big D, then Presbyterian is the place to go.

On January 8, 1991, a decade after the furor over who shot J.R., Dallas as a whole still reeled from the economic disaster of the late eighties. The city had yet to evolve from the heady concept of being rich into the stark reality of being poor, but it was well on its way. Park Cities housewives, many of them in their forties and for years accustomed to nothing more thought-provoking than ringing for the butler, were for the first time in their lives learning to job-hunt, cook, and run the washing machine. The war drums that rolled through the Persian Gulf stirred faint hope in the breasts of devastated oil men; that very morning crude rose a whopping two bucks a barrel. The excitement was to be short-lived, the fluttery recovery in oil prices as brief as Desert Storm itself. By midyear, many of the oil guys would be relearning the business from the ground up, pouring the black stuff into the crankcases of paying customers and standing in line for a meager check at the end of the week.

The eighth of January was a Tuesday. The Giants, Bears, Redskins, and 49ers received modest local coverage as they prepared to square off on opposite coasts in the second round of the NFL playoffs; since the Cowboys had seemed a certain playoff team with two games left in the season and then had blown the opportunity, most of Dallas couldn't have cared less what ball club made it to the Super Bowl. An event of greater local interest than professional football occurred around one in the afternoon on that fateful Tuesday, in the far North Dallas suburb of Richardson, when a troubled teenager placed the barrel of a .357 Magnum against his forehead and pulled the trigger before thirty stunned classmates. The year 1991 was to bring, by a whopping number of inches, the greatest annual rainfall in the history of the area, but as of January 8 the first drop of the infant year had yet to fall. The forecast called for cool to cold and partly cloudy with no chance of rain until Thursday, but experienced Dallas-ites had learned to rely, in predicting the weather, equally on meteorologists and on the state of the rheumatism in Grandma's ankle.

And, in fact, as darkness fell over the city, cloud banks gathered and faint thunder rolled. By eleven, as most of the residents packed off to bed, a cold mist drifted down to wet the rooftops and encircle the streetlights with damp and eerie halos. Dallas kept a watchful eye on the thermometer; a drop of a couple of degrees would coat the roads with ice. Luckily for nighttime travelers, the temperature sank to thirty-three and went no lower.

Around midnight, in the western half of a Park Cities duplex located a block from Southern Methodist University, a young man named Richard Lyon prepared to take his stricken wife, Nancy, to the hospital. She'd had cramps, diarrhea, and fits of violent nausea since early afternoon, and the prescriptions that her doctor had phoned in to the nearby Eckerd's Pharmacy weren't helping. Richard arose from the down mattress in the upstairs bedroom and dressed himself. He checked on his daughters, ages two and four, who slept across the hall in the nursery. He then carried his remote intercom receiver, which he used to monitor the sleep noises made by the little girls, downstairs and out onto the porch. There he stood in the icy drizzle and rang the bell to waken his next-door neighbor. After a few moments, Gayle Golden cracked open the door and peered outside. She was a petite and comely young free-lance writer who, along with her husband, Chris Worthington, a *Dallas Morning News* sports editor, were Richard's tenants in the duplex. While in many neighborhoods a midnight knock on the door is something to fear, this was Park Cities. Gayle smiled a greeting and said hello.

Richard explained his problem quickly—he didn't think that anything truly serious was wrong with his wife, but one couldn't be too careful these days with the flu going around—and asked if Gayle could keep the remote receiver by her bed in case the girls cried out while Richard and Nancy were gone. Nancy hadn't been really well of late, so her illness wasn't all that surprising. Gayle eagerly agreed to help and murmured sleepy concern over Nancy's well-being.

His daughters' safety assured, Richard returned to his bedroom and wrapped Nancy in a blanket. Though a short man, he was quite strong, and he carried his wife downstairs with little effort. On the way he passed framed photos that hung beside the landing: Richard and Nancy in wedding clothes beside a huge three-tiered cake; Richard in enraptured roughhouse with the little girls, Allison and Anna; Nancy in business dress with legendary developer Tramell Crow on her left, Barbara Bush, silver-haired and handsome, on the other side, and a personal inscription from the First Lady herself underneath. As Richard arrived at the bottom of the staircase and carried Nancy around the banister, polished hardwood creaked underfoot.

By the time Richard had borne her down the drive and deposited her in the front seat of his Alfa Romeo, Nancy was nearly unconscious and her breathing was ragged. Windshield wipers thunking monotonously, Richard drove cautiously down Dickens Street to Lovers Lane, and east on Lovers to the northbound entry ramp to Central Expressway. Southbound traffic paraded by in the opposite direction with headlights reflecting on rain-slickened pavement. The freeway going was a crawling forty miles an hour, partly due to the misting rain and partly due to the rows of construction barriers that blocked the outside lane; Central, an ancient and outmoded expressway, is, has been, and will be under repair or renovation to the ends of time.

When Richard finally exited on Walnut Hill Lane and made the winding climb toward Presbyterian Hospital, it was almost one in the morning. Nancy's classic head reclined against the back of the seat. She was deathly pale and gasping for breath. As the Alfa Romeo entered the hospital drive and moved through misty blackness toward the emergency room, the rain increased in volume and beat steadily on the auto's roof. Thunder rolled in the distance and lightning illuminated the edges of sooty cloud banks, the cold rain and faraway rumblings creating the perfect backdrop for a tale of infidelity, secret incest, and, ultimately, allegations of murder most foul.

The processions begin in mid-December, just after sunset, as the autos merge from all directions to create honking bottlenecks at North Central Expressway off-ramps on the southern fringe of Highland Park. A few drivers manage to duck the freeway snarls, sneaking through side streets near Oak Lawn Avenue, but once inside Park Cities it's impossible for anyone to avoid the traffic jam. The processioners are families mostly, riding in plain-Jane-and-Joe Fords, Chevys, and minivans. Mothers and dads sit in front while tykes gang up in back, the children jockeying against their brothers and sisters for nose-pressing room, pointing and giggling and *oh*-ing and *ah*-ing. Mom and Dad tour in silence for the most part. Occasionally Mother will gasp in appreciation or even envy. Dad wonders about the electric bill.

Many join the parade near the intersection of Hillcrest Avenue and Beverly Drive, proceeding west on Beverly at a snail's pace. The mansions are there on both sides as always, massive hulks against a blue-black sky, but on mid- and late-December nights they seem hidden in the background. It is the light show that the folks have come to see: dazzling in a word, blinding in another, fifty-foot trees wrapped from trunk to twig in shimmering points of fire, illuminating perfectly clipped lawns like noon daylight. In a few places Neiman-Marcus reindeer of burnished bronze soar among the treetops, forelegs bent, hooves sparkling and reflecting in the blaze. There are color schemes. Some of the trees have their trunks wrapped in sparkling white, their branches in dazzling green. There is an occasional Santa, to be sure, laden with gaily wrapped packages, standing on a majestic verandah with mechanical arms waving to and fro, but even Santa seems to mock rather than to beckon. Dad's thumb is sore, and throbs when pressed against the steering wheel; he suffered the injury while nailing his own meager string of Christmas lights above his doorway. Beverly Drive decorations are hung in minutes by casts of thousands.

In the final days of 1990, Park Cities Christmas cheer seems hollow, gaudy, and even a bit symbolic of the economy as processioners in the they-got-it-and-we-don't parade move in awe past the mansion home at 3517 Beverly Drive, the Robert B. Cullum estate. "You remember ol' Bob, doncha?" Dad says to Mother. "Tom Thumb Supermarkets, huh? Helped build this town from the ground up, ol' Bob Cullum did." As he cruises slowly past the lighted Christmas tree in front, he humbly bows his head.

Farther down Beverly Drive—right next door, in fact, to the hallowed fairways of Dallas Country Club—elms and sycamores wrapped in candy-cane patterns of red and white lights blast into view. It's Ed Cox's place, Dad thinks. First National Bank, that was the Coxes' baby, now that was a bank, I'm tellin' you. First National is now gone with the wind along with its big-buck competitor, Republic Bank. Once enduring symbols of Dallas Progressive, the two giants were late-eighties victims of soaring interest rates, vicious dips in real estate values, and, some say, bloodthirsty meddlers from FDIC. But the brief stretch of Ed Cox, Jr., in the federal pen after First National's closing hasn't dimmed the yuletide brightness in his father's yard one iota. Processioners gape, pause to gape again, and turn south on Lakeside Drive.

It's a short run in bumper-to-bumper traffic on Lakeside Drive to Armstrong Boulevard. The brief Lakeside jaunt carries ogling processioners past even grander homes with grander, neck-popping light displays, the wide, still waters of Turtle Creek to the west reflecting the brilliance like Disneyland Lake at fireworks time.

At Armstrong Boulevard, Dad steers to the west and crosses the bridge over Turtle Creek. The barest of trickles in late summer, the creek is swollen with heavy December rain and flows sluggishly downstream toward the Trinity River. By now the youngsters in back have tired of the game, their *oh*'s and *ah*'s turning to whines of let's-go-home. Mother threatens bottom-whippings. Dad moves grimly on, determined to see it all.

Armstrong Boulevard crosses Preston Road and widens into a parkway where two mammoth pecan trees sit majestically in the center island. The decorating of the Armstrong Parkway pecans has been for decades a Park Cities tradition, as city crews come out in early December to drape the trees in red and green lights, even to the topmost branches. When Dad was a boy, the sighting of the Christmas-y pecans was a major event, but Dad's own children barely notice the enormous trees. The light shows from neighboring yards have all but obliterated the Armstrong Parkway pecans, the steadily glowing red and green lights bobbing among the trees' branches pale by comparison to smaller trees wrapped in fiery white points. A life-size nativity scene is set near the curb; the Santa who kneels beside the baby Jesus seems somehow out of place. Close to the nativity scene is a huge doll house, draped in light and encased in glass. The glitz goes on and on. J. Fred Schoellkopf, the downtown real estate baron, lives on Armstrong Parkway, in the forty-two-hundred block. So, in 1990, does Dmitri Vail, the celebrity artist whose paintings of the famous once adorned museums from coast to coast. Now his mansion home sits dark as Dracula's castle. Within months Dmitri Vail will die in poverty, and his house will become the spoil in a tangled lawsuit between a lawyer who claims rights to the painter's work and the younger woman who comforts Dmitri in his declining years.

Rheims Place slants off Armstrong Parkway a couple of blocks east of Preston Road, and processioners pass the intersection with barely a glance. There are a few light shows on Rheims Place, but nothing to write home about. A mere block from the light shows, Rheims is ominously dark on either side. No blazing Christmas displays here, no waving mechanical Santas. The mood is dismal. The mammoth homes are silent in the blackness.

The Rheims Place neighborhood is a million miles removed from Our Town America. There's no friendly barber across the street, no Mr. Jones the butcher down the way. Beaver Cleaver never lived here, and the residents throw few block parties. John D. N-N-N-Neuhoff parks his Mercedes at 4300 Rheims, goes inside, and prays that bacon will rise again. One of the few employees in the neighborhood bunks at 4340 Rheims. He's Ward Huey, Chairman and CEO of the Belo Corporation. This Christmas, Belo's pup companies offer both good tidings and bad tidings: the *Dallas Morning News* can drive its competition, the *Times-Herald,* out of business before '91 draws to a close; on the downside, though, Channel 8 faces massive losses in a lawsuit brought by Vic Feazell, the former McClennan County D.A. who was smeared in a Channel 8 news campaign. Before Christmas next the *Times-Herald* will indeed give up the ghost, and Feazell will win the largest slander judgment in U.S. history—a whopping fifty-eight mil—and settle for half of it. Also on Rheims Place, Charles P. Storey, the resident at 4400, has a few streets named after him. In 4456 resides Ted Zale the jewelry man. In the decade past Zale's has closed hundreds of stores.

The modern two-story at 4465 Rheims Place is set back from the street and is practically hidden behind leafy evergreens. It's where the Dillards live. The real estate guy, not the department store guy; in Dallas, the names are often confused. Like his nearly hidden home, Bill Dillard keeps a low profile among the movers and shakers, and likes it that way. This Christmas there is some cheer at the Dillard place, emphasized by the sprinkle of lights above the doorway and the nativity scene adorning the window. Nothing gaudy, of course, a bit of yuletide glitter to greet visiting family, not enough brilliance to divert the processioners from Armstrong Parkway. The economy has hit Bill Dillard as hard as some and even harder than most, but there are a couple of things to celebrate. The lone surviving Dillard son has completed a year of sobriety, no mean trick based on past performance, and the youngest Dillard daughter's marriage, on the rocks for quite some time, seems about to come together again. So the Dillards' Christmas season of 1990 gives hope, a glimmer of anticipation that bad things will come to an end. It is a false hope, however. Though the season provides little warning, within a scant two weeks the entire Dillard clan will be immersed in tragedy and, eventually, awash in a spotlight cruel beyond reason.

Christmas comes and goes and Baby '91 toddles in, rosy cheeks puffed out in a smile and eyes glistening in naive excitement. The yuletide lights along the Highland Park Corridor go into mothballs until the next season. Eight days pass with much smoke but no fire as Bush and Hussein glare at each other from opposite corners of a troubled world. On the ninth morning of the year, Rheims Place residents wake up in a cold and lonely drizzle.

Things happen early in the Dillard home. Though past seventy, William Wooldridge Dillard, Sr., moves, acts, and thinks like a man many years younger. His prolonged youth is no accident. He keeps in shape with the same rigid discipline with which he conducts his business affairs, rising at the crack and going full steam while others have yet to open an eye. Jogging eventually destroys the joints, so running is out, and walking is a bore, so Bill Dillard gets his exercise in other ways.

The Masters Swim Club splashes into the Dallas Country Club pool bright and early so that its members will have the bulk of the day for business affairs. The members are professionals, doctors, lawyers, and corporate chiefs who congregate every weekday morning to loosen muscles, tread water, and labor through rigorous freestyle laps, finally emerging to face the day with blood coursing through unclogged veins. On January 9, Bill Dillard leaves the house before the eastern horizon grays with early, cloud-filtered light. He won't eat until after his swim.

He hustles out to his car with mist dampening his cheeks, and shivers a bit under his overcoat, an intense man with thin gray hair, a straight Roman nose, and a businesslike thrust to his lower jaw. Pale, intelligent eyes move in his head as his gaze darts from side to side, taking in all, missing nothing. His complexion is fair, his skin smooth and unwrinkled. His family calls him Big Daddy, but that is misleading; at just over five-foot-seven, Big Daddy isn't big at all. His shoulders are square, his bearing confident. If he promises, he delivers. If one crosses Big Daddy, one regrets.

He pauses for a moment to insert his key in the car door, and glances up and down the street. Though it is a damp and dreary morning, all seems well, fine homes stoic behind soggy well-kept lawns. As he climbs in to start his engine and back out into the street, Bill Dillard's thoughts are on business. The devastated economy shows no sign of turning for the better; unlike the oil operators, Big Daddy sees no relief in the brewing Middle Eastern crisis. His fortunes turn on real estate values and, in peace or war, land is still land. His posted properties aren't moving at any price, his stagnant joint ventures mired down and subject to vicious interest payments. As he cruises down Rheims Place and turns east on Armstrong Parkway, he thinks about advertising for rentals on some of his properties. It would be a desperate move. Good tenants are scarce.

Just a few miles away, Bill Dillard's youngest daughter fights for breath. Her blood pressure is dangerously low, and there is no letup in her violent nausea. The puzzled staff at Presbyterian has moved her into ICU, and now contemplates life support. As Big Daddy heads for his morning swim, his thoughts riveted on the economy, he is mercifully unaware of the unfolding tragedy.

While fathers' thoughts are filled with making a living, mothers think constantly about their children. So it has been and always will be, and Sue Stubbs Dillard is no different in this respect from other moms.

Though Bill Dillard, Sr., is Big Daddy to the family, none of the Dillard clan would dream of calling Sue by the obvious counterpart. Big Mama she isn't. Sue Dillard is a slender and gracious woman, like her husband appearing to be many years younger than she is, firm of chin and erect of bearing. She is a quiet but commanding presence, her voice soft, her manners perfect. She is without pretentious vanity; her wealth of rich brown mixed with dove gray hair is prettier in its natural state than it could be made by a herd of cosmetologists. In her own way, Sue is just as industrious as her husband, and the family's financial success is as much about Sue as it is about Big Daddy. In an era when changing partners has become as common as moving one's residence, Sue's marriage has endured for going on fifty years. She has borne four children. On January 9, once Big Daddy has gone for his morning swim, Sue has time to herself. She sits in her fine home, has her breakfast, and thinks of her offspring.

Susan, Sue's own namesake, is the oldest, and like many elder siblings seems the most stable. Susan lives a hundred and fifty miles to the northwest, in Wichita Falls, and has her own enduring marriage to an orthodontist named Billy Hendrickson. Susan has her own life, her own friends. She visits occasionally, mostly on holidays, and has brought a great deal more pride than grief to her parents. There is very little cause for Mom to fret over Susan, and, motherlike, Sue Dillard thinks only fleetingly of her stable eldest daughter. Sue's mind turns quickly to her other kids, because with them there is a great deal more cause for concern.

As always, when Sue Dillard remembers her youngest boy, Tom, there is a sharp pang of grief. In many ways Tom was the brightest of the Dillard children. Certainly he was the most outgoing and friendly, popular with his classmates, quick to laugh, eager to extend a helping hand. Tom's true potential was never known; brain cancer killed him when he was only thirty years old. Though it's been more than five years since Tom died, the death of a child is a tragedy from which no parent ever quite recovers. Sue sheds a tear for her baby boy, then goes on to thoughts of her other kids.

Big Daddy's moniker, of course, is straight from Tennessee Williams, and the similarities between the Dillards and the haunted clan of *Cat on a Hot Tin Roof* don't end with Bill Sr.'s nickname. The Dillard family also has its Brick and its Maggie the Cat. Fans of the play will recall that Brick is the prodigal son, the object of undying affection from Big Daddy even though Brick has gone out of his way to reject his father's love. William Wooldridge Dillard, Jr., could play Brick to a fare-thee-well.

On the cold, rainy morning of January 9, Bill Dillard, Jr., is forty years old. He is slim, straight, and handsome as a movie star, with close-cropped brown hair and a ruddy complexion. Like all of the surviving Dillard kids, he is married. His wife's name is Mary Helen, and she is a petite and pretty young woman with a wealth of staying power. Her marriage has required toughness; she and Bill Jr. have traveled rocky roads. Sue Dillard knows as well as anyone that without Mary Helen, Bill Jr. likely would not have survived until now. As she sits in her fine home and reflects on her children, Sue thanks her lucky stars for her daughter-in-law.

It would be easy to dismiss Bill Jr.'s earlier troubles as rich-kid syndrome: too much money, too little discipline. He is the only Dillard offspring not to graduate from Highland Park High School, the public-but-very-private institution for residents of Park Cities. When Bill Jr. was fourteen, Big Daddy and Sue packed him off to boarding school in faraway Dublin, New Hampshire. The reason given by the family for his transfer to private school was that Bill Jr.'s dyslexia required special class-room conditions; however, in the terrible year to come for the Dillard family, what prompted Bill Jr.'s long-ago relocation will become a point of ugly contention.

What cannot be argued is that the problems of Bill Dillard, Jr., began early on, at least as far back as his college years at the University of Mississippi. He was football student manager at Ole Miss, and during his junior year was charged with theft for selling Rebel jerseys to fans and students out the back door of the dressing room. This seems a semi-harmless college prank until considered in light of his drug possession bust the following year. Bill Jr. was a wealthy student and didn't want for spending money; the secret selling of the athletic wear seems totally out of character. Unless he needed the extra money to feed a habit, of course. Whatever the cause, the outcome of the brushes with the Mississippi authorities is a matter of record. Big Daddy provided a lawyer—Darrel Dickens in this instance; in future years the list of attorneys would grow—to reduce the punishment to a wrist slap, thereby establishing a pattern that would continue for the better part of two decades: if Bill Jr. faltered, Big Daddy was there to lend a helping hand.

After college, Bill Jr. took the standard wealthy-graduate European odyssey, dallying for short periods in London, Paris, and Rome, and finally returned to Dallas ready to make his place in the world. He worked for his father for a time; then, along with two partners—and aided by Big Daddy to help swing the deal—bought one of the Dillard real estate companies. The business didn't do well; even though it was the seventies, the big-boom time for the land business, the small company's fortunes took a nosedive. Though there could be any number of reasons for the failure, one problem stands out. For Bill Jr. and his partners, the company was more of a sideline than anything else. Bill Jr. and his friends liked to play. Did they ever. And play they did.

Like all major cities, Dallas has its trust-fund society. The group consists of heirs to vast estates (with a few pretenders thrown in, of course, though they normally can't keep up the pace for very long), kids born with silver spoons in their mouths—and more than a few of them sporting even smaller silver spoons, hung from chains around their necks as nose-candy paraphernalia—and Texas-society marquee surnames who jet-set, golf in the seventies, and burn the candle into the wee small hours. Some masquerade as writers, others as restaurant owners, and some make no pretense of doing anything at all in the way of earning a living. Some are straight, others gay, and some go in either direction depending on the heat of the moment. All play hard. Some go to prison for drugs, serve short sentences, and burst once again into the limelight as though nothing had happened. Some mature and settle down, others die in the fast lane before maturity ever comes to them. In the trust-fund crowd, Bill Dillard, Jr., fit right in.

He drank heavily and did drugs: cocaine, uppers, downers, the works. He flew an airplane and invested in nightclubs. One such venture, the Starck Club, was located in Dallas' trendy West End District, and in addition to Bill Jr. claimed Blake and Blair Woodall (for whose family an east-west downtown freeway is

named), among others in the trust-fund crowd, as active partners. The club was quite-quite private-private, members-only
with enforcers at the door, and in the mid-eighties became the
target of a drug investigation spearheaded by the Dallas Police,
Texas Department of Public Safety, and federal DEA. The investigation culminated in a 1:00 A.M. takeover of the premises during which the authorities gave the customers an opportunity to
rid themselves of any drugs in their possession before the law
conducted a systematic search of the tables and surrounding
areas. Pills, vials, and needles hit the floor in bundles; according
to witnesses there were so many drugs on the floor that it was
impossible for the cops to step around the containers in order to
conduct the intended search. Shortly thereafter, the Starck Club
closed its doors. Rumor has it that the closing was part of a deal;
for whatever reason, the drug investigation ended with the shutting down of the club. It was Bill Jr.'s last venture into the night-
club business as an entrepreneur. As a customer, though . . .
well, that's another story.

Once exiled to Dallas' sleazy ghetto and industrial areas, topless bars during the eighties took on a certain respectability. The
new image was in a large part due to a simple name change; instead of "titty joints," the topless establishments now referred to
themselves as "gentlemen's clubs," and relocated from the dusty
far reaches of Harry Hines Boulevard, or near downtown on the
shadier blocks of Industrial, to the more upscale neighborhoods
of North Dallas. The change in image began in 1983, when a
former barroom pool hustler named Donald Fuhr leased out his
entire string of sawdust-floored topless joints—there were several, including Dandy Don's and Gino's on Harry Hines, and a
spot located on a secluded stretch of Highway 157 known as
Baby Doll's—and sank his profits into a gentlemen's club called
the Million Dollar Saloon, smack in the middle of a row of upscale Greenville Avenue restaurants.
Instead of truckers who parked their rigs 'round back and
came in with fistfuls of greasy twenties, Fuhr's new customers
were men with razored hairstyles who wore five-hundred-dollar
suits and brandished American Express and Visa cards. The Mil-

lion Dollar Saloon's girls discarded chewing gum and garish makeup, had their hair done at Neiman's, and in between acts entertained in special rooms for special customers while wearing dresses with Saks and Lord & Taylor labels. By the mid-eighties, according to figures of the Texas Alcoholic Beverage Commission, the Million Dollar Saloon was the state's number one liquor merchant.

Bug-eyed over Fuhr's success, other topless bar owners followed suit and opened upscale gentlemen's clubs as well, and Fuhr's mysterious and unsolved 1988 murder (one homicide detective joked, two years after Fuhr's death, that the case had been narrowed down to "around 2,500 suspects or so") didn't slow the topless bars' upgrading movement one iota. As the decade of economic despair for most businesses neared its end, gentlemen's clubs complete with valet parking and image-building names such as Caligula XXI, Deja Vu, and the granddaddy of them all, Cabaret Royale, flourished up and down Northwest Highway, on Greenville Avenue, and in the restaurant area fronting Stemmons Freeway near the Walnut Hill Lane exit.

The Cabaret Royale is a spectacular assault on the sensibilities of even the most blasé of flesh fans. Six elevated stages, each complete with its own dazzling light display, encircle a room large enough to seat three hundred customers, and there is nonstop action on each platform. On every side of the showroom, superbly formed young women whirl, gyrate, and wiggle provocative fannies, displaying a mind-boggling array of silicone-hardened breasts, supple muscular thighs, saucy hips, and situp-tautened pelvic areas. Stage-side spectators may reach over the footlights and poke paper money between g-strings and hip or buttock. For an additional fee—ten bucks during the day, twenty after six o'clock—a girl will come to the customer's table and dance scant feet away. The law forbids touching; the girls are experts at wriggling and gyrating just out of reach of frenziedly extended fingertips. Special customers—with special quantities of money, of course—can join the dancers in secluded hot tubs.

With the new-wave movement in topless clubs came a new breed of exotic dancer. No longer do the Candy Barrs from a bygone segment of Texas lore consort with mobsters, swill whiskey straight from the bottle, shoot estranged husbands in the crotch, and perform their dances on worm-eaten stages with alcoholic comics as warm-up acts. New Age strippers have class. Not only are they beautiful and shapely, they have brains as well. Gone are the hootchy-koo bumps and grinds; these girls are magnificently trained athletes and marvelous dancers. Many are university students—the old "working her way through college" saw is no longer a joke—and more than a few are legal secretaries and housewives during the day. They read Michener and Saul Bellow and take calculus. Off-duty, they dine at Old Warsaw and Chateau, arriving in chauffeur-driven limos and gliding through the entryways on polished gentlemen's arms.

At this particular topless club, the girl is known as Crystal. She's Dawn at another place, Tigress at still a third. She's a survivor, having lived on the dancers' circuit for ten years. In 1992 she's thirty, though under the muted blue and red lights she's still a raven-haired baby doll. During peak times she'll earn three thousand dollars a week, but she's not kidding herself. She has two more years, three at the most. She has money saved, a leg up on ninety percent of the topless dancers, and in the past five years she's earned a degree in marketing. She's proud of her education, and even prouder that two years ago she kicked a heavy cocaine habit. To do her wanton dancing act, she now gets high on alcohol. She worries that drinking will hook her in the same way that drugs once did, but has decided that whiskey is the lesser of the two evils. When she retires from the topless circuit in a couple of years she hopes to go into sales. With the proper dress and makeup, her looks will open many customers' doors.

Now she wears a filmy see-through black pantsuit over a g-string and push-up bra, and she hugs herself as she leans close to a small round table. Visible behind her, a petite blonde in a pink g-string and white western boots does high kicks and bring-it-on pirouettes to "I Shot the Sheriff." Throughout the club, men cluster about more small tables. In the far corner, a cigarette glows hot red, then dims.

She glances nervously around the club, and tosses her head to move her bangs back away from her eyes. Her hair is shoulder-length and done in ringlets. "I don't want to get anybody in trouble," she says.

"You won't," the interviewer says. "All the trouble anybody's going to get into over this thing, well, they're already in it."

She lowers her lashes. "I'm talking about Barbara." Her voice is soft, and one has to lean close to hear her over the pulsing music. Her chin is pointed with a small cleft.

"She's on record," the interviewer says. "She was on the defense witness list."

"She didn't testify."

"It doesn't matter. The list is part of the record. Besides, she's got another life now." The interviewer feels a pang of impatience. "Look, we've talked about this." It's their third meeting in their third topless club. The girl known here as Crystal has gone from hot to talk to lukewarm to demurely hesitant. The interviewer himself wonders why anyone wants to talk to writers; it's a mystery to him. Something about everyone's chance for five minutes of fame, though Crystal has suddenly decided at this meeting that she doesn't want her name in print. The interviewer has agreed to that; it's Barbara Moore that he's interested in.

"That's it," she says. "If she was still in the business I wouldn't worry about it. Those people out at that fancy college where she's going, they'd take a dim view of this."

The interviewer leans back and folds his arms. "It's up to you. You want me to leave?"

She raises an eyebrow in thought. "I don't guess. I'm just nervous is all."

"Just remember, you're not hurting Barbara. She's going to be part of this story regardless. I don't blame her for not wanting to talk about it, but I've got a job to do."

A short brunette waitress saunters over to deposit Cutty and water in front of Crystal, plain soda in front of the interviewer. The interviewer pays and tips generously. He briefly wonders how much he's spent in drinks and cover charges as he's chased Crystal from club to club. The thought passes; spent money is water under the bridge.

"Last time," the interviewer says, "we talked about how you and Barbara got to be friends. You don't see her anymore?"

She smiles shyly. "Not since she quit. They, you know, go on to other things and then they don't know us anymore. Two or three years, I lose track of time. Every day is pretty much the same."

"You haven't seen her since she left to go to college?"

Her smile saddens in shadowy dimness. "Not once. That last night, she said we'd have lunch and things. I guess she lost my phone number."

The interviewer tries to quicken the pace; he's learned from experience that Crystal's time is limited. In another fifteen minutes she'll have to dance again. The dancers make the circuit, beginning on center stage, then moving in sequence to the various platforms around the room as other girls take their places in the center. The circuit takes about an hour and a half. If the interviewer doesn't finish with Crystal during her break, he's stuck in the club until past midnight. "Let's talk some about Dillard now," he says.

She hesitates. "I guess since it's all over . . ."

"It's over. The case is on appeal, but . . ."

"It's over, then," she says.

"Right. You told me before, that was two nights ago, you told me he was different."

She nods, more direct now, having made the commitment to talk about it. "A lot of these guys, older, they're in here because they like to play around and maybe don't have the looks or whatever to get women other places. That's what we're here for."

"That wasn't the story with him?"

Her forehead puckers in thought. "This is just my observation. Barbara is the one that knew the guy. But, yeah, he seemed, like, driven or something. This was a good-looking guy, not the type we usually run across. You know, older guys. Him and his crowd, they spent money like, wow. Sure, a lot of men pay for table dances, but they'd have, like, two or three girls at a time. More, even." She looks nervously around her, over at the bar, where the manager is watching. He knows what this conversation concerns, and doesn't want the other dancers or customers to get interested in the couple at the table. There are certain customers to whom the presence of a writer would mean an early exit. "I told you, didn't I, that until all that stuff was in the papers we didn't know who he was," she says.

"You mean, he didn't give the right name?" the interviewer says.

"No, he gave his name, Bill. It's just that, well, he told everyone around here he was part of the department store family. You know, Dillard's? It wasn't until, that trial, I guess, that any of us knew differently."

The interviewer already knows this from information he's gotten in court records. It's interesting, but not important, that some customers in topless clubs want their true identity kept secret. It's the same thing in reverse, the identical reasoning, that causes this girl to be Crystal at this club and Dawn at another. "And it was Barbara," the interviewer says, "that was his main girl."

"You have to understand," she says, "that nobody in here was anybody's real girl. Barbara had her own boyfriend. But in the club she was his favorite. He bought her drugs."

"Cocaine?"

"Yeah, mainly. Takes a lot of money for some of these girls. He went to her place some."

"Her apartment."

"Yeah. A few times I think he paid the rent, but I'm not sure about that. I know about the drugs, though. A couple of times she gave me, you know, a couple of twenty-five-dollar papers. They came from him."

"He was keeping her," the interviewer says.

"Not like you'd think. I told you, she had this boyfriend. Still did, last time I saw her, she lives with this guy."

"What about," the interviewer says, "when Dillard came over? The boyfriend . . ."

"It would be during the day. Her boyfriend would be gone and they'd . . ."

"Now, don't say anything you're not sure of," the interviewer says.

"Well, I never saw any of this in person."

The interviewer thinks it over. "She was trading him sex for drugs," he finally says.

"That was the really strange thing about that dude," she says. "That's what you'd think, and there's sure a lot of that going on in this business. But him, she told me that guy didn't seem all that interested in sex. He just wanted somebody to get really out of it with, is more like it."

"To get high with him?"

"Man, if that's the word for it. Blasted is more like it. He had a habit, that's for sure. Came in these clubs, drank and took dope at the same time, and I'm here to tell you from experience that's a dangerous combination. You see a lot of addicts doing what I do, you know, working these clubs, but with him there was more to it. Like an obsession."

"You think he was obsessed with her?" the interviewer says.

"With Barbara?" She flashes an even smile that looks wholesome in spite of her dress and the surroundings, the nude dancers all around writhing to throbbing guitar music. "No, not with her. She told me that dude used to get zonked and then go on these real crying jags, talk about his wife a lot. Barbara could never really understand what he was up to. He was crazy about his family, but there was something driving this guy. When all that stuff first came out, about what that defense lawyer was saying, a few of us went, Hey, you think maybe it was Bill that did the murder and not the other guy?"

The interviewer sits closer to her. He's listening carefully, thinking he might be about to get something really big. "You mean," he says, "that Dillard did or said something that made you think he might be guilty himself?"

She shakes her head. "Nothing he said, or did, really. But I'll tell you something, and this is from Barbara. This was one tortured dude. Probably he's never killed anybody, but this guy has some kind of terrible guilt complex." She seems to search for words, frowning. She licks her lips. "Something back in his past, you know?"

On the morning of January 9, 1991, there are a lot of things that Sue Dillard doesn't know about her surviving son, but she's certain that whatever problems he's had, the troubles aren't entirely his fault. Addicts simply aren't responsible a great deal of the time. But Bill Jr. now seems to have shaken his addiction—or at least to have put the addiction into remission—and his mother is ecstatic for him. He isn't out of the woods as yet, not by any means, but one day at a time he's making progress. Sue crosses her fingers and says a silent prayer for her boy, and then turns her thoughts to her younger girl.

In the Tennessee Williams play, the cat on the hot tin roof was Brick's beautiful, restless, and ambitious wife. Though the two are brother and sister rather than husband and wife, if Bill Dillard, Jr., is the family's Brick, Nancy is its Maggie the Cat. So the pretty and resourceful brunette has always been. When she graduated from high school, Nancy forsook the familiar Dallas confines for Hollins University in faraway Virginia. She got her B.A. at Hollins, then moved on to Washington, D.C., to work in a museum for a couple of years, a time that she found unsatisfying. Nancy wanted a career in landscape architecture, so headed for the U. of Pennsylvania's School of Design as if drawn by a magnet. At Penn, Nancy's grades were right in line with her irresistible obsession to excel. From Penn she went on to graduate school at Harvard, and her marriage to another Crimson graduate student named Richard Lyon didn't slow her ambition a farthing. After earning her master's at Harvard, Nancy returned to Dallas with her husband in tow. Her job with prestigious Tramell Crow Industries came about as a result of Big Daddy's connections, but Nancy's progress with the company was her own doing. She worked long, hard hours, and the brief interruptions in her career to bear two daughters were mere interludes, nothing more. At twenty-nine, Nancy became the youngest partner in the history of the Crow Companies and supervised construction of a multimillion-dollar subdivision. In her off time, she served on the board of the Dallas Historical Society, did high-profile charity work, and rubbed elbows with governors and the president's wife. Her dark brown eyes set in steely determination, there seemed to be no limit to Nancy's blossoming career.

For her husband's part, Richard seemed content to stay in the background. He had his own Harvard credentials, of course, but whereas Nancy seemed driven to succeed, Richard was happy with a lesser niche. He was more of an artist, sensitive and caring. Whereas Nancy reveled in the limelight, Richard seemed embarrassed by any attention showered on him. As of January 1991, in the eight years since his marriage to Nancy and subsequent move to Dallas, Richard had held three different jobs.

Given their widely different perspectives, it was hardly surprising that at some point Richard and Nancy would drift apart, but the nasty rumors that began in late 1989 were a shock to Sue Dillard. Sue's quiet son-in-law had never seemed the type to take up with another woman, but he had. And the affair with a flashy blonde was anything but run-of-the-mill. Richard had flaunted his infidelity, showering his lover with expensive gifts, taking her to New Orleans, going skiing with her in Taos. Finally Richard had moved out of his and Nancy's duplex and taken up residence in his own apartment. Not only had Richard forsaken his wife, he had publicly embarrassed her.

Almost as shocking as Richard's infidelity was the sudden change in Nancy as her marriage soured. Heretofore, she had seemed so strong. But with Richard's alienated love and eventual departure, Nancy became despondent and childishly nervous. The problem affected her work to such an extent that she was eventually replaced on her job. She went nights on end without sleep. So frantic with fear of losing her husband did Nancy become that she went on starvation diets and even dyed her hair blond to match Richard's new lover's hair. She pursued Richard endlessly; even after he'd moved out of the duplex she would call him late at night with pleas that she was violently sick and needed him at her side. Even her own mother wondered if Nancy imagined—or possibly even fabricated—her constant illnesses in order to draw Richard to her. During the year-long separation, the Nancy that Sue Dillard observed shrank within herself, lost weight to the point that her limbs resembled twigs, and became a hollow-eyed and haunting shell.

Then, when all hope for Nancy's marriage seemed in vain, in the fall of 1990 Richard seemed to regain his senses. Word came to Big Daddy and Sue that their son-in-law had quit seeing the other woman, and that he and Nancy were on the verge of a reconciliation. Nancy's parents listened to the news with tightly crossed fingers; in November, when Richard and Nancy withdrew their divorce petition from the courts, hope seemed about to become reality. To Sue's and Big Daddy's joy, Nancy brightened. Just before Christmas, Big Daddy made an early morning drive to DFW Airport to take Richard and Nancy to catch a plane to Connecticut, where they spent part of the holidays with Richard's folks. In January, Richard was scheduled to vacate his separate quarters and return once again to the Park Cities duplex. On the day after New Year's, he moved part of his things back into the duplex and planned to bring the rest of his gear, piece by piece, throughout the remainder of the month.

So on the morning of January 9, Sue Dillard is full of happiness for her two middle children, one having apparently beaten his addiction, the other having sunk to the depths over her marriage and now seemingly on the brink of recovery. Though wide the differences between the two middle Dillard kids, both have cause for celebration.

Sue thinks it fitting that these two seem to be bringing their lives into focus at the same time. As the two Dillard children closest in age, Bill Jr. and Nancy had the most to share while growing up. Only two years separated them, so they had friends in common. Bill Jr.'s friends dated Nancy's friends in high school, and brother and sister attended school functions and parties together. Mary Helen, Bill Jr.'s wife, was a classmate of Nancy's. Bill Jr. and Nancy had been well-adjusted teenagers for the most part, wealthy kids with the brightest of futures.

Once there'd been a problem.

Sue Dillard doesn't like to think about it. All mothers for all time have had a tendency to forget the bad things that happen to their children and concentrate on the good. It's human nature to dismiss one's children's shortcomings, even classify their problems as insignificant. Besides, the problem with Nancy and Bill Jr. was years and years ago. In 1991, the problem is ancient history. As adults, Bill Jr. had an addiction, but that, too, has passed, and Nancy was driven to succeed, survived a stunning blow to her self-confidence, and now seems about to put her life back together again. On the morning of January 9, 1991, Sue

Dillard sees only the good side of things. The years-ago problem could have nothing whatsoever to do with the troubles that Nancy and Bill Jr. have had as adults.

Or could it?

As the phone rings, Sue puts the years-ago problem out of her mind and concentrates once more on the happy things. As she reaches for the receiver, the kitchen clock shows 7:00.

The voice on the other end of the line belongs to Richard Lyon, and his words assault Sue's inner peace like jackhammers. Richard has been up all night with Nancy at Presbyterian Hospital. Nancy is terribly sick with diarrhea and uncontrollable vomiting, and the hospital personnel can't seem to figure out what is wrong with her; in fact, even as Richard uses the corridor pay phone, the Presbyterian staff transfers Nancy from the emergency room into the intensive care unit. It's probably nothing really serious, Richard says—both he and Sue are painfully aware of Nancy's many illnesses during the past year—but he thought that Sue and Big Daddy should know of their daughter's whereabouts.

As Sue hangs up, she is shrouded in gloom. Just as Nancy's life seemed about to come together, this has to happen. She fights to control her emotions, and forces herself to think rationally. What should she do? She must notify the rest of the family, of course. Bill Jr.'s wife will be home, and that's who Sue decides to call first. She'll ask Mary Helen to contact Susan, the elder Dillard daughter, up in Wichita Falls. Once she's talked to Mary Helen, Sue Dillard will then have to phone around and try to locate her husband; Bill Sr. will have already left the Masters Swim Club by now and will be going about his business. At this time of the morning, Big Daddy might be almost anywhere.

3

Later there would be wide disagreement as to exactly what went on during Nancy Cooke Dillard Lyon's treatment at Presbyterian Hospital. In fact, the only thing consistent in the recollections of those present in the emergency room, and later in the IC unit, is that there was a great deal of confusion; not surprising in a big-city hospital, where Chinese fire drills are the norm rather than the exception.

Richard Lyon entered Presbyterian's emergency unit through the double-door parking lot entry within ten minutes, either way, of one in the morning on the ninth of January. The seats in the waiting room were nearly all occupied; though the temperature outside hadn't dropped enough to freeze the drizzle on streets and sidewalks, weather conditions were still pretty nasty. Two of the patients in Emergency were there for car wreck injuries—one with fearful lacerations on the left side of his face and neck, an-other with a fractured pelvis and crushed ankle—while a third, a twelve-year-old, had suffered a concussion from landing on his head when his skateboard upended in his parents' rain-slickened driveway. Additionally, in the patient area beyond the waiting room and reception desk, there was an elderly man who'd come in complaining of severe chest pains; before the night was over the man would spend several hours on a heart monitor before the staff discovered that he'd swallowed a chicken bone. A woman with cramps, nausea, and diarrhea wouldn't be considered a high-priority case; Nancy Lyon would have to wait her turn.

Richard was dressed in jeans, a tan Harvard sweatshirt underneath a waterproof windbreaker, and worn Nike running shoes. The female nurses in the hospital would remember him well. It is true that once the story became a public event, chronicled on television and related in the newspapers under screaming headlines, others would also suddenly remember Richard (some of the refreshed memories are suspect, since the recalling parties weren't within miles of the hospital on that fateful night), but that the women at Presbyterian noticed Richard Lyon isn't particularly surprising. With his dark Middle Eastern good looks—his mother is Lebanese—easy smile, and athletic manner of moving about, he is an eye-catcher with an authoritative way about him. At the time he wore a thin, neatly clipped Omar Sharif mustache.

Although the time of Richard's arrival at the hospital is pretty well established, his demeanor was to become a matter of controversy. Depending on which description one accepts, Richard either strolled casually through the waiting room, winking and grinning at every woman in sight and casting hungry glances at each feminine chest and thigh (prosecution version); or (defense's story) dashed hurriedly around the waiting room couches and chairs like a messenger from the Alamo in frantic search of reinforcements, took a white-knuckled grip on the edge of the reception counter, and announced breathlessly, "Someone help me. My wife is ill." Whatever Richard's posture, the duty nurse sent a male attendant with him into the parking lot, and the two men rolled Nancy through the entry in a wheelchair.

While Richard's outward attitude in the waiting room is pretty well up for grabs, Nancy's appearance is not. Her pretty brown short-cut hair was disheveled, her complexion pale, her mouth slack in discomfort and pain. Her brown eyes appeared glazed over; her lids drooped at groggy half-mast. At close intervals her body shook as she retched and gagged, and in between gagging and retching she uttered a series of moans. At one point, Richard encircled her upper body with a cloth strap in order to keep her upright in the wheelchair. The hospital staff allowed Nancy to sit in the waiting room in this condition for better than three-quarters of an hour while waiting-room occupants glanced nervously at the young woman in the wheelchair and exchanged disturbed looks among themselves. The delay was in part due to staff availability, and in part due to Richard's slowness in the filling out of the hospital's medical history and insurance forms. Hospital emergency room records show that by the time Presbyterian was assured that it was going to get its money, thus clearing the way for the deathly ill Nancy Dillard Lyon to enter the patient care area behind the reception desk, it was 1:55 in the morning.

However Richard acted at the hospital, his fill-in-the-blanks on Presbyterian's medical admittance forms are a matter of written record. Additionally, Nancy had been a patient at Presbyterian several times in the past—as far back as 1974 (for a teenage pregnancy that ended in a medically approved abortion), and as recently as two weeks earlier for a bout with the flu—and the hospital had an extensive file on her. Richard's notation in the allergies portion of the hospital admittance form agrees with a doctor's previous observation in Nancy's hospital file. Both Richard and the doctor stated in writing that Nancy had experienced past violent reactions to Compazine, which is the most common drug used to combat nausea. The doctor's note, in fact, is quite a bit stronger than Richard's: according to the doctor, Nancy's reaction to Compazine resembled a cerebral palsy attack. Whatever Richard's notations on the admittance form, and whatever the doctor's entry on her hospital records, when Nancy arrived, retching and pale, in the emergency treatment section, her temperature and blood pressure were duly noted and a blood sample routinely drawn (though for some unexplained reason the blood sample remained in Emergency until 2:55 the following afternoon, at which time the staff finally sent some of Nancy's blood off to the lab for a poison-detecting toxology screen). The early formalities out of the way, one of the staff then juiced up a hypo and pumped the new patient full of Compazine.

In later critical courtroom testimony there would be a great deal of disagreement and finger-pointing as to which doctor ordered what drug for Nancy—and, indeed, as to the exact degree of her previous Compazine allergy—but it is abundantly clear that the Compazine injection administered in the emergency room delayed Nancy Lyon's treatment by several hours. Immediately after the injection, her skin turned the color of red plums, and her pulse raced and slowed like a berserk Geiger counter. Instead of receding, her nausea drastically increased. Her blood pressure dipped to a near-critical level. Her eyes rolled back in her head to the point that only the whites showed, and her eyelids twitched. She drew her legs up on the receiving table into a fetal position and wouldn't respond to verbal commands. Nancy remained in this near-comatose condition for quite some time while the now frenzied staff applied dopamine to raise her blood pressure and various inhalants and injections in an attempt to bring her around.

It isn't clear just when the staff checked Nancy's records and realized that she had had a severe allergic reaction, but some time around three, she received Benadryl to counteract the Compazine. The Benadryl revived her to the point that she could sit up partway and murmur groggy responses to questions. Understandably, the hospital people then assumed that the Compazine had caused the problem, and continued to treat Nancy for diarrhea and nausea. During Nancy's initial twelve hours at Presbyterian there was no mention of poisoning, accidental or otherwise.

The same group of nurses and attendants who were on duty in the emergency room when Richard arrived remained at their stations until the seven o'clock shift change. All remember Richard as interested and properly concerned (as previously stated, there was one witness in particular who recalled the exact opposite, that Richard's attitude was flippant) and also recall his attempts to help the staff figure out what was wrong with Nancy. He seemed greatly puzzled, the nurses and attendants remember, and went to great lengths to tell everything he knew about his wife's condition. He spoke in an authoritative, slightly nasal voice with a distinct New England accent, and gestured often with his hands to emphasize his point. Richard Lyon, as everyone associated with the case was later to learn, liked to explain things.

"I've been gone all day," he said. "Business trip. One-day turnaround to Houston and back on Southwest Airlines. I'm a project supervisor, this work my company's doing on the Pavilion Shopping Mall down there, and we had a tenant complaining that the ground underneath his space was sinking. Some kind of underground water leak's turning the dirt into a quagmire, and I had to go down to, you know, take some soil samples.

"So anyway," Richard said, "I had to get up early, six, six-thirty, and while I bathed and dressed, Nancy went downstairs to fix the kids' breakfast. When I came down she had my coffee ready, and we sat and talked a minute. Hold on." Here Richard's eyes widened and he snapped his fingers. "That coffee, you think maybe . . . ? It tasted awful. Nancy and I both had to add milk before we could drink the stuff. I told her it was terrible even with the milk, and I poured mine out in the sink. When I left, Nancy was drinking hers. I told her I didn't understand how she could swallow it, that's how bad it was.

"I left home a little after seven," Richard said, "and drove to the Love Field Garage, ran my credit card through the automatic dispenser for a round-trip ticket, and took the eight o'clock Southwest flight to Houston. Hobby Airport. I rented a car down there to get around, ate lunch with a couple of guys out on, Post Oak Road, I think, and by the time we were through I had to catch the four o'clock back to Dallas. Got home five-thirty, maybe six o'clock, and found Nancy so sick that she couldn't get out of bed. She was supposed to go to a meeting to-night that she had to call and cancel. I've tried everything, even had her doctor phone a prescription into the Eckerd's Drug on Mockingbird Lane, but those suppositories they gave me didn't seem to help. By midnight I was pretty sure she wasn't going to get well on her own, and that's when we came to the hospital. Damn, that coffee. You think that's what it could be?"

Richard offered to go home and return with the suspect coffee grounds for testing. The doctors agreed that he should. With the turmoil in the emergency room that night, none of the staff had time to reflect on the amount of detail that he'd included about his Houston trip, but later they were to wonder why Richard had gone to such lengths to establish his whereabouts during the day. It was his story, though, and through all future questioning sessions he would stick firmly to his guns.

Richard returned to his Shenandoah Avenue duplex sometime after three in the morning, shortly after the hospital people had revived Nancy by using Benadryl to reverse the disastrous Compazine injection. Even though there was to be a real donnybrook at trial over Richard's attitude and demeanor at the hospital, it's well established that he didn't leave Nancy's side until advised to do so by the staff. Now that she was awake, the doctors felt that it was only a matter of time until she fully recovered. Having the patient's husband fidget in the waiting room would serve no purpose; besides, Richard should be home when his little girls awoke. So he returned to the duplex, got a couple of hours of sleep, and woke his daughters early and arranged for their care. The hospital staff anticipated that when he returned, it would be only to check Nancy out and take her home with him. They were very wrong.

It was also during his initial trip home and back that, according to Richard, he brought the coffee with him to the hospital. He recalls leaving the soaked grounds—still cached inside the filter ring—along with the remainder of the coffee in its original container, with one of the doctors or nurses. He doesn't remember specifically which hospital person received the coffee, and with the number of white-uniformed nurses and attendants scurrying here and there around the emergency room, his memory lapse isn't particularly surprising. However, in light of the staff's later meticulous recording of certain other items brought from the duplex to the hospital, that the coffee wasn't isolated and tested seems somewhat odd. Nonetheless, the whereabouts of the suspect grounds and partially full container remain a mystery to this day.

When Richard arrived once again in the emergency room,

sometime around six-thirty in the morning, Nancy's condition had worsened. She'd lapsed once more into a coma, and this time nothing that the staff could do was bringing her around. She drifted in and out, her eyelids fluttering uncontrollably, and always there was the intense abdominal pain. Her blood pressure bottomed once again, and a second dopamine injection proved useless. Doctors watched Nancy's vital signs with intensely furrowed brows; there simply wasn't any reason for this healthy young woman to respond as she was. Finally, a few minutes before seven o'clock, a worried gastrologist on duty gave Nancy's husband the word. Her condition had the hospital staff totally puzzled, and the consensus was that she should be moved upstairs to the Intensive Care Unit. While the staff made ready to load a now unconscious Nancy onto a gurney and roll her to the elevators, Richard went to call her parents. The duty nurse remembers that he stood in front of the pay phone, head bowed, for several minutes before lifting the receiver. At the time she thought he was merely shocked and worried about his wife, but later decided that he may have been mentally rehearsing what he was about to say, choosing his words like a man selecting ripe fruit.

Among any group whose members are in competition, there's a lot of backstabbing and behind-your-back gossip. The medical community is no exception. With its status as Dallas' "society hospital," Presbyterian is the target of more barbs than most of the other institutions around town, and the word at crosstown Baylor Medical Center—which is in a low-income, deteriorating neighborhood—is that "Presbyterian is the only place in Dallas where they issue practice permits based on who the doctor is married to rather than where he went to medical school." Be that assessment true or false, the staff at Presbyterian recognizes money when it appears, and treats the customer accordingly.

In the mid-morning hours of January 10, as the Dillard clan gathered to stand vigil while Nancy fought for her life in Intensive Care, hospital eyebrows lifted in respect. The London Fog topcoats, Armani suits, and the women's Neiman's- and Saks-labeled dresses that trooped in and out of the waiting room during the following days were signs that these were the kind of people to whom Presbyterian caters. And cater Presbyterian does. Between January ninth, when Richard made his early morning call to Sue Dillard, and the fourteenth, when the Presbyterian staff turned off Nancy's life support, the main waiting room outside Intensive Care became a nearly exclusive stronghold for Nancy's relatives and friends; on occasions, when the Dillard group grew so large that it spilled out into the corridors, friends and families of other patients were asked by the staff to proceed to the smaller waiting room downstairs.

The Dillards arrived in ones and twos. Sue came with Mary Helen, and the two women set up anxious camp outside the ICU unit. Bill Jr. checked in shortly thereafter, his handsome face set in concern, and along with his wife and mother made a family circle around Richard Lyon in the waiting room. Finally Big Daddy himself arrived, walking fast, his gaze darting from side to side as if he could chase his daughter's sickness away by sheer determined will. Elder daughter Susan made the drive down from Wichita Falls alone; her dentist husband had patients to see. Susan is a composite of her parents; she has Sue's classic mouth and nose and wealth of lovely brown-streaked-with-gray hair, but her height and sturdy build are more from Big Daddy's side of the family. With her arrival at the hospital, the group was now complete. Since Nancy could have visitors only once each hour, and then only two at a time, the group huddled around Richard and made quiet but serious small talk. The Dillards as a whole hadn't been fond of Richard during the previous year while he'd been separated from Nancy, but—for the time being, at least—crisis caused the family to rally around. However, Richard's closeness with his in-laws wasn't to last throughout the day.

Sometime during the morning Susan and Mary Helen had a private conversation. Both women had the same nagging fear on their minds, and as they stood apart from the rest of the anxious group, the two talked over some things that Nancy had told each of them during the previous months. Disturbing things. Stories that they'd both dismissed as Nancy's fantasies, but now they weren't sure. Moreso, they were even less certain whether they should let other family members in on what Nancy had said. The doctors and hospital staff seemed totally in the dark as to the cause of Nancy's condition, but Susan and Mary Helen thought that between the two of them they might have the answer. Because of the implications contained in what Nancy had said, their hesitancy to discuss the matter with Big Daddy and the rest is easily understood. As Big Daddy, Sue, and Bill Jr. gathered around Richard in close conversation, Susan and Mary Helen looked helplessly at each other and wondered what to do.

It was also mid-morning when Mary Henrich learned that Nancy was in the hospital, and she had a great deal more than a passing interest in Nancy's condition. Ms. Henrich is a pleasant and gentle woman whose looks are deceptive. She's a society divorce attorney, specializing in the special kinds of divorces had in Highland Park, and she goes after well-heeled, soon-to-be exhusbands like the Lord himself after the Temple's money-changers. She'd represented Nancy Lyon before she and Richard had withdrawn their divorce petition just a few months earlier, and also had more than a passing acquaintance with Big Daddy. Mary Henrich was and is a devoted participant in the Masters Swim Club, and had seen Big Daddy at the country club early that day. Like Susan and Mary Helen, Mary Henrich had heard some troubling stories from Nancy during the past year, and like them, Mary wasn't certain whether she should come forward with what she knew.

Legal ethics had a great deal more to do with her hesitancy than did concern over the implications to Richard, because during her association with Nancy the divorce attorney had developed a dislike for Richard that bordered on hatred. Mary was worried about attorney-client privilege, though, because Nancy had told her lawyer some things in confidence that now might have a bearing on whether Nancy lived or died. It is a no-no among lawyers to give out confidential information without the client's permission; in fact, divulgence can be grounds for disbarment. But Nancy wasn't in any condition to give her consent at the moment, so Mary Henrich's consideration with legal ethics was brief indeed. Her chin firm, she picked up the phone and called the hospital.

★ ★ ★

At just about the same time that Mary Henrich picked up the phone, Susan and Mary Helen reached a decision. They simply had to tell. Susan was hesitant to be the newsbearer, but not so her sister-in-law. Mary Helen Dillard is made of some pretty stern stuff; she's held together a marriage that, with a woman of lesser pluck, would have floundered years ago. Her features set in determination, Mary Helen approached the family group, pointedly ignored Richard, and pulled Big Daddy aside.

Dr. Ali Bagheri, though raised in the Middle East amid scenes of babbling confusion, wasn't ready for the furor surrounding his patient, Nancy Dillard Lyon. It was bad enough that she was losing ground by the minute in the battle for her life, and that the Intensive Care Unit staff—cardiologists and neurologists, assisted by medical aides, in addition to a parade of no-nonsense nurses who moved around ICU with stockinged legs flashing like pale white pistons—couldn't figure out what was wrong with her. To top it off, by noon on the tenth of January, her family had squared off in the waiting room in two opposing camps. Nancy's husband, along with what few supporters he could muster, had taken up residence on one side of the waiting room while her parents and siblings were grouped on the other side, the two opposing factions glowering at each other like fighters in their corners waiting for the bell to ring. And the poor doctor, Bagheri thought, is squarely in the middle.

An olive-complexioned man with a neat mustache, groomed like a stallion and handsome enough for a Valentino role, Bagheri was a third-year resident at Presbyterian and a graduate of Southwestern Medical School. Just hours after Richard had brought Nancy into the emergency room—and after she'd survived the disastrous Compazine injection, and then had failed to respond to every known remedy for cramps, vomiting, and diarrhea—the emergency room staff had transferred her to the intensive care unit, and it was in ICU that her treatment came under Bagheri's supervision. As the ICU staff tried one futile treatment after another, Nancy's blood pressure dropped by the minute and her pulse alternately raced and slowed. Bagheri realized that the hospital had its hands full just with keeping her alive.

As he was quick to point out in later courtroom testimony, none of the errors made in Nancy's treatment was his fault. As a resident, he made no decisions as to treatment. Those diagnoses were up to the practicing physicians—eventually seven different doctors were to sign off on Nancy's hospital record—and the resident's responsibility was merely to see that the prescribed treatments were adhered to. But the Compazine injection plus later problems with Nancy's treatment in ICU? No way was anyone going to lay that blame on Dr. Ali Bagheri.

But the burden of keeping Nancy's loved ones abreast of her condition did fall on Bagheri's shoulders, and it was in performing this duty that he had problems with her family's attitude. Families, the doctor knew, needed unity in times of crisis. But not only were Nancy's loved ones not pulling together, they were practically at one another's throats. Her husband huddled on a bench, all alone except for an occasional supporter who came by to wish him well, while Nancy's parents and siblings grouped together on sofas and chairs, talked in guarded whispers, and shot icy glances in the husband's direction.

Businesslike to a fault, Bagheri assumed that whatever rifts existed within the family were none of his affair, but the breakdown in the family created double duty for the doctor. In Nancy Lyon's case, the husband would demand to know what the staff was doing on her behalf—and then sigh in indignation after Bagheri had told him as much as the resident doctor knew, or in one instance shout, "Look at these dummies. They don't even know what she's allergic to," when he learned of the emergency room Compazine shot—and then Nancy's father or sister would ask the exact same questions of Bagheri, and the doctor would have to go over it all a second time. In addition to monitoring Nancy's condition and keeping track of the cardiac arrests, mangled bones, and terminal cancer cases also under ICU's care, having to duplicate his reports to Nancy's family was a waste of time as far as he was concerned. Why, Bagheri thought, can't these people learn to pull together?

If Bagheri had taken sides, he would have favored Big Daddy

and the rest of the Dillards. For one thing, Sue, Mary Helen, Bill Jr., and the rest were right in line with Bagheri's idea of what distraught loved ones should be. Ever since the Dillard clan had gathered at the hospital they had remained attentive and somber in the waiting room, existing on soft drinks, cookies, and sandwiches brought in by a seemingly endless host of friends, occasionally interrupting their vigil with brief trips inside the IC unit to sit beside Nancy when hospital rules permitted. Nancy's husband, though, was an entirely different matter; for a number of reasons real and imagined, Dr. Ali Bagheri simply didn't like the man.

It was Bagheri who was to testify at Richard's trial that his hospital attitude was somewhat flippant, and whether or not the doctor's view was slanted is an interesting question. Richard Lyon can be a pushy guy, though his pushiness at the hospital is a perfectly normal reaction be his motive concern or cover-up. In his view, the hospital people simply weren't doing much for Nancy, and given the circumstances, there's nothing odd about his flying off the handle. While at Presbyterian, Richard stormed at doctors and nurses alike, demanding to know what they were doing for Nancy, and Bagheri himself more than once drew the brunt of Richard's anger.

Aside from Bagheri's resentment of Richard's raking the doctor over the coals, there is the matter of culture. The doctor recognized Richard's dark Lebanese good looks to be of Middle Eastern origin like Bagheri's own. Unlike Texas good old boys, who meet in a foreign country and embrace like brothers, Middle Easterners who are strangers are slow to buddy around together. Pakistanis dislike the Arabs, who dislike the Israelis, who can't stand the Iraqis, who don't particularly give a damn for anybody. Friendship between Middle Easterners doesn't come easy, and although Richard had never been farther east than Boston, Dr. Bagheri was inherently suspicious of him.

Also, people's attitudes when seen through others' eyes are after all a matter of perspective. Bagheri is a no-nonsense, nose-to-the-grindstone type who studied like a Trojan to be a doctor, and who takes his profession as seriously as he does the strokes and heart attacks he treats. Taking his overall views into consideration, his opinion that Richard Lyon at the hospital acted more like a man on a lark than a husband with a gravely ill wife might be a bit of overkill. Nonetheless, in Bagheri's eyes, Richard spent his time laughing and joking with the nurses—actually flirting, Bagheri thought—and the idea that Richard's outward breezy attitude might be a front, a cover to keep him from going bananas with worry, cut no ice at all with Dr. Bagheri. Your wife is very likely dying, man, Bagheri thought, the least you can do is appear concerned.

Such was Bagheri's view when Big Daddy stopped the swarthy, handsome doctor in the hallway near the intensive care unit. Bagheri halted, his manner attentive; William Wooldridge Dillard, Sr., is a man who commands respect. Bagheri waited patiently for more questions about Nancy's condition.

But when Big Daddy spoke, his tone was low and urgent. "Have you checked her for poison?" He glanced cautiously about to be certain that no one else was listening. Richard was visible inside the waiting room. Nancy's husband had his back turned.

The question stunned Bagheri. Toxic shock syndrome, yes, the staff had considered that, a jolt to Nancy's system that could have come from a lot of different things. But the rash which normally accompanies TSS was missing from Nancy's skin. Incredible as it may seem, Presbyterian does not routinely run poison tests on patients admitted in Nancy's condition; nor, to be fair, do other hospitals in the Dallas area. Nancy's blood sample— ordered by emergency unit personnel on her admittance— hadn't even gone to an out-of-state lab for a toxology screen until 2:55 P.M. on January 9, fourteen hours after her arrival, and the result wasn't available as Bagheri stood with Big Daddy in the corridor. In fact, the tox screen results wouldn't arrive at Presbyterian until after Nancy had died, and, because of the speed with which arsenic works its way through the body, would reveal only minimal traces of the poison in her blood. So the answer to Big Daddy's question was no, they hadn't tested Nancy for poison, which of course wasn't Dr. Bagheri's fault. Residents only carry out orders. Resignedly, Bagheri shook his head.

"Well, you need to test her," Big Daddy said. "Nancy's lawyer called, and her sister-in-law confirmed it to me. We've got reason to suspect that Nancy's husband poisoned some wine and gave it to her. We think he may be trying to kill her." The bombshell dropped, Nancy Lyon's father waited for the doctor to speak.

Bagheri was now in a dilemma. The seriousness of what his patient's father was saying wasn't lost on him, and neither were the possible consequences to the hospital and, for that matter, to the doctor himself. If Nancy's husband had indeed poisoned her, it was up to the hospital to preserve records to turn over to the police. It was a situation the likes of which Bagheri had never before encountered, and prior to taking any action he wanted to talk the matter over with his superiors. For the time being, Bagheri would only listen. He bent his head nearer Big Daddy, and the two men engaged in a brief, hushed conversation. As they parted company and went their respective ways, Dr. Bagheri's expression was rigidly grim.

By any set of standards, arsenic is nasty stuff. It's one of the elements, bearing the chemical symbol *As,* and you can find it in the makeup of just about any surface rock lying about on the ground. Most of its known uses have to do with killing things, and that even includes a major industrial function: a small amount of arsenic increases the surface tension of molten lead so that it's easier to mold the lead into bullets. Researchers have tried other things with arsenic; it's been an experimental pesticide and even an ingredient in medicines. Neither trial use worked because the arsenic posed just as great a danger to those persons using the bug killer or medicine as it did to the insects or viruses. Other than its use in the manufacture of lead shot, arsenic has only one other purpose. It kills things. Combined with hydrogen, arsenic forms a poisonous gas; mixing one part arsenic with three parts oxygen forms a deadly liquid.

Big jolts of arsenic kill quickly, within an hour or two, and rapid death is preferable for the victim. Those who take smaller doses survive over a period of as much as a week, and grow short of breath as the poison slowly paralyzes the respiratory muscles. Sores develop on the brain and the victim loses the ability to think clearly. The dizziness, excruciating stomach pain, and vomiting go on and on without interruption. The hands and feet burn as if on fire, and the skin grows so sore that the barest touch brings screams of agony. Flinching in pain, breathing in piteous gasps, Nancy Lyon clung to her life at Presbyterian Hospital for six torturous days.

Once the Dillard family's suspicion of Richard Lyon came to light, an odd game ensued. A game of pretend. No one wanted to alert Richard that he was the prime suspect, but at the same time, any scrap of food or drink in which Nancy could have gotten her fatal dose needed to be brought to the hospital and categorized. Since Richard lived in the duplex, bringing anything from the Lyon home without his knowing about it was going to be well nigh impossible.

As it turned out, other than the coffee that Richard himself brought to the hospital—and which mysteriously disappeared—and some food, suspect items from the duplex were never examined. In fact, the police didn't search the Lyon home for over a month. In the interim many things were to vanish from the duplex, and the source of Nancy's poisoning was never found. While hindsight is roughly twenty-twenty, it's easy to see why no one ransacked the duplex in search of tainted food or drink during those panicked January days while Nancy lay dying. A search of the Lyon household was deemed unnecessary because the Dillard family thought they knew what had poisoned Nancy, and one of the many strange twists surrounding the death of Nancy Dillard Lyon is that the source of her family's belief was Nancy herself.

One of the troubling stories that Nancy had told involved an event the previous September. At the time, Richard and Nancy had been separated for over eight months, and he was living in an apartment in the far North Dallas suburb of Richardson. Although there are small differences in their telling, the memories of three women—sister, sister-in-law, and divorce attorney— regarding Nancy's tale are essentially the same.

★ ★ ★

According to Nancy, one warm September afternoon she returned from a shopping trip, parked in front of the duplex, and made her way across the lawn to the front porch. Near the porch she paused. Sitting side by side in front of her door were a tinted bottle of white wine and a large, tub-shaped plastic container. An envelope was attached to the neck of the bottle, secured by a ribbon. Nancy stepped up on the porch, undid the ribbon, and opened the envelope.

The note and envelope are yet more items never found during the investigation, but according to Nancy the one-line message went something like this: "Nancy, you're one great lady." There was no signature. Nancy told no one whether the note was printed, scripted, or typed, but however the note was crafted, Nancy stood on the porch and read it over. Puzzled, she let the note and envelope hang loosely from her fingers as she bent to examine her other gift, the plastic container.

The container was full of what Nancy assumed to be vitamin capsules; along with a large percentage of the rest of yuppie America, Nancy Lyon was a vitamin junky. Whatever their contents, the brown cylindrical objects inside the container were standard, inch-long gelatin caps. It was a strange present indeed, and just as strange was the anonymity of the giver. Had Richard left the wine and pills, possibly as a token of his love? Nancy hoped that the gifts were from him; she'd made no secret of the fact that she hated the idea of separation and liked the thought of divorce even less. But by this time, after eight months of loneliness, there were other men in Nancy's life as well. Had some bashful suitor left the presents? She didn't know. Still baffled, a smile of wonder touching her lips, Nancy Lyon picked up the bottle and the plastic container and carried them inside.

By the following morning Nancy was no longer pleased with her gifts, at least as far as the wine was concerned. On the evening that she found the gifts on her doorstep, she poured herself a glass of the wine to have with her dinner. According to her, the taste was bitter, and when she'd finished the meal she became sick to her stomach. Her experience with the wine disturbed her enough that she called Mary Henrich the following day and told her lawyer what had happened from beginning to end.

To hear her peers tell it, if Mary Henrich has a fault in the practice of law, her shortcoming is that she gets too involved with her clients. Mary would disagree; in anything so agonizingly personal as a divorce proceeding, the more a lawyer can fit into the client's shoes, the more zealous the pursuit of the client's best interests becomes. In the months that Mary had acted as Nancy's divorce lawyer the two had become fast friends, and though they shared many feelings in common, they were at odds on one particular subject. While Nancy still professed a deep love for Richard and hoped against hope for a reconciliation, Mary Henrich would think no more of completely destroying Richard Lyon than she'd think of stepping on a revolting bug.

Nancy Lyon may have been unsure of the source of the anonymous gifts, but the second Mary Henrich heard that the wine had made her client sick, she knew who'd left the items on Nancy's porch as well as she knew her own name. The wine and capsule tale wasn't the first troubling story that Mary Henrich had heard from Nancy. Moreover, even if Richard wasn't the culprit, the suspect wine and pills were evidence that someone had attempted to harm Nancy. Mary's advice to Nancy: Bring the wine and capsules immediately to her office, and Mary would have them tested and examined for fingerprints.

Surprisingly, Nancy refused. She said that she'd be embarrassed for anyone to know she suspected Richard, and that she'd dispose of the wine and pills herself. Mary Henrich was appalled that Nancy would let Richard—or anyone else—get away with the evil stunt, but the final decision was, after all, up to Nancy. So, grudgingly, Mary Henrich accepted her client's decision.

But on the bleak January day when she learned that Nancy was in the hospital, the wine and pill incident popped into her mind like a TV replay. Immediately she called the hospital to be certain that the Dillard family knew about the wine and pills, and that the doctors checked Nancy for poison. Her warning didn't fall on deaf ears; both Susan Dillard Hendrickson and Mary Helen Dillard had heard the identical story from Nancy, and Mary Helen had related the tale to Big Daddy. So as the hospital staff and the Dillard family set about building a case against Richard Lyon, the suspect wine and pills were the main things on their minds. Moreover, the wine and container of capsules were in a place where they would be easy to get without sidestepping Richard to enter the duplex.

The items were in fact in an auto-repair shop, locked in the trunk of a car. The car belonged to Lynn Pease, who'd been Nancy and Richard's nanny for three years, and who was yet another party who could corroborate Nancy's story. Lynn is a gentle New England girl, a professional nanny who'd come to the Lyons with references from several prominent families, and during the time she'd worked for Nancy and Richard, Lynn had become practically a member of the family herself. She adored the Lyon children, and though she'd resigned as the Lyon nanny for health reasons—Lynn suffers from multiple sclerosis—and also because Nancy no longer worked and was home full-time, Lynn continued to call on Nancy and the children while the Lyons were separated. She often took the kids shopping and out to the movies. The Lyon girls, Allison and Anna, were crazy about Lynn as well, and loved to ride in her old heap of a car, which the kids had dubbed the Zoomobile. On one of her drop-in visits, Lynn had found Nancy in bed, so sick she could barely move, and on another occasion Lynn came by within a day or two after Nancy had found the wine and pills on her doorstep.

"The pills were on a low table," Lynn remembers, "just outside Nancy's bedroom, great big capsules like horse medicine. I told her, 'You know the kids might get into those,' and that's when Nancy told me where she'd found them. She said she thought Richard had given them to her. When I said, you know, about the children getting into them, Nancy picked up the box, container or whatever, and took me downstairs with her. The bottle of wine was on the dining room table. She carried the pills and I took the wine, and we went out to my car. Nancy asked me to hide them in my trunk, so that's what I did." Here Lynn flashes an infectious grin. "Guess it's lucky I did that, huh?"

Lynn was in the group who'd joined the Dillards at the hospital, and it was the items in her trunk on which the secret plan-ners zeroed in. Any hesitancy on the part of the Dillard family to try to implicate Richard was gone now that Big Daddy had taken firm control of the situation, and it's fortunate for the later police investigation that Big Daddy was in charge. In his business or in his private life, William Wooldridge Dillard, Sr., never goes off half-cocked. While he shared—or *personified,* actually—his family's feelings that if Richard had harmed Nancy, then he was going to pay for his crime, Big Daddy maintained the presence of mind not to zealously muddy the investigative water. If he was going to engineer a campaign against Richard Lyon, he was going to do it up right.

No one involved will say exactly what was the source, but it's obvious that from the outset the Dillards had help in building their case. After all, neither the hospital staff nor the Dillard family are criminal lawyers, but the careful manner in which these laymen went about dropping a noose around Richard's neck reeks of legal assistance. Technically, the Dallas Police Department had no cause to get involved at that point because, first of all, the Dillards had no concrete evidence that any crime had occurred. Furthermore, the hospital didn't have Nancy's blood sample back from the lab as yet, so for all the police knew she could merely be having a bout of indigestion. But whether the cops supplied behind-the-scenes instructions to the Dillards—as is often the case when the police are without cause to investigate, but nonetheless suspect foul play—or one of the many private attorneys at Big Daddy's disposal furnished advice, it's apparent that the private investigation which went on during Nancy's final hours in the hospital wasn't any amateur affair.

There is a portion of every criminal trial through which spectators and jurors alike generally doze. This excruciating proceeding is known as chain of custody testimony, and consists of a seemingly endless string of witnesses—policemen, ballistics experts, forensics people, and private citizens—who take the stand, look at a gun, knife, or other article that the prosecutor shows them, and tell where they've seen the item before, how it came into their possession, and what they did with the item when it left their custody. It's boring and rather silly, but chain of custody testimony is a vital part of the criminal justice system.

Without precise knowledge of where each piece of evidence has been since its discovery, and through whose hands the evidence has passed, there's no way to know whether the evidence has been tampered with, or indeed if the piece on display in the courtroom is the actual evidence at all. Defense attorneys do their damnedest to shoot holes in chain of custody testimony because unless the prosecution has done its homework, the evidence might not be admissible. Under Big Daddy's guidance, and playing by the rules furnished by legal experts unknown, the Dillard family and hospital staff proceeded to build an evidentiary case against Richard Lyon that would be the envy of the finest professional investigator. It is somewhat ironic that the wine and pills—which everyone assumed at the time to be critical— were handled so carefully and expertly by amateurs, while the later police investigation allowed other evidence against Richard to slip between the cracks like so much hourglass sand.

Physically retrieving the wine bottle and the capsule container from the trunk of Lynn Pease's car wasn't going to be a problem. While Nancy's mother, father, sister, and sister-in-law kept Richard occupied with meaningless conversation in the waiting room, Bill Dillard, Jr., and Lynn Pease secretly left the hospital.

Bill Jr. was sober and alert, as he had been for over a year at the time, and more so than the rest of the Dillard clan, he had reason to prove himself. For one thing, he had the recovering addict's feeling of remorse over his past conduct, and for another, his distrust of Richard was nearly as strong as his concern for his sister. If Big Daddy was to be the voice of reason in the relentless pursuit of Richard Lyon over the following year, Bill Jr. was to be its driving force. It was his chance to make some amends, and he wasn't about to let the opportunity get away from him.

Lynn and Bill Jr. went to the repair shop, where her old heap lay in drydock with a haywire alternator, retrieved the key from the attendant on duty, and found the Zoomobile parked at the rear of the shop on bald, dusty tires. Bill Jr. inserted the key in the trunk and turned. Rusty hinges creaked as the lid rose crankily upward. There the wine and pills were, behind some cardboard boxes of God-knows-what; Lynn is an incurable hoarder and the trunk of her car contains things that would drive Fibber

McGee bananas. Slowly, carefully, using latex gloves so as not to disturb any prints, Bill Jr. and Lynn carried the wine and pills back to Presbyterian Hospital. In order to be certain that they wouldn't bump into Richard by accident, the two used the downstairs emergency room entry to carry the items inside.

Kim Grayson, a pert redheaded R.N. with an elfin spray of freckles across the bridge of her nose, was on duty in the intensive care unit when Lynn and Bill Jr. arrived, and Kim well knew what was going on. Carefully avoiding the waiting room where Richard still sat near his wife's family, Kim stole downstairs. She took the wine and capsules from Lynn and Bill Jr., then toted them back up to ICU. With Misty Don Thornton, another registered nurse, as a witness, Kim carefully labeled the items "Room 103—Do Not Touch," and placed them in a storage cabinet in ICU. There the wine and capsules were to remain until after Nancy died, when the police would take them in for testing. Kim Grayson, Misty Don Thornton, and Lynn Pease were to give chain of custody testimony in regard to the wine and capsules at Richard Lyon's trial, with Bill Jr. available for backup in case anything should happen to Lynn.

Also while Nancy Lyon was at Presbyterian, two old school chums of hers brought various portions of food from the Lyon duplex, but these items were only those that Richard had selected and pointed out. The police lab later ran the foodstuffs, wine, and gelatin caps through a series of tests. None of the carefully preserved items revealed the barest trace of arsenic.

In hearing the story of any criminal investigation composed of intricate legal maneuvering, the after-the-fact listener inevitably finds portions of the tale hard to swallow. Just as suspects make clumsy attempts at cover-ups—the results of which are often the suspects' undoing—the gymnastics performed by police and prosecutors in firming up their cases are sometimes less than Olympic quality.

Much later, at Richard Lyon's trial, Dr. Ali Bagheri was to testify as to what he had done once Big Daddy had clued Bagheri in on the Dillard family's suspicions. While very possibly accurate as a Swiss timepiece, Dr. Bagheri's recollections tend to give the imagination somewhat of a hernia. If one gives the doctor the benefit of the doubt and assumes that his testimony is right on target, then one must also wonder if Bagheri, under the pressure of the investigation going on in the unit where he worked, completely took leave of his senses. The most logical explanation of the doctor's testimony is that he received legal advice from the same source as the Dillard family—more than likely from the police or district attorney's office, though neither had officially entered the case as yet. Like the Dillard family's handling of the evidence against Richard, Dr. Bagheri's activities were choreographed as if he spent the entire day thinking of ways to make his future testimony admissible.

Anyone who's watched one of a thousand TV courtroom dramas knows that when a lawyer leaps to his feet, nostrils flared, and shouts, "Objection. *Hearsay*," this generally means that the other side is pulling a fast one. Even the greenest neophyte understands that courtroom witnesses are supposed to testify only what they *know*, and may not tell what they've *heard* someone *say*. Simple rule, what? Now, anyone who believes that the hearsay rule is simple will please line up to purchase some Kennedy motorcade maps, autographed by Mr. Lee Harvey Oswald himself fifteen minutes before he made his fatal walk into the muzzle of Jack Ruby's gun.

Basically the rule goes something like this: If A tells B that C buried Jimmy Hoffa underneath Trump Tower, B can't testify against C in court unless A is also present so that C (who by this time will be in a world of hurt) can have his lawyer cross-examine the originator of the statement. The inadmissibility of hearsay testimony is a basic defendants' right. In the Lyon case, Nancy would be A, and no one who'd heard her stories about Richard's suspicious behavior in the months preceding Nancy's death could tell these stories in the courtroom because Nancy, of course, wouldn't be there for Richard's lawyer to cross-examine.

Since hearsay evidence is a real hurdle for the prosecution in a murder case (the victim is *never* present in the courtroom, of course, so the statements of the victim are hearsay), policemen and district attorneys have spent decades developing methods for evading the rule. Quite a few of these methods have won the ap-

proval of the appellate courts; therefore in today's murder prosecutions, in addition to the hearsay rule we now have a list of
exceptions whereby hearsay statements of the victim are made
admissible. In the modern courtroom, hearsay ain't hearsay until
the judge says it is.

So the best way to make Dr. Bagheri's testimony effective at
Richard's trial was to coordinate his movements so that (1) what
he had to say fell under one of the exceptions to the hearsay rule,
and (2) there would be no one to refute the doctor's story. The
first problem wasn't a problem at all; two exceptions to the hearsay rule are deathbed statements of the victim (so that when the
policeman rushes in to find the store clerk dying of a gunshot
wound, and the clerk—heard only by the policeman, of course—
identifies his killer, then the policeman can point the finger in
court) and medical testimony of those treating the victim in the
final hours (Doctor: What's wrong with you, Willie? Willie: [gasping
for breath] Old Joe, he done blowed me away with a shotgun). Dr.
Bagheri's testimony, if properly coached, could fall into either
category.

But making certain that no one could refute the doctor's testimony required having Bagheri talk to Nancy when no one else
was present. All during her hospital stay, people were constantly
at Nancy's bedside. Though she could receive outside visitors
only once an hour, Richard had free access to his wife, and except for the time he spent in the waiting room talking to family
and friends, Richard hovered over Nancy at all hours.

The above lengthy discourse aside, there is no evidence whatsoever that Dr. Bagheri's story on the witness stand was
stretched in the slightest, nor is there any evidence that the good
doctor received any coaching in reconstructing the events as they
happened. It's just that, assuming that he is telling it as it is—and
also keeping in mind that he had no legal training—his actions
were . . . well, quite convenient for the prosecution in the case to
be entitled The State of Texas v. Richard Allan Abood Lyon. What
follows is Dr. Ali Bagheri's story exactly as related in the courtroom.

It was late morning when Big Daddy stopped the doctor in the
corridor to relay the family's suspicion that Nancy was the victim

of foul play. There was almost a hundred percent chance that Richard had poisoned Nancy, Big Daddy said, and the stories that Nancy had told her divorce attorney, sister, and sister-in-law were critical to finding out exactly what had made Nancy sick. The situation was urgent, and while she was still in a coherent state, someone needed to hear her story from her own lips. Something Nancy knew could be the key to saving her.

Armed with the knowledge that his patient probably wasn't suffering from toxic shock syndrome at all, but had likely fallen prey to intentional poisoning, for the next ten hours Dr. Bagheri proceeded to do exactly nothing in regard to Nancy Lyon. He didn't run to his supervisor with the news, and he didn't call the police. He didn't hail the nurses aside, indicate Richard Lyon from afar, and whisper, "Watch that guy. He may be a wife poisoner." So unconcerned was Dr. Bagheri, in fact, that he continued on his normal rounds for the balance of his shift, making certain that all other patients in ICU *except* for Nancy received the various medications and treatments that their attending physicians had ordered. At the two o'clock shift change, Dr. Bagheri went home, bathed, had his dinner, and got a few hours' rest before returning to duty at eight. The graveyard shift was more than an hour along before Bagheri decided that it was time to pay Nancy a visit.

When Richard's attorneys questioned Bagheri at trial, the doctor's explanation for the time lapse between his conversation with Big Daddy and his visit with Nancy was that he was waiting for an opportunity to see the patient when Richard wasn't around. That may be so, but there were numerous times during the day and evening when Richard left his wife's bedside. Bagheri himself complained that Richard was bugging the staff constantly about Nancy's condition (at one point, when Richard asked what the hospital was doing for Nancy, Bagheri replied, "We're running tests." When Richard pursued the issue, saying, "Such as what?" Bagheri turned and walked away without a word), and it's quite doubtful that Richard could effectively "bug" the staff without leaving Nancy alone.

There are a couple of explanations for the doctor's testimony other than that, on hearing that Nancy may have been poisoned, he went blithely on his way, and in analyzing the case that the state later brought against Richard, both alternatives bear some thought. The first possibility—that Bagheri was in reality waiting for instructions from the police and district attorney as to the proper method of questioning Nancy—is rather harmless in the scheme of justice. Since the authorities had no probable cause—no evidence of foul play—to investigate at that point, that the police might issue behind-the-scenes instructions is both understandable and proper. This is particularly true if Richard had indeed murdered his wife.

The second explanation for Bagheri's testimony—that the entire scenario was constructed after the fact so that Nancy's stories could be told in court through the doctor's lips, and that Bagheri's meeting with Nancy in fact never occurred—is, of course, something that those dependent on the justice system for right don't even like to contemplate. That Dr. Bagheri, the only witness available to the prosecution whose testimony about Nancy's stories would be admissible, had an eleventh-hour conversation with the victim must be simply the luck of the draw. Dr. Bagheri is, after all, a man of medicine, with no bone to pick on either side, and has no motive to fabricate anything.

Or does he? That's something we'll get to later on.

Nonetheless, to continue with Bagheri's story, after he'd returned to duty on the late shift, he entered the darkened room where Nancy Lyon lay on death's doorstep. Since Nancy had entered the hospital she'd undergone a transformation that wasn't pretty. A slim, attractive woman only a day earlier, Nancy was now puffily swollen. (The bloating effect was partially due to the poisoning, but another sad part of the story of Nancy's death is contained in hospital records. Because the patient couldn't keep any liquids down, one of the staff had inserted a catheter directly into her body for fluid transmission, and a doctor's remark on Nancy's bedside record takes note that the catheter was dangerously close to her heart. The catheter did in fact eventually puncture the vena cava—the large vessel leading to the heart—and cause internal bleeding, and Nancy's swollen condition was for the most part due to the blood leakage inside her body.) She couldn't speak above a whisper. Dr. Bagheri bent over Nancy's bed and gently asked if she could tell him anything that might lead her to believe that she was the victim of poisoning.

According to Bagheri, Nancy told him in a faint, halting voice about the wine and pills left on her doorstep, and she told him another story as well. She said that the previous September, Richard had taken her to see the movie *Pretty Woman*, and during the show he'd left the darkened theater and brought her a Coke. The drink was so bitter that Nancy took a mouthful and then spat it out, at which time Richard became enraged and told her to drink the soft drink regardless of how it tasted. Nancy told Dr. Bagheri that she'd noticed a white powder floating on the liquid's surface, and that she refused to drink any more of the Coke in spite of Richard's anger. Also, according to Dr. Bagheri's testimony, Nancy said that she was violently sick all night after the movie. The Coke-in-the-movie story, in addition to the tale about the wine and the capsules, were both stories that Nancy had told her attorney, sister, and sister-in-law.

Having heard Nancy's tale, Bagheri then left the patient. According to him, as he reached the door, Nancy called out, "Oh, please, Doctor. Please don't let me die." Those were the last words that anyone was to hear from Nancy Dillard Lyon.

Despite Nancy's tearful revelation, according to Bagheri he continued on his rounds. He didn't prescribe any poison treatment, and he didn't request a hurry-up on the testing of the blood sample drawn from Nancy in the emergency room. The toxology screen results, in fact, didn't arrive from the out-of-state lab until January 15, one day after Nancy died.

There is another facet to Dr. Bagheri's testimony that gives one pause, this having to do with the records according to Nancy's duty nurse. By the nurse's written record, she entered Nancy's room around 4:00 P.M., several hours before Dr. Bagheri's visit, and found the patient thrashing about on the bed. Nancy had pulled the breathing tube from her throat and had cast her oxygen mask aside, and at the time the nurse found her, Nancy constantly kicked her feet off the side of the bed and begged, nearly incoherently, to go home.

The nurse made the decision that, for Nancy's own protection, the patient needed restraint. With an orderly to assist her, the nurse then shackled Nancy's hands and feet and tied a strap around her middle to keep her in the bed. Finally the nurse put Nancy's breathing tube back in place and replaced the oxygen mask over Nancy's mouth and nose.

A short time after the doctor's visit, also according to hospital records, Nancy's vital organs began to fail. Around nine-thirty in the evening, the night doctor on duty ordered Nancy placed on life support. She was to remain on such life support until January 14 when, with consent from the family and the advice of the attending physicians, the staff mercifully pulled the plug. When the staff placed her on the life-support machine, hospital records note that they removed her oxygen mask and breathing tube. Other than the conversation to which Dr. Bagheri later testified, there is no written record of Nancy speaking a word after the nurse placed her in restraints. Therefore, once again assuming that Nancy did tell the doctor the Richard-damning stories in the darkness of her room, the entire conversation took place while she had a breathing tube down her throat, and while her mouth and nose were covered by an oxygen mask.

Nonetheless, there can be no doubt that Nancy told the stories to her lawyer, her sister, and her sister-in-law, and that the stories alone were plenty of reason to suspect Richard of murdering his wife. Whether or not the doctor's testimony was accurate is a matter for the conscience of the justice system.

It isn't clear just when a hospital gathering of concerned friends and relatives becomes a death watch, but there is a time when the mood changes. Waiting-room voices diminish in volume and all attempts at humor cease. Conversation slows. Men jam their hands into pants pockets and stare dully at the floor. Women show vacant smiles.

All members of the Dillard clan have a trait in common. They don't show outward emotion. Big Daddy is Big Daddy regardless of the circumstances, polite to a fault, majestically businesslike. His smiles are quick to appear and even quicker to fade. The rest of the family follow his example; even Bill Jr. accepts good fortune and faces adversity with the same demeanor. It hasn't always been so with him, but now that he has the upper hand over drugs and alcohol, he grows more like his father every day.

So the mood change among the group gathered in the waiting room at Presbyterian Hospital was a bit harder to recognize than in most such gatherings, but the shift in attitude was there nonetheless. On the morning of January 11, when word spread that

Nancy was now on life support, gloom set in. The family continued to visit Nancy once an hour, two at a time, but whereas they'd previously offered her words of encouragement and even played tapes of her children singing and talking to their mother, bedside callers now stood mutely by while the tireless machine breathed in and out, in and out, pumping air into helpless lungs.

The woman who lay silently in a coma as her life ebbed away was not the same vivacious Nancy her friends and family remembered. The puffy face hidden behind the breathing mask was barely recognizable; for the three days that Nancy was on life support she never woke up, never spoke a word. Just a few miles to the north, two lonely little girls wondered when their mother was coming home. Children Allison and Anna's age have no real understanding of death. They would ask about their mother for many months to come; likely for the rest of their lives, they will never understand why their mother left them.

During the early parts of the vigil, the Dillard family's attitude toward Richard Lyon had changed from concern (when they'd first learned that Nancy was sick) to coldly aloof (when their suspicion of Richard had grown) to outwardly accepting (as the gathering of evidence behind Richard's back went into full swing). Now that it was apparent that Nancy was going to die, the Dillards became stoic toward Nancy's husband. It was as if they wanted to devote their attention only to Nancy during her final hours, leaving whatever they had in store for Richard until she was gone.

For Richard's part, he now had his own gathering of loved ones. His father, Allan, and his mother, Rosemary, had flown in from Connecticut to be with their son, and the Lyon family set up their own private watch in a separate waiting room downstairs. Allan Lyon is a short man with a slight middle-aged paunch and curly graying hair. Richard's mother is small and dark, obviously the source of Richard's good looks. Like Allison and Anna, Richard's parents will never quite understand what happened. As the tragedy unfolded, they did what they could to be a comfort to Richard. Other than stiffly formal greetings, few words passed between Richard's folks and Nancy's family, but that had little to do with the gravity of the situation. The two groups of in-laws had not been close during the entire marriage.

So as afternoon moved into evening and another dreary day passed, two opposing factions sat in different hospital waiting rooms. They had two more days of gloom before Nancy died.

On January 11, one well-wisher dropped by who was not particularly welcome—at least not to the Dillard family. The visitor was named David Bagwell, a slender brown-haired man who'd attended the same high school as Nancy. Later he'd worked with her. The Dillard family had reason to be distrustful of the man; in fact, it was somewhat of a surprise that Bagwell would visit the hospital at all.

After his visit, as he was leaving, Bagwell encountered Richard just outside the waiting room. The two men shook hands and engaged in serious conversation as they walked together down the hallway to the elevators. They continued to chat as Bagwell pressed the Down button, and Richard waited until the elevator doors closed with Bagwell inside the car before returning to the waiting room.

It was a harmless meeting, a supporter comforting a bereaved husband in time of need, but Richard would remember the incident. In the year to come, in fact, David Bagwell's name would surface many times.

During the time that Nancy fought in vain for her life, there was yet another Bagwell moving about the corridors of Presbyterian. This Bagwell is named John. He is a doctor, and he is David Bagwell's older brother.

John Bagwell is a cancer specialist, and he doesn't normally practice at Presbyterian. Crosstown Baylor Medical Center is his usual stomping grounds, though he does duty at Presbyterian occasionally under another doctor's contract. His presence at Presbyterian during Nancy's final hours was pure chance, nothing more; there's no official record that John Bagwell ever paid a visit to Nancy Lyon's room at any time. But just as David Bagwell's visit was indelibly etched in Richard's memory, John Bagwell's presence at Presbyterian struck home to Richard as well. Along with Bill Dillard, Jr., the Bagwell brothers were to become odd-shaped pieces to a puzzle that Richard Lyon would frantically strive to assemble in his own defense.

The thirteenth of January fell on a Sunday, and as church pews filled for morning services all over Dallas, a duty doctor paused in Nancy Lyon's room at Presbyterian. He stood at the foot of her bed for a few moments, his expression gentle as the life support's air pump moved up and down in a series of hisses and the monitor beeped in toneless monotony. Finally the doctor sighed, adjusted his pale green smock, and stepped to the bed-side table to examine Nancy's chart. He thumbed through the clipboarded pages, his brow knotted as he searched in vain for the answer. There was no answer. He sadly shook his head.

Finally, reluctantly, the doctor began to write. He noted Nancy's current vital signs, noted the different procedures at-tempted over the past five days, then paused to gaze once more at the still form beneath the covers. Nancy's chest rose and fell in rhythm with the breathing apparatus, but otherwise there was no movement, no reflexive eyelash flutter, nothing. One corner of the doctor's mouth tugged reflectively to one side as he bent his head to write once more. His final entry on her chart was brief but caring: "There is nothing left for us to do but offer our con-dolences to the family." Before he left, the doctor duly noted the time: 10:42 A.M.

Big Daddy flew into an uncharacteristic rage around three o'clock in the afternoon, when he came to Nancy's bedside to find nurses and staff surrounding her, and Richard alone in one corner of the room. "My son says you're turning off her life sup-port," Big Daddy said. He swept the room with a cold-eyed gaze.

Nurses and attendants watched the floor and, vacantly, so did Richard. "Who authorized this?" Big Daddy demanded.

One of the nurses spoke up timidly. "Her husband," she said, nodding toward Richard. "Mr. Lyon over there."

Big Daddy angrily pointed a finger. "You don't touch her. You don't remove her life support until you get the okay from her mother and me." The tremor in his voice was tempered with helpless grief.

The hospital staff and the nurses looked futilely at one another. Richard was Nancy's husband and, officially, removal of the life support was Richard's call and his alone. Big Daddy ignored Richard and continued to glare.

Finally the head nurse nodded in agreement. At her order the staff people left Nancy's bedside and went out into the hall. Richard and Big Daddy were alone with Nancy for a moment. They didn't exchange a word. At long last Richard also left, his eyes downcast. Big Daddy stood by the bed, his head bowed, and finally reached out to pat Nancy's hand. Then he moved on, his stride determined as he walked the corridors in search of the doctor in charge.

As it turned out, Big Daddy had only postponed the inevitable. That evening, Nancy's family—including Richard, but by now no one in the hospital doubted who had the final say—met with the doctors who'd treated Nancy. Somberly, tearfully, Nancy's parents and siblings listened to the physicians, one at a time, outline the helplessness of the situation. The doctors had tried everything, every treatment, every medication. Nancy's liver and kidneys had failed, and her other vital organs showed no responses. While the machine continued to pump air to her lungs and blood through her body, Nancy was in fact already clinically dead. Big Daddy listened to the report, conferred with Sue and his children, then agreed that all hope was lost. Nancy's life support would be removed the following day.

Grieved though they were, the Dillards hadn't been idle. Bill Jr. and Big Daddy had already had private conversations with the hospital staff and, unbeknownst to Richard, the county medical examiner stood ready to perform an autopsy. Bill Jr. had received some private instructions from the M.E., and once Nancy was officially no longer among the living, Bill Jr. knew exactly what to do. Even as the Dillards sadly accepted the doctors' words, the legal processes against Richard shifted into high gear.

The following morning, Monday, January 14, the fight for Nancy Dillard Lyon's life came to an end. Quietly and efficiently, with Richard, Big Daddy, and Bill Jr. standing nearby, the staff disconnected Nancy's life support. The form within the bed ceased to breathe and became still for all eternity.

Once the disconnection process was over, Bill Jr. stepped to the bedside. Gently but firmly, using scissors borrowed from a corridor nurse, he cut his dead younger sister's hair and carefully stored the clippings in a plastic bag. If anyone present wondered what he was doing, they didn't ask questions.

Nothing in life hurts like the loss of a child. No parent whose son or daughter has died can explain the depths of the aching emptiness, the constant pain of living on once a child is gone. People expect their mother and dad to someday die. But their son or daughter? Never. As Nancy lay forever silent at Presbyterian, Big Daddy and Sue felt the agony for the second time in less than a decade. Younger son Tom's death had been devastating, but Tom had been a cancer victim. Nancy's senseless dying at the peak of her life hurt even more.

The official hospital record attributed Nancy's death to septic shock, but that was only a temporary finding until the county medical examiner's report. With regard to the pending autopsy on Nancy's remains, the hospital staff had a problem. Without permission of the next of kin, autopsy could happen only by court order, and the time required for such a process would likely call for exhumation since Nancy's funeral was only two days away. Ironically, the only person who could give approval to send Nancy's body to the medical examiner was the prime suspect in her death. Hesitantly, fully expecting him to decline, hospital personnel asked Richard to sign the consent form.

Surprisingly, he didn't hesitate. His expression stoic, he signed his permission on the consent form without batting an eye. It wasn't the last time that he would fail to act like a guilty man; however, even though he approved the autopsy and was well aware of its existence, in the months to follow he was never to inquire as to the medical examiner's findings, and his lack of curiosity about the cause of Nancy's death would contribute greatly to the case against him. Next of kin's permission granted, the hospital detoured Nancy's body to the medical examiner en route to the funeral home.

After Richard had signed the autopsy form, he rode home to his duplex with his good friend and business associate, Gary Perkins. Perkins, a raw-boned, no-nonsense subcontractor who'd met Richard on one of the many construction jobs that he supervised, has no doubt that Richard's grief over Nancy's death was real. During the ten-minute drive, Richard sat morosely in the passenger seat and cradled Nancy's running shoes in his lap, his gaze vacantly on the passing landscape. Richard was crying, and his voice broke as he spoke of his wife as if she were still alive. When Perkins parked in front of the duplex, Richard sat for a moment and stared at the floorboard before finally climbing down into his yard. Before he went inside, he wondered tearfully what to say to Allison and Anna. Gary Perkins had no answer for his friend.

Back at the hospital, Big Daddy moved into action. He was totally convinced that Richard is guilty, just as many who know Richard quite well are certain of his innocence, and as long as there was breath in Big Daddy, he would do everything within his power to see that his daughter's murderer paid for his crime. Big Daddy had a brief meeting with Bill Jr., and father and son planned strategy. In spite of his wealth of energy, Big Daddy was getting on in years, and in the time to come he was to lean heavily on his one remaining son for support. Bill Jr. was not to let his father down. Once the two surviving Dillard men had finished their talk, Big Daddy called the Dallas Police Department and asked the operator for Homicide.

* * *

Although Nancy died within the city limits of Dallas, the Lyon duplex where she presumably received her fatal dose is in Park Cities, and these two facts presented a problem of venue. Park Cities—or the Town of University Park, to be exact, which along with its sister city Highland Park combines to form the Park Cities—is a separate municipality with its own fire and police departments, and like any ghettoless wealthy community, University Park has a very low crime rate. Murder is a rarity, rape nearly unheard of, drug busts generally limited to a few hand-rolled joints in the pockets of experimenting teenagers. Under flexible Texas law, either the University Park or Dallas police could have headed the investigation into Nancy's death. Though not having the homicide experience of the grittier Dallas force, the University Park police would have had more time to devote to the case, but pinpointing the exact location where Nancy took the poison was going to be difficult. What if, for example, Richard had slipped his wife an arsenic-laced drink en route to the hospital after he'd crossed the boundary line? With that problem in mind, the University Park police took a back seat and left the bulk of the investigation up to the more burdened Dallas cops. Whether or not it was fortunate that the City of Dallas became the lead investigative unit in Nancy's death is a point of contention.

Dallas, a city that constantly sticks out its chest over its progress, continues to treat its police department like an unwanted stepchild. A mile to the southeast of the glistening new city hall and public library, law enforcement labors on in the same surroundings it has occupied since the thirties. The underground police garage through which Jack Ruby walked to his rendezvous with destiny thirty years ago is still in use, and so is the old city jail.

Main police headquarters, next door to the jail and garage, is a four-story building of ancient stone block on the eastern edge of downtown Dallas, surrounded by storefront single-stories that house boxing gyms, bail bondsmen, and stand-up barbecue restaurants. The chiseled inscription, "Municipal Building," has weathered to the point that the words are barely discernible, and the once majestic steps leading from street level to the second-floor main entry are littered with trash and pigeon droppings. In fact, the main entry is seldom used anymore, and is often pad-locked. Visitors and officers alike generally enter and leave the building through the basement, descending a dusty stone stair-case through two sets of double doors. At night the basement steps are an ideal sleeping place for druggies, drunks, and drift-ers. At times, depending on the mood of the current police chief—the office of the main city law enforcement mogul has, in recent years, contained a revolving door—night-duty personnel vigorously keep the homeless at bay, but on other occasions per-mit street people to snore on uninterrupted and step over the slumbering bodies on their way in and out of police headquar-ters.

Rundown as is the exterior of Dallas' main police headquar-ters, the inside of the building is even more in need of a face-lift and, some say, even poses a health hazard. The walls are loaded with cancer-causing asbestos; in places there are holes in the sheetrock. Clerical personnel make do with gray government-issue desks and metal chairs, and store records in old green steel file cabinets. The computer system is modern and up-to-date, though the furniture on which the monitors sit is anything but, and the sharply creased navy blue uniforms of the officers seem out of place in the delapidated surroundings.

Stone-faced plainclothes detectives report to the third floor, where they work in one of two divisions: Crimes Against Prop-erty (investigating theft and burglary mainly) and Crimes Against Persons. Crimes Against Persons handles just what the name implies, and within the division are further breakdowns: Assault (including rape), Robbery, Homicide.

Of the several thousand felonies committed annually in the city of Dallas, less than four hundred involve murder. Drunken barroom shootings and stabbings are the bulk of the lot, followed by husband- or wife-killings and murders committed during rob-beries. In recent years a disturbing number of teenagers have been involved, mostly black underprivileged kids with a boiling anger against the society that has deprived them. Park Cities poisonings are definitely outside the norm.

Case assignments in Homicide are the luck of the draw, and often depend on which detective happens to be lounging in the office when the call comes in to the lieutenant-in-charge. *Lady found a stiff in the alley behind the Drop Inn Bar, Harry. Get off your ass and get out there.* The original inquiry into the death of Nancy Dillard Lyon wasn't a high-priority item because, first of all, there wasn't any concrete evidence that there had been a murder at all. There was no disfigured corpse, no bloody hatchet, no smoking gun. With hundreds of active homicide investigations in progress, the Dallas police were naturally to place a *possible* murder on the far back burner. Whatever preliminary inquiries were made into the Lyon case went on the department's assignment sheet under the already burdensome case load of Homicide detective Donald Ortega.

Don Ortega is a short, round-faced man with smooth olive-complexioned skin. He is given to light-colored suits and ties and speaks in a soft and pleasant tenor with just the barest trace of a Hispanic accent. Ortega doesn't joke much, and regards the world through heavy-lidded, I'm-suspicious eyes; as a twenty-year murder cop he's seen 'em come and seen 'em go. He is a private man, both in his personal life and in the cases he investigates. He doesn't like newspaper people and lets it show; other than his public testimony from the witness stand he has no comment for eager reporters. Up until he handled the Lyon investigation, Ortega had shunned publicity like the plague. He didn't know it as yet, but as he was assigned the death of Nancy Lyon, Don Ortega's life was about to change.

Crime victims make good prosecutorial props, tearfully outlining their devastation in front of sympathetic jurors, but the cold, hard fact is that victims receive little comfort from the system. To detectives with an impossible load of cases, inquiries from victims are often considered bothersome hindrances in the process of getting the job done. When Big Daddy's call came in on January 14, Ortega had little to go on and said so. Without the medical examiner's report—and with the hospital staff's official finding that Nancy had died from septic shock—the Dallas Police Department was without cause to officially enter the case at all.

With most crime victims, Ortega's statement of his lack of cause would have ended the issue until the M.E.'s report—which wasn't to come for eleven weeks—but William Wooldridge Dillard, Sr., is far from your normal victim. Putting Big Daddy off where his little girl's murder was concerned, the police were to find, wasn't going to be easy. Big Daddy was insistent. He had information for the police, and he wanted action *now*. Somewhat reluctantly, Ortega agreed to meet with Big Daddy on the following day. Gazing about the homicide office, at the old desks and chairs, at the gashes in the sheetrock, Ortega decided that main police headquarters wouldn't be the best place to meet with a distinguished citizen from Highland Park, and set up his initial conference with the victim's father at the department's central substation.

The central substation is the nearest Dallas police facility to Big Daddy's office at 2001 Bryan Tower, and while its interior is newer and in better condition than main police headquarters, the neighborhood isn't any more exclusive. The big white buildings of the substation sit beside Thornton Freeway just north of the state fairgrounds, and on a certain October afternoon each autumn the roar of the Texas–O.U. crowd in the nearby jam-packed Cotton Bowl assaults the visitor's ears. Glass double doors lead from the parking lot into a wide, pleasant lobby. The station's interior is spotless, done in greens and beige, easy on the eyes. Detective Ortega met with Big Daddy in a small conference room off the lobby just after noon on January 15, even as Nancy's body lay with the medical examiner. Her funeral service was scheduled for the following day.

"I got to tell you there are a lot of problems here," Ortega said. "It seems like a lot of red tape, I know, but we can't even say right now that Mrs. Lyon died from poison. That's what the medical examiner's for."

Big Daddy raised a hand, palm out. "I know you have your rules. But if somebody doesn't do something, he's going to have time to cover things."

Ortega sighed. He wished there weren't so many details himself. His job could be so much simpler. But building a murder case against someone is about ten percent action and ninety percent attending to details. "Mr. Dillard, we know the longer this hangs fire, the less chance there is of finding what we're looking for. Most cases if you got no answer within a few days, the trail gets cold. But I can't help it. To look for anything on Mr. Lyon's property, we got to have a warrant. To get the warrant we got to have probable cause to conduct a search, and without a finding that a murder's happened we're helpless." The detective sadly shook his head. "I'm sorry. I really am."

"He was having an affair," Bill Sr. said. "We know he bought poison."

Ortega's interest picked up. "How do you know that?"

"We have canceled checks."

Ortega frowned and leaned back in his chair. "His personal checks?"

"Drawn on a joint account," Bill Sr. said. "His and Nancy's."

"I got to tell you, sir. A man planning something like that, it's not likely he'd give a check. Especially not a check that his wife's going to see." Skepticism is what makes Ortega a good detective; someone has to show him.

Big Daddy's expression was drawn, his eyes red from lack of sleep. "It's what we have to go on. And this other woman—"

"Mr. Dillard. Look, I know this is killing your family. If it was my daughter . . . well, I'm not sure what I'd do. But a lot of men have affairs. It's not that much to build a case on, not these days."

"What about the wine and pills, the things he left on her doorstep?"

"We can analyze those," Ortega said. "Since they're at the hospital, we need no warrant. But how do we know Mr. Lyon's the one that left them? Anybody see him?"

Big Daddy lowered his gaze. "No."

"That's what I'm talking about. Even if the stuff is loaded with poison—"

Big Daddy clenched his hands into fists. "There's got to be something we can do."

Ortega studied the older man. Homicide cops see grief on a regular basis, but Big Daddy's was tempered with a steely determination. Noting the thrust of the smooth-skinned jaw and the slight trembling of the thin upper lip, Ortega thought that if Nancy's husband had in fact murdered his wife, then Ortega would hate to be in his shoes. Big Daddy was the type not to give up. "From the beginning," Ortega said. "And take your time, sir. Detail for detail, tell me why you think your son-in-law did this."

Big Daddy thought for a long time. Finally he said, "He's always depended on her, ever since they were married."

"And how long is that?" Ortega said. "Please. Don't leave anything out. Any detail can be important."

Big Daddy's gaze shifted slightly upward. He was remembering. Finally he said, "Well, they met at Harvard, when they were both in graduate school. Is that too far back?"

Ortega smiled. "It might be and it might not be. You never know. Whatever, it's a start. Yeah, why don't you begin with that?"

If there is an ideal place in this land of ours for a couple of future yups to meet and fall in love, it's a half-hour hop on the T northwest of downtown Boston. The Park Street station is within easy walking distance from Central Boston hotels, and tourists who fail to spend the buck to ride the T out to Cambridge are missing one of the cheaper treats in the birthplace of freedom. The train runs underground for a time, then emerges to cross over the majestic River Charles, clicks softly through pleasant New England countryside dotted with homes like American history textbook prints, and eventually deposits the passenger in Cambridge near the intersection of Massachusetts Avenue and Boylston Street. From there it's a two-block stroll past delicious-smelling bakeries, a couple of ice cream shops, and a bookstore with the intriguing name of Wordsworth's—which displays copies of Spenser mystery novels by Boston's own Robert B. Parker in its windows—to the main entrance at Harvard. There's a well-kept Revolutionary War graveyard at the campus entry, surrounded by a low iron fence (just as there is a Revolutionary War graveyard every block or so in the rest of the Boston area), and to the first-time visitor who's only heard of the place, the university itself is somewhat of a surprise.

The legacy of Harvard conjures up images of ancient red brick walls choked with twisting English ivy, scowling bearded professors whose expressions look as though a smile would shatter their faces, and harried students laboring through the night by kerosene lanterns in Oliver Twist cubbyholes. The reality of the campus is quite, quite different from the myth. There are wide expanses of perfectly clipped and sculpted lawn, straight tall trees overlooking the classroom buildings and dorms like watchful palace guards. Handsome young men and lovely young women wrinkle cheerful noses at one another as they pass on the sidewalks. Students dress down; there are pea coats, hiking boots, khaki pants, castoff army shirts. In sunny weather, joggers exhibit long and muscular legs in drab gray running shorts as they loosen up on the campus trails, and bluebirds hop and twit among well-pruned branches. From nearby courts echo the muted *k-pop*'s of tennis games. There are a few old fuddy-duddies left at modern Harvard to be sure, but they are only statues, and even the stone faces of the Oliver Wendell Holmeses and such scattered about display a kinder set to their mouths than one would imagine. Such was the scene in the warm early fall of 1979.

A bonus to students at schools like Harvard—and a good excuse for college recruiters to use in explaining tuition rates that would drive a Rockefeller into shock—is that classes are small. As opposed to state universities, where professors lecture in auditoriums with audiences the size of crowds at Broadway hits, Harvard classes are quite intimate. Twenty students, twenty-five at the most is the norm. With Harvard's limited enrollment, professors are easily accessible for out-of-class coaching, and the students get to know one another. At a larger college Nancy and Richard might never have met. As it was, the dark-eyed brownette from Texas caught the studious Connecticut boy's eye on the very first day of school, in their very first class together. Before the opening lecture was halfway done, the soon-to-fall-in-love young couple were shooting furtive glances at each other across the classroom.

Richard Allan (for his father) Abood (his mother's Lebanese maiden name) Lyon had traveled a far different road to Harvard than had Nancy Dillard. Richard was from rural northeastern Connecticut, having alternated the years of his upbringing between the towns of Willimantic and Mansfield, honest little burgs that lie a stone's throw apart across cleared farmland and heavily wooded areas. Allan Lyon sold life insurance to support his family of five (Richard is the eldest; he has a younger brother and sister). Although the Lyons never wanted for much, in order to meet ends it was necessary for Rosemary Lyon to work as well, as a teacher's aide. Prosperity was to come to Allan Lyon later on, after he'd opened a nursing home called Lyon Manor, but as Richard sat in 1979 classes at Harvard, any sort of wealth in store for his father was still some time in the future.

In highly publicized criminal cases, book writers and TV movie scripters generally have field days delving into the defendant's deep, dark past to show reason for sociopathic behavior. Mother domineered while Father lay around drunk all the time. Aunt Lucy took the murderer to bed during his formative years, after which Uncle Herman beat the youngster senseless with fists and coat hangers. Those in search of such things to explain Richard Lyon had best look elsewhere than his childhood.

Richard was an adventuresome kid of sorts. There were some dark and spooky woods near the Lyon home where he and a neighborhood boy named Jeff Cariglia used to roam, hiding behind trees and jumping out to scare the tomfool out of each other, and through the forest a wildly rushing river flowed. Mansfield Hollow Dam was actually little more than a mud-and-mortar fence that spanned the river, and the two lively little boys used to dare each other to crawl across the dam in springtime while the river rapids frothed swiftly below in a raging, eardrum-shattering torrent. Often Jeff would chicken out. Richard never did.

The oldest Lyon boy isn't and never has been much of a jokester. He was brought up to be self-sufficient, and from the age of twelve and on through high school was the best lawn-mower-for-hire in the Mansfield area, using his profits to buy his own clothes, pay for what few dates he had, and stash the balance away for rainy days. While Big Daddy generously financed Nancy's education—and supplemented her various detours from same—Richard made use of savings, grants, scholarships, and the government loan program to make it through college.

In a community the size of Mansfield-Willimantic—Richard's 1975 graduating class from E.O. Smith High, which is in Storrs, a nearby town whose high school services the entire community, was a shade under two hundred strong—just about everybody knows everybody else, and while still in his early teens Richard gained a reputation as a talented artist. And talented he was. He liked to do caricatures, and his cartoonish drawings of friends and neighbors were of newspaper politico-satire quality. He became a fair to middling guitarist as well; as opposed to the belting rock 'n' roll that most of his generation preferred, Richard liked to strum and sing ballads. The Lyons were Sunday regulars at St. Joseph's Episcopal, where Richard played guitar accompaniment for the choir.

Like many with rural backgrounds, Richard was brought up as a sexual conservative. *Ultra*-conservative, some might think; he's become a whole lot more tolerant of gays in recent years, but the truth is that anything he views as a sexual perversion sends shudders up and down his spine. It's an ingrained attitude. Of all the traits that he developed growing up, his sexual conservatism is probably the most important thing to remember about him. His rigidity in matters of sex would someday cause many problems.

But most of all, Richard liked to tinker and invent. He took small engines apart and put them back together; confronted with anything mechanical, he wanted to know exactly what made the thingamajig tick. Once he'd learned how the gadget worked, he'd make alterations to improve its operation. And as jurors and spectators in a packed Texas courtroom were to learn years later, Richard loved to tell about his findings.

After high school he took his sterling transcript and upper-nineties-percentile SAT scores and packed off to UMass, a three-hour drive from Mansfield in Amherst, Massachusetts, which is about as close to Richard's hometown as in-state UConn. There was another kid from E.O. Smith High at UMass, a classmate of Richard's named Peter Reynolds, and the two small-town boys roomed together. Peter, later to become a successful lawyer down in Hartford, found that he had a lot in common with Richard. The two played chess—at which Richard can beat the pants off of most people—organized pickup soccer games—a sport at which Richard is only fair as a player, but as a strategist is the equal of most professional coaches—and became bench-press and sit-up partners in the weight room. Richard has a propensity to go to fat if he doesn't exercise and watch his diet, so he does so with rigid discipline. His close friendship with Peter Reynolds was to last until near the end of their sophomore year, when first true love entered the life of Richard Lyon.

Where women were concerned, Richard was never a field player. For his first two years of college he didn't date much at all, spending most of his out-of-class time hitting the books, and a three-point-plus grade average was the result. In the spring of his second year at UMass he met a beautiful Hawaiian girl named Dawn Minai, and before the school year was out romance was in full bloom.

That Richard didn't go out with many girls before he met Dawn certainly wasn't for lack of opportunity. He was a strikingly handsome young man, polite to a fault with perfect manners, and just the type that coeds' mothers are wild for their daughters to meet. But Richard's studiousness and outward lack of interest where most girls were concerned masked a certain shyness. The truth was that he was painfully timid with the forward, if-you-don't-call-me-I'll-call-you breed of young woman that developed through the seventies, which made Dawn Minai's quiet allure all the more attractive to him.

Dawn has a wealth of glistening hair the color of dark mahogany, and soft, flawless, Brandy Alexander skin. Her gentle almond eyes are tilted just so, as though she is perpetually about to ask a question. She is soft-spoken and intelligent, and in a male-female relationship never the type to take the lead. Dawn was brought up to be the pursued and not the pursuer, and whatever the strength of her technique, it worked perfectly where Richard was concerned. From near the end of his sophomore year at UMass on through his graduation, there was no other woman for him.

During the next two and a half years, Dawn and Richard had separate addresses for appearance's sake—particularly for the occasions when Richard's folks would drop in from Mansfield—but for all practical purposes they lived together. Though they never made official wedding plans, during the time they were together they both considered their eventual marriage a given.

When Richard learned of his acceptance to the Harvard School of Design just before his spring 1979 graduation, he and Dawn thought that his pursuit of a master's degree in Cambridge would fit their future plans perfectly. Dawn had another two semesters left at UMass, and although the thought of being separated for any time at all saddened the young couple, Boston-Cambridge was just a three-hour drive from Amherst and they could easily spend their weekends together. They continued to see each other throughout that summer, and once September rolled around, bade each other a sweet but temporary farewell. So as Richard sat in his first day of class at Harvard and admired the comely Texas girl Nancy Dillard from afar, his interest was merely to look and not to touch. Richard was, after all, spoken for.

For Nancy's part, she didn't come to Harvard looking for love. She certainly was taken with Richard's looks—as many women are—but on the warm fall day when she first gazed on him, romance was the last thing on her mind. Nancy came to school in Cambridge to pursue her ambition, and for no other reason. Just what fueled Nancy Dillard's desire to succeed is something she herself likely didn't know. In the year before she died, Nancy may have come to suspect the origin of her driving force, but in 1979 she knew only that her ambition was there.

The younger Dillard girl first saw the light of day in New York, as did Susan and Bill Jr., before Big Daddy migrated to Dallas. William Wooldridge Dillard, Sr., lived in a number of places before settling down in Highland Park. He is originally from Memphis and was born into wealth, and as a young man lived all over. He met Sue Stubbs on an airplane. She was a stewardess in the days before flight attendants' rights, back when a stew was considered over the hill at thirty and marriage signaled instant termination of an airline hostess's job. Even today Bill Jr. will jokingly chide his mother, "Mom, you're still someplace up in the air." After Big Daddy wooed and married Sue, the couple settled in New York for long enough to spawn their three eldest children, and finally joined Big Daddy's brother down in Texas. In 1957, when the family of five took up residence on Highland Park's Normandy Street, about a mile south of their current Rheims Place home, Nancy was four years old.

The Dillard children were no more nor no less spoiled than the rest of the Highland Park neighborhood kids, each having their own car as soon as they were old enough to drive, spending their summers lounging by the pool at Dallas Country Club or going on long vacations with Sue and Big Daddy. All attended John S. Bradfield Elementary School and Highland Park Junior High School. As was common in Park Cities, from the time the Dillard kids were toddlers on through early adolescence, they reported to a series of nannies while Sue and Big Daddy attended to business and social commitments. Highland Park nannies came with the highest of references, of course, but no matter how earnestly children's clothes are washed and ironed, and no matter how promptly their meals are prepared, a nanny-for-hire generally regards children as only part of the job. More than one Park Cities family whose child has become delinquent or near so has learned that the relationship that places domestics between parents and their kids is missing an important ingredient. Left for the large part to their own devices, the Dillard offspring became quite close. In some ways, perhaps, they were too close, too dependent on one another for love.

Nancy's emergence as the family's restless and ambitious Maggie the Cat didn't come to pass until after she'd graduated from high school. Throughout her adolescent years she was quiet and reserved. She had good grades and spent a lot of time by herself, and although her quiet beauty attracted a number of boys, she didn't show much interest in relationships. She wasn't particularly shy; most of her high school friends remember her as the outgoing, take-charge type. For a girl as attractive as Nancy not to want to date was considered unusual by some. Maybe even downright strange.

Nancy's college plans were rather limited in scope, since only certain universities meet acceptable standards for educating Park Cities children. In order for the college of choice to receive cocktail-party approval, the Highland Park High School grad must be discerning indeed. The University of Texas is the only public school to receive consideration—though attendance at any UT branch other than the Austin campus is thought a bit pedestrian in Highland Park—and even the approved private colleges are limited in number. SMU is adequate, though since it's located right in Park Cities it's considered more of an extension of high school; Stanford is all right if one can't be accepted in the Ivy League. For young ladies there are several D.C.-area–Virginia institutions that pass muster: Randolph-Macon, Washington & Lee, Holyoke, Hollins. Nancy chose Hollins, and enrolled in the classy girls' school in the fall of 1971.

Though their curriculums have expanded in recent years, private women's universities are still primarily geared toward liberal arts degrees. Translate that: Proper Wife Diplomas; although schools like Hollins have the highest academic standards, they actually have little to offer the career-minded young woman. A popular trend is for ladies who want professional training in business, medicine, or law to transfer at the end of their sophomore year. Nancy didn't follow the trend; she remained at Hollins and received her bachelor's degree in 1975. Her undergraduate grades were above average, her career at Hollins unremarkable.

Or unremarkable in most respects. In 1974, during her junior year, Nancy had a secret abortion. After her death the hidden incident would come back to haunt.

Embarking on life with a liberal arts degree wasn't as much of a problem for Nancy Dillard as it might be for many young women struggling to survive. Secure in the knowledge that Big Daddy would foot the bills she couldn't cover herself, she could afford to work for peanuts. Whether the job was fun was more of a factor than salary, so Nancy took a job with a museum in Washington. For the next two years she conducted walk-throughs, pointing out the more riveting aspects of cavalry swords and Civil War uniforms to tourists who dropped by on their way to the Lincoln Memorial or Washington Monument. Not surprisingly, after the novelty had worn off, Nancy's museum job bored her to tears.

During the time she worked in D.C., Nancy decided that, career-wise, the time she'd spent at Hollins University had been pretty much a waste of time. Her liberal arts training simply hadn't prepared her enough, she thought. At that time in her life Nancy had no thoughts of marriage anytime soon, and she certainly wasn't willing to spend the rest of her life as a museum guide. If she wanted to excel in any profession, she was going to have to go back to school. With continued education in mind, Nancy began to look around.

With family resources to back her up, she could afford to take her time about choosing a career, but she didn't take long in setting a course once she'd decided to return to school. Landscaping fascinated her. She seldom passed one of the grand homes in the finer Washington suburbs without having an idea that would improve the exterior looks of the place. Some grading here, more trees there, perhaps a row of hedges. During the latter portion of her second year at the museum, Nancy took a trip home to Dallas during which she let Big Daddy know of her desire to become a landscape architect. Her father liked the idea—though it's likely that, where his younger little girl was concerned, Big Daddy would have thought it marvelous if she'd decided on a circus career or anything else that had popped into Nancy's mind—so in the fall helped her move to Philadelphia and enrolled her in the Penn School of Design. Two years later, bolstered by a B-plus average in undergraduate school, she continued on to do work at Harvard.

On the hot September day when Nancy first laid eyes on Richard in a Harvard classroom, she was twenty-six years old, having already completed four years at Hollins, two years with the museum, and two more years at Penn. Richard was four years younger than she, though he looked much older. Their love affair would be well along before she confessed the difference in their ages.

Though the two felt instant chemistry, Richard and Nancy

didn't actually date for several months. Richard was involved with Dawn, of course, though the relationship was doomed to go the way of many college long-distance loves, and Nancy simply didn't seem interested in going out with anyone. While otherwise a self-confident and assertive young woman, Nancy actually seemed frightened of men. On more than one occasion she accepted invitations for dates and then, at the last minute, backed out. At other times she would go, and suddenly during the middle of an evening would invent excuses to be taken home.

One chilly November Saturday she went to the Princeton–Harvard football game with a law student named Douglas Meems and three other couples. The group planned to attend a party after the game down in the Boston Bay area, all four young couples deciding to pile into Doug's ten-year-old Lincoln for the drive.

"Talk about an attitude reversal," he says. "I mean, this was a sharp and attractive girl. I'd heard some stories that she could be a little bit weird, but, man, this I didn't expect. From the outset, when I picked her up and we headed for the game, she just sort of bubbled over. Talked my freaking ear off, told a few jokes, and up until we got seated with the other people we were meeting I was having one helluva good time. Then, whammo.

"It was pretty cold, damn cold, I guess, for your part of the country"—Doug Meems is a Manhattan lawyer, and was speaking long-distance to Dallas—"but something we all get used to up here. Anyway, I spread a blanket over us, and I had a little flask and all, and there we sat watching the ball game. All of a sudden, and I don't know if it was the drinks or my body odor or what, but all of a sudden she just clammed up. Would barely speak to me, and every time I'd try to start any kind of conversation it was like I'd done something wrong.

"Around the middle of the third quarter, I guess it was, Nancy just up and disappears. I can't remember if she said she was going to the bathroom or what, but all of a sudden there I am, just me and these other couples. I went out and hunted all over for her to no avail, and after the game even went by her place looking for her. I don't mind telling you I was more than a little pissed, and I had to let this other guy borrow my car because I couldn't, felt like I couldn't, go along with the others without a date. And guess what? The next time I saw her on campus she runs up with this big friendly grin like nothing was wrong. No apologies, no nothing. I'm telling you, as far as I was concerned, the lady *invented* weird."

As much as Nancy was taken with Richard's looks, her attraction to him had equally to do with his attitude. She knew that Richard was next to engaged, and that any relationship he had with a fellow student was going to be platonic. And in the beginning, Richard's association with Nancy was a just-friends thing and nothing more. They studied together often at the library and went for long campus walks during which their discussions centered on classwork. They became lab partners in one course and undertook projects together. Though many on campus thought of the two as an item early on in the school year, the truth was that they rarely saw each other away from the campus. Nancy confessed to close friends that if being seen with Richard kept other college men at bay, then that was just the way that she preferred the situation.

And though Richard admitted to a strong attraction to Nancy from the beginning, any romantic plans he may have had were well hidden. There would be many, years later, to say that Richard's primary interest in Nancy had to do with Big Daddy's finances, but for the first half year of their relationship, at least, he didn't even know she was wealthy. She made good small talk, was an excellent study partner and campus friend, but Richard's heart at the time was three hours away, back at UMass with Dawn. As the school year progressed, though, that was going to change.

There is nothing unusual about college romances falling apart when sweethearts attend separate schools, and Richard's relationship with Dawn Minai wasn't much different from the norm. Back in Amherst, with Richard away in Cambridge, the lovely Dawn began to develop other interests. She never wanted for attentive young men, before or after her romance with Richard, and the temptations were more persuasive once Richard was gone from sight. During the fall of 1979, her calls to and from Richard slacked off, and his visits to Amherst became more and more infrequent. By the Christmas break of that year, in fact, the relationship was more off than on. When Richard returned to Harvard in the spring, he considered himself a free man. His unattached days were to be numbered indeed.

With his romance involving Dawn at a close, Richard began to see Nancy in a far different light. During that spring they went on picnics together and attended campus outdoor parties where Richard would strum his guitar and other students would join in and sing. They had much in common; both enjoyed movies, both were reserved, and both were immersed in their studies. And sometime during the following months, when they eventually went to bed together, they found that both in their own way were pretty much sexual novices.

Since Nancy was older, that she wasn't more experienced in making love was surprising to Richard, but his own inexperience turned out to be just what she needed. He was slow with her, and understanding as well, and tentative as their first encounters might have been, Nancy soon lost all hesitancy with him. By the end of that semester in school, she was hopelessly in love, and her devotion to Richard would one day become an obsession that would border on the psychotic.

It is somewhat surprising to many, given Richard's good looks and his allure to women, that there wasn't more romance in his life before Nancy, but his only lengthy relationship up to that time had been with Dawn. People tend to take on patterns in their love lives, and Richard was no different. For the balance of the time that he and Nancy attended school at Harvard, they kept the outward appearance of living apart, just as he and Dawn had done during their years at UMass, but in reality Richard and Nancy spent most of their nights together. They slept in a twin bed at Richard's for much of the time, studying together into the wee hours and then crawling off to sleep entwined in each other's arms. They arranged to take the same classes whenever possible, and even took great pains to have similar handwriting patterns. They practiced for hours, writing sentences over and over until even trained experts would have trouble telling Richard's writing from Nancy's, and vice versa. That two people would consciously strive to have their writing patterns indiscernible seems strange at first glance, but apparently there was a method to the madness, at least from Richard's point of view.

Herb Wagner was a landscape student at Harvard, from up-state New York, and currently heads his own construction firm in the Dallas suburb of Garland. "Sure, I followed the case," he says. "Who in this area didn't? That handwriting business didn't really surprise me, and I'll let you in on a little secret. All the country-boy gee-whiz aside, Richard was a user. He was always borrowing class notes from somebody because his own weren't really that good, and once he had Nancy, school really got to be a snap for him. She was a real whiz in the classroom, and I'll tell you that those last two years in school at least, if Richard ever did an assignment on his own, I'd be surprised. She used to sit up half the night and make two copies of all her assignments, in longhand, mind you, while he sat around and watched TV or played the guitar. The next day he'd hand one copy in and she'd hand in the other. That was what those handwriting sessions were all about, pure and simple. Rich was a friendly and likable guy, don't get me wrong. And he may have been nuts about Nancy, I'm not saying he wasn't. But the guy was a user. Don't make any mistake about it."

Although Richard wasn't aware of the extent of Nancy's wealth when he first began seeing her, he wasn't long in finding out. Big Daddy kept up with his little girl. For a long time he and Sue had been concerned about Nancy's lack of a love life, and when the stories began to filter back to Park Cities—some through Nancy's friend Alice Eiseman, a Highland Park girl who roomed with Nancy when she wasn't staying with Richard, some through Nancy's brother and sister, and some, though told rather timidly, from Nancy herself—about Nancy's new Harvard beau, Mom and Dad were bursting with curiosity. Just about any Harvard man is automatically an eligible suitor for the daughters of Park Cities, but once the eligibility is established, there are certain other criteria to be met before final acceptance. What are his bloodlines? Does he wear well socially? Is he ambitious on his own, enough so that he is potentially able to support one's daughter in the manner to which she is accustomed? With these and other questions in mind, Big Daddy and Sue decided on an eyeball-to-eyeball meeting in the fall of 1980.

The leaders of the Dillard clan chose New York City for the meeting place, partly so that Big Daddy could combine the Richard-examination journey with business, and flew to the Big Apple to check into the Hilton. Nancy and Richard came down from Cambridge, and for the next three days the Dillards and their prospective son-in-law (though no official wedding plans were in the works at the time, Sue and Big Daddy certainly saw Nancy's eventual union with Richard as a definite possibility) got acquainted. The foursome went out to dinner at some of Manhattan's posher establishments, took in a Broadway show, and caught a concert at Carnegie Hall, and during the daytime Sue took Nancy shopping while Big Daddy and Richard did lunch and visited.

For Richard, the whole thing was an eye-opener. Though he had an uncle who was a member of a prestigious Manhattan law firm, the kid from Mansfield-Willimantic had never really observed the life-style of the wealthy firsthand before, and he definitely liked what he saw. He put forth his maximum effort where Sue and Big Daddy were concerned, and by the time the visit was over, Nancy's parents were thoroughly enchanted.

Once during the Manhattan sojourn, Nancy and Richard had a midnight tryst. Silently they crept from their separate beds into the Dillard suite's parlor, and there made passionate love that lasted far into the wee hours. Nancy was later to confide to friends that never before that night, or ever again in their entire relationship, was Richard more attentive to her physical needs. It was as if pleasing her on that evening with Sue and Big Daddy slumbering nearby, and making the encounter one that she would remember always, was at that moment to Richard the most important thing in the world.

Though the Manhattan trip gave Richard an inkling as to the Dillards' extensive wealth, it was the following summer before he was to see the empire firsthand. During the summer recess from classes he flew from Boston to DFW International

Airport, and was the Dillards' guest for a couple of weeks in their magnificent Rheims Place home. During the visit Richard toured the length and breadth of Park Cities with Nancy as his guide. The couple lunched in the Highland Park Shopping Village and shopped at Northpark Mall, and as Big Daddy's guest had dinner at Dallas Country Club. Big Daddy gave Richard the cook's tour of his own fine offices at 2001 Bryan Tower and introduced the Harvard lad around to some of the Dillard business cohorts, among them then Texas Rangers owner Bob Short, and then Dallas Cowboys owner H. L. (Bum) Bright. The mansions along Rheims Place and Beverly Drive set Richard's mouth agape, and on his return to Harvard the next fall his Dallas trip and the grandeur of the Dillard life-style were all that he could talk about.

It was also during Richard's initial visit to Dallas that he first met Bill Jr. By this time Nancy's older brother had graduated from college, completed his European odyssey, and along with a partner named Joe Bowers had bought into one of Big Daddy's real estate companies. Bill Jr. was then at the height of his party-time career, and Richard found the older Dillard son's manner more than a little offensive. Nancy's quiet and reserved posture was the exact opposite of Bill Jr.'s, and her brother's hard-drinking, raucous carrying-on was something that Richard simply couldn't tolerate. Bill Jr., on the other hand, seemed to interpret Richard's lack of interest in burning the candle at both ends as some sort of character flaw. The conflict between the two, husband and brother, would carry on throughout Richard's marriage to Nancy. The friction was still there on the day that Nancy died.

"It was about that time," the convicted drug dealer says, "when we used to call the guy 'Cabbagehead.' Wasn't behind his back or anything, it was just his nickname. You'd go, Cabbagehead this, or Cabbagehead that, and everybody'd know who you were talking about."

"Jesus Christ. *Cabbagehead?*" the interviewer says.

"Yeah, this was late seventies, around then. Time before last for me."

"You mean, two incarcerations ago?" the interviewer says.

"Yeah. I'm telling you this is the last go-round, too. I'll shovel shit before I'll get into that again."

"I'm not throwing stones," the interviewer says. "I'm not in any position to."

It is Sunday noon. The visiting room at the Federal Correctional Institute, Big Spring, Texas, is packed to the gills. The visitors are for the most part harried-looking wives who clutch at the moment, desperately holding hands with prisoners who wear castoff air force garb: fatigues, pistol belts, khaki short-sleeve permanent press shirts. The inmates' clothing was original issue back in the sixties, when the prison was a strategic air command base. The interviewer and the convicted drug dealer share a table. Both sit in hard plastic chairs, and lean close to each other to be heard over the shouts of visiting children and the hubbub of nearby conversation. Some families have bought vending-machine sandwiches and spread lunches on the tables under the ever-watchful eyes of guards who stand here and there about the room.

"It was his hair," the drug dealer says. "Man, like a big round head of cabbage, that's just what it looked like."

"You met him doing a deal?"

The dealer grins. He is a slender, balding man, and wears fatigues along with black hard-toed boots. "I guess you could say that. The statute's run on anything back then."

"You knew him well?"

"I guess about as good as I knew any of those guys. A lot of those rich kids used to come around, money was easy back then. I tell you I didn't know anything about his sister, though, or any of the rest of his family."

"In the late seventies she would have been in school back east. I don't guess you ever knew Richard, either," the interviewer says.

"Never laid eyes on the guy. What I know about that deal, the murder, is exactly what I read in the paper, just like everybody else."

"But you knew his name was Dillard?"

"Later I did. First, though, he was just Cabbagehead to me."

"And aside from your—your business, you really didn't know him?"

"Now, I didn't say that," the dealer says. "You get to know these guys. If you're going to be careful, you find out everything you can, the people you're doing business with." He glances around the visiting room. "Don't guess I was careful enough, huh?"

"You had him pegged as an addict?" the interviewer says.

"Well, more than that. Most of them were addicts in one form or another. Anybody buys illegal drugs, they're hooked to a certain extent. But old Cabbagehead, it was more than that with him."

The interviewer frowns. "Oh?"

"Give you an example. We went hunting one time. Listen, you know what a doe permit is?"

The interviewer shrugs. "I don't hunt. Never been in my life."

The dealer gestures with his hands, flattening his palms. "It's a deal from the Parks and Wildlife. When you get your license. You're only supposed to kill a certain amount of does."

"Has to do with prolonging the species."

"Right. There's permits you can buy to attach to the license, and if the game warden catches you with more does than you got permits, it's a big fine. A bunch of us, we went down on this guy's deer lease."

"Who is 'we'?" the interviewer says. He readies pad and pencil.

The dealer raises a hand. "Hold on, this is supposed to be about Cabbagehead. None of those other guys might want to—"

"Their names aren't for publication," the interviewer says. "But face it, some of this is pretty inflammatory. If I can't verify the story, I can't use it."

"Look," the dealer says. "This was ten, fifteen years, and I didn't know all of those guys that well."

"Just a few will do," the interviewer says. "Enough so in case I have to . . ."

Hesitantly, skeptically, the dealer rattles off three names. The interviewer jots the names down, then watches with lifted brows as the dealer continues.

"The guy's lease," the dealer says, "he rented hunting rights, you know? We were up there in doe season, and the deal was that none of the other game on the property were we to touch. Or if we did shoot, say, a buck or any birds or anything, we were supposed to pay the guy so much a head for anything except doe."

"He was trying to preserve the other game," the interviewer says.

"Right. Or get paid for any other game that anybody killed. We were only paying for the right to hunt doe, in season. Anything else was extra.

"So anyhow," the dealer says, "you know most of these guys didn't really give a shit about hunting anything. Those hunting trips were just an excuse to get snorted up, shot up, whatever. Why the hell you think they invited me along? They stayed up all night, watched a few porno movies, and did more than a few lines, you know, and the next morning off they go. Except for me. If you think I was about to go tromping around in the woods while a bunch of coked-up bastards waved shotguns around, well, you're wrong is all I can tell you.

"So Cabbagehead, he'd done about twice as much dope as anybody else, which was about par for the course for him, and the first thing you know he's wandering around out there blowing the shit out of everything there was. Fence posts, trees, beer bottles, you name it. Didn't take long before even the doped-up guys came back in, they were so afraid Cabbagehead might shoot one of them. There was this one other guy stayed out there with him, don't ask me why, and first thing you know Cabbagehead shoots this buck. And instead of bringing the carcass in, he takes and buries the fucking thing under a brush pile, so's the guy that has the lease won't know that old Cabbagehead's killed something which ain't a doe. Hides the carcass and then leaves the deer lease, even though in the shape he was in I don't see how he made it home driving."

"Funny way for him to act," the interviewer says. "How much was shooting the buck going to cost him?"

The dealer snorts derisively. "Shit, fifty bucks. Wasn't any money, the way real estate was going in those days. The fifty dollars had nothing to do with it. This guy used to do dope till he was so zonked he'd do just about anything, lie, cheat, anything else. Other guys were addicted, sure. But there was more to it with Cabbagehead, let me tell you. He was on the world's longest guilt trip about something. Ask anybody that knew him then, that guy had problems that the rest of us wouldn't even want to think about. All that coke and booze, I think the guy wanted to forget some things."

It was late 1981, during their third and last year at Harvard, when Richard and Nancy firmed up wedding plans. Both were soon to receive their master's degrees, and decided that the ideal marriage date would be in early 1982. Nancy so notified Sue and Big Daddy, and the Dillards set about arranging a Dallas wedding for their daughter that would be an event to remember. Richard told his own folks back in Willimantic of his upcoming marriage, and Allan and Rosemary Lyon scurried to make friends and relatives aware, and to firm up travel plans.

During the months before their wedding, Richard and Nancy had a disagreement of sorts over where they wanted to live. Harvard graduates, particularly those with master's degrees, have their pick of the jobs just about anywhere in the country. Nancy wanted to stay on the East Coast, preferably in Boston, for a number of reasons. She was still a history buff at heart, a throwback to her museum days, and what better place for a history nut to live than the birthplace of freedom? Also, like many young women striving for independence Nancy didn't want to live in the same town with her family; she confided in friends that she'd just as soon not spend her entire adult life under Sue and Big Daddy's thumbs.

Richard, though, had other ideas. Ever since the first time he'd made the Dillards' acquaintance, and particularly since he'd had the tour of Highland Park, Richard had wanted to move to Texas. As the wedding approached, he and Nancy spent many long nights debating their future place of residence. Richard told his future bride that while the East Coast was in a slowdown, things in Texas were booming. In 1981 Richard's argument didn't quite hold water; at that time the entire nation was on a financial upswing. Nonetheless, slowly and doggedly Richard wore down Nancy's resistance, and she finally agreed that wherever he wanted to move would be fine with her. For the balance of her shortened life, Nancy was to give in to her husband's wishes over and over again.

Just before Christmas of 1981, Richard called Big Daddy at the office. He told his future father-in-law that he and Nancy had decided, between them, that they wanted to live in Dallas, and he wanted to know if Big Daddy could be of any help in finding them a place to live and a place to work.

Big Daddy didn't give his answer at once. First he had to contact Sue, to find out whether she concurred that it would be nice to have Nancy and her husband living nearby. Big Daddy needn't have worried; Sue, of course, was delighted. Big Daddy then called Richard back, and told his future son-in-law to come on down. And if the young couple had any problems in getting settled, Big Daddy would be glad to lend a helping hand.

Debate rages, both among those who "know" and among those who only followed the case in the newspapers and on television, as to precisely who or what caused the death of Nancy Dillard Lyon, and more than one speculator points the finger at Park Cities itself as a contributing factor. That any one neighborhood or any one area could be in part responsible for a tragic death seems unthinkable at first, but Park Cities has a personality all its own. To some, the townships of Highland Park and University Park represent dreamed-about Camelots, places where most would like to live but could never afford, and many Dallasites regard the social antics of Park Citizens with envy and even faint amusement. Events within the townships' boundaries take on more significance merely because of where they occur. In Oak Cliff, Bluff View, or any one of a dozen other Dallas neighborhoods, Nancy's death would likely have received a quarter column in the obits, nothing more, and would have been soon forgotten.

A squatter named w w Caruth began the legend in the latter

half of the nineteenth century. Whether he was far of vision or short of bankroll begs a question; the fact is that the center of fledgling Dallas sprang up near the Trinity River—just as all major cities were born near the waterways and spread outward from there—and at the time Caruth built his home place near what is now the intersection of North Central Expressway and Southwestern Boulevard, his farm was out in the toolies and far to the north of Big D proper. While Reconstruction land hawks did battle for the downtown acreage, Caruth quietly went about acquiring countryside property in wholesale lots; the land was cheap and the bidders few in number. At the turn of the century it was a full day's wagon ride over rutted and washed-out trails from Caruth's front door to the Dallas cornerstone cross streets of Main and Akard, and the single largest landowner in Dallas County was largely unknown to—and completely unnoticed by—the big cigars down in the financial district. During World War I, the Caruth image underwent quite a face-lift.

Actually, the Methodists had more to do with the growth surge in Park Cities than did the war. The Methodist Church has always been one of the leading proponents of higher education, and by the time the war began they had already established their flagship Texas college, Southwestern University, in Georgetown, only a few highway miles north of Austin. The state capital is centrally located on the banks of the Colorado River, and up until the turn of the century was thought of as the state's main center of population. Neither educators nor growth-center analysts were prepared for the explosion in the Dallas–Fort Worth area— the Trinity is hardly navigable, and even today Dallas continues to defy the rules to remain the largest city in the world not located on a major body of water—but by 1913 the Methodists realized that there was a need for a second university to service the large number of Wesleyans who'd settled beside the Trinity. During the next two years several college scouting parties came to tour the area, and in 1915 the Methodist Church settled on a plot of Caruth land on a pleasant grassy hilltop, constructed a now famous domed building known as Dallas Hall, and founded the now even more famous college that they christened Southern Methodist University. Southwestern U. even lost its president to the new institution when Dr. Robert S. Hyer made the trek north to become SMU's first mentor, and although Dr. Hyer's name remains on a couple of college buildings and one University Park street even today, his granddaughter Martha went on to even greater fame as the beautiful and wholesome blonde who brought out the best in Frank Sinatra in the sixties hit movie *Some Came Running.*

Although the sale to SMU was the most important transfer of Caruth land, it was not the first and hardly the last. Anyone who wished to subdivide in the north central area of Dallas County had to deal with the Caruth family, and by 1915 a few residential neighborhoods had taken birth. But the founding of the college brought about an intriguing name for the newly formed township: University Park. A prestigious campus in the area meant the construction of homes for faculty and staff, new shopping areas, and new public schools for younger children associated with the university to attend. As the years rolled by and university enrollment increased, the residential neighborhoods that appeared around the college grew as well, so that by 1950 every available foot of space in University Park was subdivided into shopping centers or lots occupied by middle-class homeowners. It was a nice place to raise a family.

Whereas University Park grew as a modest college community, its sister township of Highland Park catered to the wealthy from its very beginnings. Before World War I, Dallas' rich lived for the most part in one of two areas, either along Forest Avenue south of downtown or close to Swiss Avenue, which lay directly to the east of the financial district. Two wide boulevards, Gaston Avenue and Akard Street, provided the wealthy easy access to the center of the city, but around the turn of the century the two main thoroughfares also became the primary streetcar lines. The rich had no need for public transportation because they could afford the newfangled motor cars, and the super-elite Texans of east and southeast Dallas found the clanging trolleys and the bumpy auto rides along streets rutted with streetcar tracks more than a little annoying. So, during the same period when the Methodists scouted for a college location, Dallas' wealthy sought out a more peaceful place in which to live.

The City of Highland Park provided the answer. Not only did the tributary of the Trinity River known as Turtle Creek provide a majestic, tree-shaded setting in which to build one's mansion, the fledgling township offered a more attractive tax base than did the City of Dallas. It was the golden era of silent pictures, and it was no accident that the main street that wound its way through Highland Park and skirted the banks of Turtle Creek was christened Beverly Drive. Highland Park wanted the wealthy to come and build their movie-star mansions, and the town soon had its wish. As Dallas moved into the Roaring Twenties, the grand homes along Beverly and Lakeside Drives became tourist mustsees.

The event that forever cemented the bond between Highland Park and its more modest college-community neighbor, thus identifying the two townships forevermore under the joint title of Park Cities, was at the time considered somewhat of a coup for Highland Park. The cost of living on or around Beverly Drive naturally dictated that the population was sparse, and therein lay a problem in the formation of schools. The price per head of public education exclusive to Highland Park children was prohibitive even to its wealthiest citizens, so in forming the Highland Park Independent School District, the township invited University Park to join. The addition of University Park's population to the district kept school taxes at a manageable level, and for almost four decades the two townships, one super-wealthy and the other middle-class, lived peacefully a stone's throw apart while their children attended classes and buddied around together. In the meantime the City of Dallas grew to the north and completely encircled the Park Cities, so that Highland Park and University Park had no expansion room. For a long time no one thought the fact that the Park Cities had no more space in which to expand bore much significance; though the townships had their own mayors, police, and fire departments, they were considered by most to be mere extensions of Dallas proper. Then, in 1958, Little Rock Central came along.

That University Park has the battle over public school integration to thank for its current wealthy status is somewhat sad, but true nonetheless. As National Guard troops escorted frightened black children to and from Little Rock's Central High in front of a national TV audience, and street rioting over the prospect of forced busing broke out from coast to coast, Park Cities residents saw the integration furor as a mere dinnertime diversion. There was no racial tension in Park Cities schools because the population was totally white. There were blacks living in Highland Park, of course, but those people occupied servants' quarters, and families with children need not apply for the Beverly and Lakeside Drive domestic jobs. Court-ordered busing had no effect on the two townships, because at the time the Highland Park Independent School District existed without federal funding, and even if the busing had been effective in Park Cities, there were simply no black children to bus. Thus while City of Dallas residents scrambled for the suburbs, and private schools burst at the seams, Park Cities residents went calmly on about their business; in effect, the events of the late fifties and sixties transformed the cities of Highland Park and University Park into Dallas County's version of Whitey's last stand.

And stand in Park Cities Whitey has done, and quite effectively. The resistance to black residents in the community isn't official, of course, but is rigid nonetheless, and the exceptions have been few and far between.

For example: For a ten- to fifteen-year period in the fifties and sixties there lived on Miramar Street, one block off of Beverly Drive, a locally notorious lunatic named Hazel Vincent. Dame Vincent was a surgeon's widow, and while unarguably nutty as a fruitcake, she possessed the financial wherewithal to keep most of her eccentricities a poorly held secret. She had a forty-foot yacht built on runners in her backyard so she could sit on the deck and pretend that she was on the high seas, and in the middle of the night her cries of "Land ho!" and her off-key rendition of the "Song of the Volga Boatmen" would keep the phone lines jammed for hours while neighbors called in complaints to the police department. Once, when served with a civil restraining order regarding her nighttime activities, Dame Vincent tore the legal paper into bits in front of the astonished constable and ordered the officer of the court into her backyard to "Weigh anchor and set sail for Galveston."

Although Mrs. Vincent's landlocked maritime jaunts were a source of amusement (for all who lived far enough away from her not to have to put up with the racket through the night, that is), the lady was far from harmless. For years she waged a one-woman war with mischievous Highland Park teenagers who, egged on, took delight in making her life as miserable as possible. Baiting Old Lady Vincent became as exciting a pastime for Park Cities kids as sneaking up on Boo Radley for the fictional children of *To Kill a Mockingbird*. Her phone number was listed in the book; the less venturesome teenagers of the area called her at all hours and had anonymous screaming fights with Mrs. Vincent, who recorded all calls and threatened the kids with intervention from the Coast Guard. The braver adolescents, mostly acting on dares, conducted raiding parties into her yard—after first casing the joint to make certain she wasn't out and about—to drill holes in her ship deck and scrawl obscenities on the yacht's bulkhead. Dame Vincent countered by sitting in her upstairs window for days, armed with a Daisy Red Ryder BB gun, keeping out of sight while the preliminary adolescent scouts peered into her yard, and then pelting the unsuspecting teenagers with BB's as they crept onto her boat like Boston Tea Party patriots.

Mrs. Vincent's final hurrah in Park Cities came about over an incident with a plumber whom she employed to fix several leaky pipes. The job took several days while the plumber—an unsuspecting man from a downtown Dallas firm who didn't have the slightest idea what he was getting into—crawled about under the sinks and beneath the house while Mrs. Vincent kept a watchful eye on him. On the third morning she accosted the plumber and held him at gunpoint, accusing him of making off with some of her jewelry. When the terrified man denied any knowledge of the bracelets, rings, and necklaces, Dame Vincent locked him in a closet and kept him on bread and water for two days, vowing to hold the man until he gave up his ill-gotten booty. Eventually the plumber's distressed family filed a missing-person report, and the police rescued the fellow unharmed, but the incident created enough of a furor that Highland Park authorities could no longer sweep the wealthy lady's activities under the rug. Commitment proceedings began, and then were dismissed when Mrs. Vincent voluntarily agreed simply to move. With the prospect of having Dame Vincent become some other community's problem, Highland Park fathers breathed a long sigh.

The relief was short-lived. Mrs. Vincent wasn't through with the neighborhood, not by a long shot. True to her word, she did put her home on the market, but added the stipulation that the only qualified buyer would be a black family with a minimum of five children, and agreed to fit her selling price to meet the family's budget. Horrified, Park Citizens held a secret meeting and, in order to quietly relocate the community thorn in the side and at the same time protect themselves from African-American invasion, quickly dreamed up a plan. One of the Highland Park family maids had a brother living in an integrated section of Dallas and, secretly backed by a consortium of Park Cities money, the brother appeared one day on Mrs. Vincent's doorstep and made her a cash offer. Mrs. Vincent accepted with a triumphant cackle and quickly made the deal. The maid's brother then immediately sold out, at double his investment, to the same Park Citizens who'd backed him to begin with. His pockets stuffed, the brother returned happily to his South Dallas digs, and Highland Park's exclusivity was preserved.

While neither politically nor morally proper, Park Cities' rigid Whiteyism caused University Park property values to skyrocket. The area now sported not only the rarity of all-WASP high school football and basketball teams, but some of Texas' most incredibly expensive houses as well. In 1950, the average University Park home cost $15,000; by the mid-sixties the figure was $45,000 and climbing. In 1980, at the height of the real estate boom, a 1,600-square-foot home heated by floor furnaces and air-conditioned by window units, located in the four-thousand block of University Park's Centenary Drive—and originally bought by its first owner in 1946 for $11,500—went for $265,000.

With the rise in home values, the makeup of University Park's population changed as well. Greeted with the prospect of instant wealth, college professors who'd originally intended to live in their homes for life gladly sold out to the newly rich and moved to country cottages. The cash-drugged yuppies who bought the old homes thought the financial boom of the late seventies so permanent that they didn't stop with the mere purchase of property. Obsessed with getting ahead of their neighbors, new University Park residents bulldozed the houses that had stood for decades on the 150-foot lots, and in their places erected castles that extended ludicrously from property line to property line. The Fords and Chevys that for years had paraded up and down Hillcrest Avenue in front of SMU were no more; Mercedes, Bentleys, and Jags were now the norm. By 1982, when Nancy Dillard married the boy from small-town Connecticut and the newlyweds came to Dallas from Harvard, to live in Park Cities was, so to speak, to die for.

Allan and Rosemary Lyon made the trek from Connecticut down to Texas for their eldest son's wedding with unexplainably heavy hearts. The trip should have been a happy occasion for Richard's parents. For one's child to marry well is a parent's dream, and Richard's betrothed came from a background which made his folks the envy of Mansfield-Willimantic. Word had spread quickly through the gossipy little burgs that Richard was marrying into millions, and more than one of the locals had greeted Allan on the square or in one of the rural Connecticut coffee shops with handshakes and backslaps of congratulation. But as the airliner touched down at DFW Airport, and as the Lyons greeted the Dillards with smiles for one and all, both of Richard's parents had misgivings about the wedding that they couldn't quite put their fingers on.

First of all, the Lyons were accustomed to friendly small-town folks who, while far too nosy at times, considered every resident of their community as part of one large family. Though the Dillards were polite, as fitted the occasion, Rosemary and Allan found Nancy's relatives to be more than a little pretentious, and even a bit standoffish. The Dillards' attitude made Allan and Rosemary uncomfortable, and to feel like outsiders whom the Dillards merely endured for the length of time required to get the wedding over with, after which the Dillards couldn't wait for the country bumpkins to take the first plane back to New England.

Allan found Bill Jr. to be particularly offensive. During the entire time that the Lyons stayed in Dallas for the festivities before and after the wedding, Allan never saw Nancy's older brother draw a sober breath. He tried to write Bill Jr.'s behavior off as that of a young man feeling his oats and having a good time, but any justification for the extent of the elder Dillard son's drinking was hard to come by. Allan noted that at all parties, both at the country club and at the Dillards' Rheims Place home, Bill Jr. never completely emptied his glass before having the help place a fresh drink in front of him. Anytime his cocktail was nearly gone, Bill Jr. assumed a look near panic, and the more he drank the louder and more obnoxious he became.

Allan attended the night-before bachelor's dinner at Richard's request, and found himself to be the only stranger in the group. Nearly all of the partiers were Bill Jr.'s friends, and Allan noted that all of the Dallas trust-fund kids at the dinner seemed to drink liquor as though there was no tomorrow, and also noted that more than one of the group would occasionally leave the party and return with telltale red marks beneath their noses.

Sometime during the evening Bill Jr. proposed a toast. He lifted his glass in Richard's direction and, his words slightly slurred, announced loudly to one and all, "Here's to my future brother-in-law. My sister is marrying a Yankee and a Yard man, but what the hell, drink to him anyway." As Bill Jr. tossed off his drink in a single gulp, the trust-fund kids at the gathering broke up in glee.

Allan Lyon didn't think the bogus toast a bit funny. As Bill Jr.'s words cut through him like a knife, Allan looked at Richard. He was smiling, but the smile appeared painted on, and his eyes were dead as flints. At that moment Allan felt like grabbing his son by the ankles and, forcibly if necessary, dragging him back to Connecticut and away from this Texas madness.

Rosemary Lyon was even more uneasy about the proceedings than her husband. She was uncomfortable around Nancy's family to begin with, and the introductions to the wedding guests, emceed by Nancy's mother, made Rosemary even more ill at ease. "Why, this is Tramell Crow," Sue would say, and then cut her eyes and whisper, "He's a *huge* developer," or "This is Bob Short," and then say softly in a condescending tone, "He owns the Texas Rangers, you know." But not only did Rosemary not have the slightest idea who these Dallas bigwigs were, she thought the whole lot of them a bunch of snobs.

The wedding mass at the Church of the Incarnation, the Episcopal cathedral that towers over North Central Expressway and keeps watch over commuters to and from downtown, had Rosemary on pins and needles. The tears she shed when Richard completed his vows and kissed his bride were much more tears of grief than of joy. During the reception at the Dallas Country Club, Richard hugged his mom and asked her to pose with him for a photo. Rosemary obliged and put on her best joyous face for the occasion, but as Richard held her close and flashes clicked, she squeezed her son's hand hard enough to leave nail impressions in his flesh. And later, as the airliner bore the Lyons back home, Rosemary couldn't stop crying. She was terrified that if Richard remained in Texas, her son would one day become a total stranger to her.

It is interesting, but neither surprising nor particularly significant, that both Nancy and Richard downplayed Big Daddy's involvement in whatever success the young couple enjoyed. "He might have given me a start, but the rest was up to me" is a typical stand taken by the Rockefeller and Rothschild heirs of the world, though the declaration sounds as credible to the working-class listener as a seminar entitled, "Making It on Your Own," conducted jointly by Nancy Sinatra and Jane Fonda.

As Richard was later to tell a packed courtroom, the newlyweds did spend their first four months in Dallas living in a one-bedroom apartment, but they were hardly roughing it. Big Daddy footed the rent. The apartment was a newly refurbished pad with a heated pool, and was only a stopgap residence while Big Daddy helped the young couple search for a house. While they lived in the apartment, Richard passed his idle time familiarizing himself with Dallas from one boundary to the other while Nancy, who'd been raised in the city and knew every nook and cranny, occupied herself with the Dallas Historical Society and joined the Junior League. The Richard and Nancy saga is hardly "Love on a Rooftop." Prudently—and at Big Daddy's insistence—the couple finally settled on an M-Street duplex.

Actually, the duplex purchase was as much an investment for Big Daddy as it was an aid to the kids. The M-Streets— McCommas, Monticello, Marquita, all running east and west and joining North Central Expressway just east of the Highland Park city limit—became trendy addresses in the seventies. They are narrow, tree-shaded avenues, and the modest brick houses in the area stood virtually unnoticed by real estate speculators for a half century or more before the restoration trend set in. Before the outset of the refurbishing stampede, M-Street homes were mostly occupied by retirees on pensions who had lived in the houses since they'd been new. No one recalls the name of the first Park Citizen, tired of the modern-but-lacking-in-personality castle in which he lived, who decided that old M-Street houses restored to their original state would make a nifty project, but by the time Richard and Nancy went house hunting in the neighborhood, retirees had already sold by the dozens. The remodeling costs were several times the houses' original purchase prices, but that didn't stop the trendsetters. The duplex that Richard and Nancy selected for their first home cost $84,500, of which the couple put up zero as a down payment. The mortgagor for the entire sum was William Wooldridge Dillard, Sr., and given the increase in property value once the old house had new floors, updated wiring, and central air and heat installed, Big Daddy's loan was well collateralized.

Once moved in, the newlyweds set about contracting for plumbers, Sheetrock installers, and roofing contractors. Richard and Nancy personally supervised the remodeling job, with Richard, shirtless much of the time, doing some of the work himself and Nancy, hands on hips, keeping a watchful eye on the construction crew.

Although the refurbishing of the seventy-year-old duplex kept Nancy quite busy, she had other things on her mind as well. The M-Street address was trendy and with-it, and quite satisfactory as a starting point, but the Park Cities boundary was still a few blocks to the west, on the other side of Central Expressway. Un-

til she'd assumed her rightful place among the Park Citizens,
Nancy Dillard Lyon wasn't going to be satisfied.

It might seem that buying a home before one finds a job is
putting the cart somewhat before the horse, but Richard and
Nancy weren't subject to the same rules as most of working
America. For a large portion of the new graduates, job hunting
consists of a series of nail-biting interviews, the careful weeding
out of a number of potentially bad choices, and finally settling on
the best position available at the time. For the Lyon newlyweds,
locating employment was simply a matter of Big Daddy holding
a few breakfast meetings.

Dallas business people have always lagged years behind established L.A. and New York City practices, so in 1982 the inclusion of breakfast and dinner, in addition to lunch, as
tax-deductible meals was still somewhat of a novelty to Texans.
How much business the moguls conduct amid the tinkling of
stirring spoons, the glassy clink of china cups on saucers, and the
hustling to and fro of jacketed waiters bearing sterling half
spheres concealing scrambled eggs, bacon, and fruit cups is subject to debate; the IRS hasn't as yet received clearance to bug the
linen-draped tables to find out exactly what is going on. Big
Daddy breakfasts often, well, and with good company; one of his
regular dining cohorts is the legendary Dallas developer Tramell
Crow.

Tramell Crow needs no more introduction to Dallasites than
Trump to New Yorkers; while Crow's personal life is not nearly
the grist for the rumor mill as is The Donald's, Crow's business
dealings are certainly more successful. Tramell Crow Partners'
office buildings, shopping centers, and huge residential developments span the length and breadth of Dallas County, and while
The Donald has battled Ivana, trysted with Marla, and played
the bankruptcy courts like lit-up pinball machines, Crow has
quietly and profitably acquired a tidy chunk of Manhattan as
well. Just as J.C. Penney built his empire by establishing his original stores as a series of partnerships, Tramell Crow believes
equally in doling out pieces of the action; he founded his business on the theory that people will work harder if their eventual

reward comes in the form of equity ownership as well as increased income. The system has proven successful; Tramell Crow Partners numbers several millionaires among its work force. So, at breakfast one morning, Big Daddy mentioned to friend Tramell that the Dillards' baby girl was out of Harvard and looking; Crow accommodatingly popped a business card facedown on the tablecloth, scribbled his hotline phone number, and told Big Daddy to have Nancy give him a call.

Actually, Crow wasn't being altogether charitable by offering his friend's daughter a job. Nancy's education credentials were, after all, on the cutting edge, and she'd been second in her class at the Harvard School of Design. Furthermore, along with all of her other attributes, Nancy was female. Being a qualified woman in the eighties—or nineties, or seventies, or at anytime within our nation's memory—translated to cheap labor. At the age of twenty-eight, as a Harvard graduate with a master's degree, Nancy's beginning salary with Tramell Crow Partners was thirty thousand dollars a year.

And if Nancy was willing to work for peanuts, Richard fared even worse than his wife in the way of salary. His own Big Daddy-influenced position was as a project-manager trainee with the Rosewood Company, which is the main business interest of Caroline Hunt Schoellkopf. In addition to having a husband who is a tycoon in his own right, Mrs. Schoellkopf is the daughter of H. L. Hunt—who in his day fought it out with J. Paul Getty for bragging rights as the world's richest man—and also is the sister of Lamar Hunt (who owns, among other things, the Kansas City Chiefs football club), and two of her other siblings, Nelson Bunker Hunt and Herbert Hunt, once dual-handedly turned the national silver market upside down. If nothing else, Richard's and Nancy's jobs put them in a position to drop a few names.

But, prestigious or not, Richard's job paid only twenty-six thousand, and coupled with Nancy's income gave the newlyweds a combined total of fifty-six per. Not a bad starting point for a couple with no children, but as the Dillards' daughter and son-in-law, they had a certain standard of living to maintain. The payments to Big Daddy on their original duplex loan exceeded a thousand dollars a month, and within two years they were to add a second duplex that would double the monthly obligation. It is true that the duplexes were partially rental property, but the rents derived from the two units didn't come anywhere near to covering the payments, and the soon-to-come recession was to make it difficult to keep the places rented at all. Additionally, as part and parcel of their social position, Richard and Nancy had to attend the right parties—and bear the accompanying expenditure for the proper clothing for same—drive the right cars, and participate in (and donate to) the proper charities. From the onset, from the day that Nancy and Richard went to work, it was apparent to Big Daddy that he had some subsidizing to do. Seven years later, when Richard and Nancy filed, then subsequently withdrew, their divorce petition, an inventory of their community property listed a debt to William Wooldridge Dillard, Sr., of two hundred fifty thousand dollars. By any set of standards, it wasn't hay.

If keeping Richard and Nancy's standard of living up to snuff was to cause some runoff in Big Daddy's resource lake, solving Bill Jr.'s problems would very nearly rupture the dam. At the time Richard and Nancy moved into their M-Street duplex, the eldest Dillard boy was at the height of his drinking and involvement in drugs. The faster the Dillard land company—which Bill Jr. and his partners had bought with a loan from Big Daddy—brought in money, the faster Bill Jr. seemed to make the money disappear. As long as business boomed, as it did in the seventies, Bill Jr.'s lack of thriftiness was a mere irritation to Big Daddy, but there were times during the real estate collapse of the eighties that bailing out his son became a near catastrophe.

So intertwined did the Dillard finances become at one point that the various trust funds which Big Daddy had set up for his children came into play. One particular rescue of Bill Jr. from the clutches of poverty required that Nancy cosign a note for her brother in the amount of $86,000. She executed the note on the Lyon kitchen table in front of her husband, and though Richard had little to say about the matter, he took precise mental notes.

Richard has a very good memory, and he would one day trot out Bill Jr.'s personal and financial problems for all the world to see.

Insufferable as Richard considered his brother-in-law, Bill Jr. was nonetheless family, and the two found themselves thrown together often. As is common among alcoholics, Bill Jr. became quite loud and abrasive when he'd had a few pops, and Richard spent more than one late evening, cold sober, as the last remaining person awake to hear his brother-in-law rant and rave. For Bill Jr., drinking time was bragging time. Since it was "just among us fellas" (and also because it gave him a chance to shock his more conservative brother-in-law), Bill Jr. let it all hang out during these sessions. He told Richard many stories of cocaine snorting among the trust-fund kids, and even made the less than wise decision, influenced by alcohol, of course, to let Richard know about the topless dancers at the Million Dollar Saloon and Cabaret Royale. He needn't have worried about Richard letting Nancy in on what he knew—thus sparing Bill Jr. the problem of having his own wife find out, since Nancy and Mary Helen were thick as thieves—because Richard was the kind of guy who could keep his mouth shut. Like his knowledge of Nancy's cosignature on the note for Bill Jr., Richard filed the information regarding the cocaine use and the topless dancers away for future reference. One day, long after he'd taken the cure and begun to walk the straight and narrow, Bill Jr. would deeply regret the times when he'd allowed liquor to loosen his tongue.

During the passage of time leading up to the final tragedy, Richard and Nancy were to move their place of residence two times. Nancy was to hold only one job while Richard was to work for three different employers. Nancy was to find success while, his declarations on the witness stand to the contrary, Richard's business career was sort of a bust.

Just how much her success vs. his lack of same had to do with his eventual rejection of his wife is known only to him. Chances are that the differences in their careers affected his feeling toward her very little; he is the type to take things as they come and roll with the punches. Whether he was the guiding influence behind her achievements (defense's position once again) or she pulled her husband along by her skirt hem (you guessed it, prosecution's version) likely didn't matter to him; Richard and Nancy lived the good life, and which partner was most responsible for bringing in the bacon, as far as he was concerned, didn't amount to a hill of beans.

There is also room to speculate as to how much Big Daddy influenced Nancy's meteoric rise at Tramell Crow Partners. Considering her meager beginning salary, her promotion to partner only a year later was the fastest climb in the history of the company, and at twenty-nine she became Tramell Crow's youngest partner ever. But exactly what Nancy achieved to deserve such rapid promotion isn't clear. One Crow associate (who remains anonymous, just as anyone connected to Tramell Crow Partners who will discuss Nancy at all remains anonymous) puts it this way: "Damnedest thing I ever saw. One day she's around here learning the ropes, the next day, bam, instant partner. It's like, last week she couldn't even spell project supervisor, the next day she is one. She must have put together a lot of deals that the rest of us weren't aware of, is all I can tell you."

But whether Nancy battled to the forefront through a series of brilliant job performances, or if Tramell Crow's original breakfast-meeting statement to Big Daddy went something like, "Tell you what, we'll put her on a starvation diet for a year or so and then jump her on up from there, and by the way, old buddy, about that two million you were going to sink in this project of mine," she did make partner in just over a year, and she did become an assistant project manager. It was likely somewhat distasteful to her that in order to assume her new duties she had to drive every day to Grand Prairie, which is about as far removed from Park Cities as one can get.

Grand Prairie is mid-cities, in between Dallas and Fort Worth, and although in the minds of many Dallasites it maintains the same blue-collar image the little town developed in the fifties and sixties, Grand Prairie has become quite progressive. Industry booms in this commuter city in between Interstates 30 and 20, and in recent years the real estate developers have realized the possibilities along Grand Prairie's southern edge. A country club community called Woodcrest began just off of I-20 in the 1970s, and when people flocked from Dallas and Fort Worth to buy out all the Woodcrest lots in record time, Grand Prairie was suddenly on the residential builder's map. Tramell Crow began his own development, Westchester, just a ways down the road from Woodcrest, a few years later. Westchester's billboards along I-20 advertised homes "from the nineties," though the nineties really wouldn't buy too much, and at the time of Nancy's hiring the new community had begun to thrive. Her first assistant project supervisor's job was at Westchester, and her instructions were to report to the partner in charge of the subdivision, a man named David Bagwell.

Bagwell—who was later to visit Presbyterian Hospital during Nancy's final hours, and also was to have a brief encounter with Richard in the hospital corridor—wasn't acquainted with Nancy Lyon before her work at Westchester, though if he'd been just a little bit younger, the two likely would have been old friends. Like Nancy, David Bagwell was a graduate of Highland Park High School, and also like Nancy, he hadn't come up the hard way. His wife is the former Suzanne Shamburger, whose older sister Lynn was married to Dandy Don Meredith of NFL and Monday Night Football fame, and whose family is worth millions in their own right. He is a man with sandy red hair, given to monogrammed shirts, tailor-made suits, and East-Coast-tycoon, small-lensed glasses, and he considered Westchester his own personal kingdom. As Nancy politely shook hands with Bagwell in Westchester's sales office, there was instant tension between the two. Bagwell was in charge and let his people know it; anything she considered domination made her hackles rise. David Bagwell and Nancy Lyon were to work closely in Westchester's management, but the friction between the two would one day set the entire project squarely on its ear.

In relating the importance of the various individual straws at which Richard Lyon grasped in setting his defense to murder charges, it is necessary to go forward a bit, shift into reverse and backtrack at times, and at other times make quantum leaps into the future. It is neither the best method in which to tell, nor the most understandable way for the listener to hear, any story, but the puzzling case involving the death of Nancy Dillard Lyon is without convenient continuity.

At the time that Nancy went to work at Grand Prairie's Westchester subdivision, David Bagwell certainly had no past to define him as a murder suspect. The events that led Richard later to point the finger in Bagwell's direction were sometime in the future, and even those events required a catalyst, some well-known happenstance to cause jurors and media alike, when hearing Bagwell's name, to thoughtfully pinch chins between thumb and forefinger and reason, "Oh, yeah. *That* guy." At the time of Richard's well-publicized prosecution, the Bagwell name with which the TV and newspaper people were familiar was that of David's older brother, John.

Like the Dillards, the Bagwell boys were well-heeled Highland Park kids. John graduated high school in the late fifties, David a few years after that, and neither boy was particularly a yearbook personality; no student council president bios, no football team notations, no Most Likely to Succeed nominations. John was quiet and studious, came and went from the high school campus virtually unnoticed, and many of his former classmates fail to recall him at all. In fact, the only memory that anyone seems to have of John, once they prod their recollections, is of his romance with the lovely, outgoing, and quite unforgettable Betsy Monroe.

It's not surprising that now middle-aged former Highland Park students remember Betsy; she was, after all, a Texas high school cheerleader. But more: her father, Dr. Frank Monroe, was the Superintendent of Schools at the time, and was the man whom the kids held ultimately responsible for the bottom-paddlings in the principal's office that were then routine. Betsy was lush of figure, sparkling of eye, and the object of many from-afar crushes, but the prospect of reporting to Dr. Frank for inspection prior to taking Betsy out on a date kept more than a few would-be suitors at bay. John Bagwell might have been the bookworm type, but he certainly wasn't faint of heart; he courted Betsy with vigor, stole her right from under the noses of the letter-jacket-wearing jockstraps of the time, and ultimately claimed the prize by making Betsy his wife.

And not only was John Bagwell lionhearted in the ways of love, he was firm of career purpose as well. Whereas a large number of his Highland Park contemporaries crammed four years into five while trudging through college, and then ultimately went to work for banks and insurance companies, John blazed through undergrad and medical school and became one of the area's leading cancer specialists. He and Betsy settled prominently into the Park Cities mainstream; while John labored ten-to-fifteen-hour days, not only with his own private practice but in helping to establish Baylor Hospital's cancer wing, Betsy bore two children, taught Bible classes, and sang in the choir at Highland Park Presbyterian Church, worked on Dallas' socially prestigious Shakespeare Festival, and joined (what else?) the Junior League. John and Betsy, in fact, had everything positive going their way when in 1981 an alluring woman named Sandra Bridewell entered their lives.

To call Sandra Bridewell a woman is akin to calling Michael Jordan a basketball player; the listener misses the total picture. She is fantastically sexy, but at the same time she drips with class. She is a magnet for men and the envy of women, the stuff of which viciously delicious rumors are made. She lists among her former lovers Norman Brinker, the ex-Steak 'n' Ale magnate and now the owner of Chili's restaurants, polo player supreme, international jetsetter second to none. While Sandra was seeing Brinker, one of his former girlfriends (it is *presumed* that the culprit was one of Brinker's exes, at least; there are those who accuse Sandra of doing it herself) broke into her home and scrawled a threat on her mirror in lipstick. The incident was the talk of Park Cities, and afterward Brinker provided Sandra with a bodyguard for a time.

Though still a young and voluptuous woman, Sandra has survived three husbands, two of whom died from other than natural causes. She was a suspect in one husband's death and, if one listens to gossip (and who in Park Cities doesn't) the principal cause for the suicide of another. She is known around Dallas as the Black Widow.

Husband number one, David Stegall, was a dentist, and so intent on becoming Dallas' "society tooth doctor" that he borrowed enormous sums of money to set up a Park Cities practice straight out of dental school. He and Sandra spent money like water, and plunged further and further into debt to the point that bill collectors sat in David's waiting room more often than patients. None of the creditor harassment slowed the Stegalls' life-style one iota; once, as David borrowed $100,000 from his father just to make ends meet, Sandra spent $45,000 remodeling the Stegall home. Apparently, attempting to cope with the financial pressure finally drove David over the edge. His lawyer thwarted his first suicide attempt by breaking into a closet, finding David crouched on the floor with a pistol to his head, and disarming the frantic dentist. The second attempt, three weeks later, was successful and David did quite a job of it. By this time he and Sandra slept in opposite wings of the house, and she awoke one morning to find him not only with his wrists slashed, but with a .22-caliber bullet hole through his brain. Sandra collected life insurance, sold her home, paid off the debts, and had enough left over to continue to live the good life.

Husband number two, Bobby Bridewell—whose last name Sandra continues to use—was the stereotype of the Dallas wheeler-dealers of the seventies and eighties. He made one fortune in real estate, lost it all in joint ventures when the market bottomed out, and then miraculously regained his chips through a unique and resourceful scheme. He talked Caroline Hunt Schoellkopf (Rosewood's owner, Richard Lyon's eventual employer) into buying a grand old Italian villa on Turtle Creek Boulevard and, under Bobby's direction, converting it into a hotel and restaurant. The Mansion on Turtle Creek remains today as the uppitiest of the uppity, and is known far and wide as Bobby Bridewell's baby. The hotel grounds cover more than four acres of pleasant lawn and shady wooded areas, and the original construction cost of the Mansion's rooms came to $143,000 per unit. The dining room features original eighteenth-century paintings, walls of soft forest green fabric, a stunning mantel over a replica of the fireplace in England's Bromley Castle, and an inlaid ceiling constructed of 2,400 individual pieces of carved and lacquered wood. Among the set that tosses off thirty-dollar lunches like Big Macs, the Mansion is definitely the place to see and be seen.

Her marriage to Bridewell gave Sandra the ultimate in visibility among the Dallas social set, and she certainly made the most of it. She lunched daily at the Mansion—at the best table, of course—and became one of the hostesses for the Cattle Baron's Ball, which in Dallas is the primary social event of the year. She made whirlwind shopping trips to Houston during which she stayed at the Remington or Post Oak Park Hotel (another Rosewood project of which Bobby was in charge) and spent thousands of dollars at the Galleria Mall. With Bobby's flair for the upscale hotel business and Sandra's penchant for glamour, the Bridewells' marriage seemed the perfect union.

At the height of Bobby's success (and of Sandra's prominence in the social whirl), however, tragedy struck. During a routine physical, doctors diagnosed Bobby as suffering from deadly lymph cancer. Faced with almost certain death, he determinedly gritted his teeth. In his fight for his life, he would settle for only the best in medical care, and the best available physician by far was Dr. John Bagwell.

Even the nosiest of the Highland Park gossips (and there are a number of contenders for the title) were never able to establish that Sandra Bridewell and John Bagwell conducted an affair while Bobby's health failed, but this much is known: As Bobby grew weaker and weaker, and finally became bedridden, Sandra was seen more and more often in Bagwell's company. It is quite possible that the numerous times when Sandra popped by Bagwell's office during the day, or joined him at the Mansion for lunch or dinner, were merely to discuss Bobby's condition, and lacking evidence to the contrary, Sandra's relationship to John should be left at that. By any stretch of the imagination, however, her actions during Bobby's last days were to say the least unusual.

During Bobby's final winter, even as he lay in a hospital bed in the Bridewell home, Sandra hired remodelers and redid the house. The heat went out in the area where Bobby stayed, but as horrified friends brought blankets and space heaters by to comfort the dying man, Sandra continued to supervise work on other portions of the house and left Bobby to shiver in a frigid bedroom. In fact, she never did anything to improve his living conditions until the following spring, when the temperature outside had climbed into the seventies and eighties, and then the warm weather brought on her strangest behavior of all. She contacted a friend of hers named Marian Underwood, explained that a new heating unit was being installed at the Bridewell house, and asked if Ms. Underwood, a retired teacher, could keep Bobby in her home for a week while the work was done. A good and caring neighbor, Ms. Underwood agreed. One day in late March, Sandra loaded Bobby and his hospital bed into a van and delivered him to Marian Underwood's house.

And left Bobby there, and never returned for him. Too weak to move, he stayed at the Underwood home for three weeks while Sandra allegedly had her heating redone. Even the accommodating Ms. Underwood finally had had enough, and at the end of the three weeks she contacted Bobby Bridewell's father. The elder Bridewell, himself a successful landowner, was furious to learn what Sandra had done, and immediately had Bobby moved into a suite at one of the Bridewell motels. There Bobby remained until, one late April day, it became apparent that his body was shutting down and the end was near. Bobby's dad then contacted Dr. John Bagwell, who had Bobby moved from the motel into the cancer wing at Baylor Hospital. Bobby died at Baylor two weeks later at the age of forty-one.

Local suspicion aside, there was never anything concrete to show that Sandra wasn't alone in the Bridewell house during Bobby's final days, and if she did move Bobby out to clear the way for a series of trysts, she conducted her affairs with the utmost of secrecy. At Bobby's funeral, Sandra was properly grieved. Two weeks later she vacationed in Hawaii. Upon her return she began to show up at John Bagwell's house on a daily basis, and more or less forced herself on John's wife, the former high school cheerleader Betsy Monroe.

To say that she forced herself on Betsy is likely putting it mildly. According to all who knew Sandra, she was the type to drop by unannounced and stay for hours, and since Betsy was never one to hurt another's feelings—particularly in Sandra's case, where the woman had just lost her husband—Betsy did her best to make Sandra feel at home. Aside from her numerous visits to Betsy, Sandra continued to drop by John's office from time to time, though whether Betsy knew that Sandra was calling on her husband isn't known. The drop-ins on Betsy continued for about a month, a time during which Sandra told several Highland Park acquaintances that Betsy Bagwell was "my new best friend."

In early July 1982, two months after Bobby Bridewell had died, Sandra called the Bagwell home one evening and, when Betsy answered, asked to speak to John. Betsy was puzzled, but called her husband to the phone. John talked to Sandra briefly, hung up, and told his wife that Sandra's car had stalled. He then struck out into the night, presumably to aid Sandra, but when he returned home a couple of hours later he seemed furious. He told Betsy that when he'd followed Sandra's directions and arrived on the scene, a policeman was already there, and that with the policeman behind the wheel, Sandra's car had started at once. John further told his wife that he believed Sandra had made up the car trouble story in order to lure him out of the house, and finally instructed his wife to stay the hell away from her. For Betsy, following John's orders not to see Sandra anymore was easier said than done.

Just a few days afterward, July 16 to be exact, Betsy had a morning call from Sandra. She told Betsy that she'd found a letter hidden in a picture frame in her house, a letter from a woman indicating that Bobby, while alive, had been having an affair. According to what Betsy told two women over lunch that day, the letter had Sandra quite upset. Betsy also told her lunch partners that she hadn't believed the story, and that Sandra was, in Betsy's opinion, a compulsive liar. Sandra has subsequently denied that she ever called Betsy that morning, and also has denied the existence of the suspect letter. Nonetheless, the following tale is from Sandra's own lips, as later told to the police.

Though she steadfastly denies that she called Betsy Bagwell on the morning of the sixteenth, she acknowledges that she did phone Betsy in the early afternoon, shortly after Betsy had returned home from her lunch date with the two women at Dallas Country Club. Sandra made this call from the Highland Park Presbyterian Church, where her car had stalled—once again—in the parking lot. By this time Betsy likely wondered why Sandra didn't get her car fixed, or at least carry cabfare money, but always one to help, went to Sandra's aid. She picked Sandra up at the church and drove out to Dallas Love Field, where Sandra was to rent a car. Once the women arrived at the car rental agency, however, another snag reared its head. Sandra had forgotten her driver's license, so couldn't get a rental vehicle. By now Betsy was likely at her wit's end as to what to do with this disorganized woman, but then drove Sandra back to the church parking lot where—shazam—Sandra's car started at once as if by magic. Sandra says she then left Betsy at the church and went to Preston Center to shop. If the story is true, Sandra Bridewell was the last known person to talk to Betsy Bagwell.

By eight o'clock that evening, Betsy was dead. Responding to a frantic call from John Bagwell, police combed the area for Betsy, and at 8:20 located her powder-blue Mercedes in the Love Field Terminal parking lot. The former cheerleader and current Junior Leaguer was slumped over the wheel with a .22-caliber pistol in her hand and a bullet hole through her right temple. There were traces of gunpowder, blood, and tissue on her hand, which led the medical examiner—lacking any concrete evidence of foul play—to rule Betsy's death a suicide. Park Cities gossips—this time with probably a great deal more insight than the police—contend to this day that the medical examiner was full of bull.

First of all (this from the grapevine), Betsy simply didn't act in the short time before her death like a woman thinking about killing herself. That very day she'd kept her lunch date at Dallas Country Club, had eaten well, and hadn't acted as though a thing was wrong. She'd even talked lightly with her dining partners about a couple of upcoming parties, and on her way home she'd dropped a dress off for alterations. Before she'd left to pick up Sandra at the church, she'd told her kids (who were out of school for the summer) not to pig out that afternoon because she was fixing dinner that evening, and to emphasize her point had left a chicken to thaw in the sink. All normal behavior. No panic in her manner, no streaks of depression. None of which, of course, proves that Betsy Bagwell *didn't* kill herself. But there's also the matter of the gun.

The case is long closed, but even today policemen hem and haw and avert their gazes when the subject of the .22-caliber revolver comes up, the gun in Betsy's hand when the law found her Mercedes. It wasn't just any gun. It wasn't your standard upper-class protection weapon, a pearl-handled Derringer or neat little

James Bond Walther PPK. The pistol in Betsy Bagwell's hand was in fact what the cops call a Saturday Night special, a two-dollar popgun. The cheap little piece was registered to an Oak Cliff man (Oak Cliff bears about the same relationship to Park Cities as the South Bronx to Midtown Manhattan, or Watts to Beverly Hills), and, on following up, the police learned that the gun's registered owner was dead. His widow remembered the .22, said her husband had carried it in the glove compartment of his car, and also said that in the mid-seventies someone had stolen the pistol. It had never been recovered. Just what connection there could be between Betsy Bagwell, late of the Dallas Country Club and the Junior League, and a stolen handgun from Oak Cliff was something that the police didn't know, and never followed up on. The M.E. had ruled Betsy's death a suicide. Case closed. On to the next open file.

Gossip. Rumor. Innuendo.

Betsy's death was, of course, big news, featured in the newspapers and chronicled on television, excitedly talked about in Park Cities clubs and at the Mansion on Turtle Creek. And for all her blossoming career and business acumen, Nancy Dillard Lyon was, after all, as subject to juicy gossip as anyone. On the day after Betsy died, Nancy couldn't wait to get home from the office and tell her husband that the John Bagwell whose wife was dead was the brother of Nancy's boss at Tramell Crow Partners. At the time Richard likely found the news that David Bagwell was related to the now famous doctor to be an interesting tidbit, but no more than that. He did, however, file the information away in the back of his mind, where, along with Bill Jr.'s carousing and Nancy's cosignature on Bill Jr.'s note, it was to remain for several years.

The beautiful and provocative Sandra Bridewell here drifts out of our story and (presumably) out of John Bagwell's life forever, but in order to understand the significance to locals when the name of the Black Widow came up during Richard Lyon's prosecution, it is necessary to look briefly at a later event in her life, one that eclipsed even the death of Betsy Bagwell in etching Sandra forever into Dallasites' memories. The event involves her short-lived union with husband number three.

After Bobby Bridewell died, and after Betsy was laid to rest, Sandra continued to live in the Bridewells' Highland Park home. She supported herself on Bobby's insurance money and what inheritance she'd gained after Bobby's death, and two years later, her notoriety had faded into the background and her life seemed on an even keel. She dated often—aside from her obvious physical beauty and infectious charm and wit, her fame made her just the to-be-seen-with companion for many of Dallas' more visible bachelors—but often told friends that none of her relationships was serious and that she wasn't looking for another husband. Then, one hot July day in 1984, a muscular hunk named Alan Rehrig walked up to Sandra on her front lawn and introduced himself.

Alan's life was a pretty good tale in its own right. He was from Edmond, Oklahoma, a four-hour drive to the north of Dallas, and in his hometown he was sort of a local legend. A three-sport all-state athlete in high school, he'd gone to Oklahoma State University to play basketball, tried out for the football team as well, and had become the first OSU jock since 1940 to earn varsity letters in two sports. In addition to the more physical endeavors, Alan was a scratch golfer as well (two of his high school buddies are currently touring pros), and once through with college he moved to Phoenix and tried to make it on the PGA tour. His try for golfdom's brass ring didn't work out, however; Alan was never able to qualify for a single tournament. Disillusioned, he returned to Oklahoma and tried the oil business. That didn't work out, either, so in the summer of 1984 he took a from-the-ground-up job with Nowlin Mortgage in Dallas at a starting salary of $24,000. At the time he met Sandra Bridewell, he was touring Highland Park in search of a garage apartment to rent. He never located a Park Cities place to live, but he did find Sandra.

It is a tribute to Sandra's allure that in spite of the age difference—Alan was twenty-nine, Sandra forty—the strapping he-man went quickly head over heels. His first date with Sandra was that very evening, and five months later the two were married in (where else?) the lobby of the Mansion on Turtle Creek.

Alan's courtship of, and eventual marriage to, Sandra, like everything else involving Sandra Bridewell, was seen from two different points of view. Alan's buddies felt that the older woman used him as a "trophy husband," while those on Sandra's side felt Alan was after her money. Shortly before the wedding, Alan told a close friend that Sandra was pregnant. Since it is well documented that, shortly after Bobby Bridewell's death, Sandra had gone in for a hysterectomy, the question is whether she was lying to Alan, or if he was pulling his buddy's leg.

The contradictions continued on into the marriage. Within weeks after the wedding, according to Alan's camp, Sandra broke the news that she'd gone to Baylor Hospital, where she'd miscarried. Sandra's side counters that she told Alan from the beginning that she couldn't have children. Even the couple's financial problems (which were many) were subject to interpretation. Shortly after the wedding, the couple sold Sandra's Highland Park home and moved into a Park Cities duplex, and the proceeds from the sale quickly disappeared. According to Sandra, Alan spent all of her money. In rebuttal, he pointed to a $20,000 bill run up on his American Express card, all by Sandra, which has never been paid. Whatever the truth, the marriage wasn't made in heaven. After only six months the couple separated. They lived apart for half a year, but neither filed for divorce. Alan said he couldn't afford a lawyer; Sandra told friends that she and Alan were planning to reconcile.

On Alan Rehrig's last day on earth, December 10, 1985, he said goodbye to friends and told them that he was headed for a mini-warehouse in Garland, a Dallas suburb, to help his estranged wife move some boxes they had stored. He drove away and never returned. Sandra maintains that Alan never showed up to keep their appointment, that she waited for several hours and finally went home.

Alan's body turned up two days later on an icy side street in Oklahoma City, a hundred and fifty miles to the north. He was in his car, shot twice with a .38. There has never been any explanation as to why he might have made the sudden out-of-state trip. For Sandra the total was now three husbands, three tragic deaths, and one strange suicide that might not have been a suicide at all.

Sandra went to Edmond for Alan's funeral, ordered the cheapest casket available, then never paid the funeral home. Eventually, Alan's parents picked up the tab. An intense police investigation followed Alan's murder, both by Oklahoma City and Dallas cops, with Sandra as the main suspect. Investigators found two statements made by witnesses very interesting. A close friend of Alan's said that Sandra called him at six-fifteen on the evening of Alan's disappearance, allegedly from the Garland mini-warehouse, and asked if the friend had seen her estranged husband, since he had never showed for his appointment. However, a second woman said that Sandra was at home shortly after six o'clock, a half-hour drive from the mini-warehouse, and that evening the woman and her husband took Sandra with them to a movie. The movie, *White Nights*, by the way, is the same picture that another friend of Sandra's says that she and Sandra had seen the night before.

Sandra retained a criminal lawyer and, on her attorney's advice, completely clammed up about the matter. She refused to provide fingerprints or hair samples when requested, and refused to submit to a polygraph. Her declination of the lie-detector exam came after she'd taken such a test arranged by her own lawyer. According to a woman who accompanied Sandra to the test, she flunked two key questions.

Lacking Sandra's cooperation, the investigation eventually closed minus any concrete evidence that could lead to an indictment. As far as any charges go, Sandra has proven to be bulletproof. After Alan's death, she deserted her beloved Park Cities and moved to California, where she remains to this day.

When the screaming headlines involving Alan Rehrig's murder came out in the paper, Nancy Lyon had been with Tramell Crow for three years and Richard was by then on his second job. Nancy's problems with David Bagwell were still three years away.

Nonetheless, Sandra Bridewell's final encounter with notoriety was the hot Park Cities dinner-table topic for weeks on end, and John Bagwell's connection to Sandra was something that Richard would long remember.

Richard likes to describe his business career in glowing terms. During his drawn-out trial testimony he would spend half of a day trotting out photos of mirror-walled skyscrapers whose construction he'd supervised, and point with pride at the multimillion-dollar budgets he'd controlled. Spectators and jurors alike were somewhat confused as to what Richard's construction expertise or lack of same had to do with the charge that he'd poisoned his wife, but one thing was for sure. Richard had seen a lot of big buildings.

He also portrayed his eighteen-month stay at Caroline Hunt Schoellkopf's Rosewood Properties as somewhat of a power struggle, and said that he finally left Rosewood for greener pastures because the company's promise of eventual equity ownership fell through. According to Richard, his services were much in demand elsewhere.

"It's all a lot of bullshit," says a thirty-year veteran of the Dallas real estate wars. "All that project superintendent stuff. Look, at a smaller outfit the job means something, but in a big operation like Rosewood a project superintendent's nothing but a glo-rified clerk. The contractor does the work, right? Then the archi-tect inspects, and if the work's up to snuff he sends his approval in to the main office at Rosewood. Then the project superinten-dent fills out a bunch of forms and puts in for the contractor's draw, and if he fills in the right blanks the contractor gets paid. You really want to know what a project super's for? Okay, look. There's times at all these megabuck stores when for one reason or another, cash flow or whatever, they decide to slow-pay all the contractors. So then the project superintendent is the guy that sits and listens to the plumbers and electrical guys bitch about getting stiffed for their money, and you know why? Because the project superintendent makes the perfect foil. He's the guy set up to take all the shit, because he doesn't have the authority to pay the contractor to begin with, so while the project super gets the headaches, all the big shots can go do lunch over at the Mansion and not have to fuck with listening to the contractors bitch and moan. That's what it's all about, if you really want to know."

The real estate vet takes a slug of his bourbon and water and goes on. "You remember what he said on the stand about own-ership in Rosewood Properties? It doesn't work exactly the way he said. Rosewood is one of these outfits where damn near ev-erybody gets to be a partner eventually. That way they can give the guy equity ownership, which he's got no way to cash in, in-cidentally, in lieu of a raise. If Mr. Lyon left Rosewood because he didn't make partner, then it's likely that the next step they had in mind for him was that he was going to get his ass fired."

For whatever reason, Richard's career at Rosewood ended in early 1984, and in order to insure that his son-in-law maintained steady employment, Big Daddy held another breakfast meeting. This time his omelet and fruit cup partner was a maverick real estate developer named Kenneth Hughes, and in the overall scheme of events leading up to Nancy's death, Richard's new job with Ken Hughes Industries would prove significant.

Hughes was one of a dozen or so Dallas loners who hit home runs during the late seventies and early eighties without resorting to alliances with Rosewood, Tramell Crow, or any other con-glomerate. This loosely knit group of overnight millionaires came along at just the right time, when federal deregulation of the savings and loan industry made megabuck financing easy to come by, and when the banks loosened credit in order to keep pace with the suddenly competitive S&L's. By the time the eighties bumped to a close, most of the fast-money group was gone with the wind (along with a high percentage of Texas banks and S&L's as well), either through the bankruptcy courts or absorption by the conglomerates, but during the time that they stayed in business they made noises heard from the Rio Grande to Chicago.

Ken Hughes was barely forty years old when he took Big Daddy's recommendation and hired Richard, and his Hughes Industries at the time was in the process of shooting office towers up into the sky like rockets. Several Hughes projects were out of town, most notably in Houston, and as a small company, Hughes Industries was to give the bright young Harvard grad a much freer rein than he'd had at Rosewood. Ken Hughes took a liking to the handsome kid of Lebanese descent—Hughes' own stunning wife is Middle Eastern, and together with her sister, who is married to the former head of publicity at Neiman-Marcus, forms as comely a sibling duo as can be found anywhere—and Richard's new job was, prestige-wise at least, quite a jump from what he'd been accustomed to at Rosewood Properties. Not only did he suddenly have virtual carte blanche on the company expense account, he had authority to make a few deals on his own, acted as liaison for the company with a number of banks, and was the company check signer on a forty-million-dollar office building constructed in Dallas' upscale Preston Center. He took trips in the company airplane, did business in Houston and out of state, and pretty well set his own schedule. The job gave Richard a new visibility, and within months he was rubbing elbows with the big boys. It would be five years from Hughes Industries' hiring of Richard until the company went down in flames, and many of the things that went on while he worked for Hughes would seal the fate of Richard's marriage. For beginners, though, as Richard accepted Ken Hughes' proposal over dinner one evening, he was in for a relatively short but heady ride.

★ ★ ★

Just how much love flowed between Nancy and Richard during their seven-year stint in the fast lane is difficult to pin down. According to Richard, very little. Nancy was, he says, always hesitant in sex, never willing to experiment, seemingly only enduring what encounters the couple did have. Nancy, on the other hand, confided in those close to her that Richard was a sex maniac, always at her, never seeming to get enough, making her feel at times as though she were his virtual concubine. As in all fragile marriages, there were definitely two sides to the story.

But regardless of whether Nancy's habit was to come to bed clad in an ankle-length shapeless nightgown, quickly douse the lights, dive beneath the covers like a gopher into its hole, and immediately feign a series of snores; or if Richard hid naked behind the bedroom door, and every time Nancy entered, thrust a hardened penis or vibrating dildo in her direction, it's obvious that the couple was into family planning. *Ding,* time to establish careers. *Ding,* time to blend into the social whirl. *Ding,* okay, time for kids.

When Nancy became pregnant in late 1985 or early 1986, her niche at Tramell Crow Partners was well established; she virtually ran the Westchester subdivision on her own while David Bagwell, by now elevated to partner-in-charge of all Tramell Crow residential developments, spent most of his time at the main office or on the road. Also, as befitted her position at the company as well as her legacy as Big Daddy's little girl, she was deep into high-profile charity work, spending many of her evenings and weekends on Junior League projects or in her capacity as chairman of the Dallas Historical Society. She was into political fund-raising as well; her acquaintance with Barbara Bush had to do with a Dallas stop-off for the future First Lady while hustling up voters during the second Reagan campaign.

And while Richard was well into the second year of his stint with high-flying Hughes Industries, he nonetheless had time for a few charitable endeavors of his own, one in particular. St. Phillip's School, located in South Dallas' ghetto area, has in recent years become one of the really "in" charities for which Park Citizens donate time and money. Through Big Daddy's recommendation, Richard had filled a vacancy on St. Phillip's board in 1984, and by 1986 acted as the board's chairman. He also pitched in as a volunteer on the Easter Seals telethon. Both of the couple's careers in apparent high gear, and both social and charitable priorities in order, it was now time to continue the lineage.

Aside from its brief interruption of her job, Nancy's impending delivery had another impact on the Lyons' orderly family plan. By this time the couple had moved into and renovated their second trendy-area duplex, this one on Llano Street, in the same neighborhood as the avenues with the M-names, but they were still across Central Expressway from Park Cities proper. With a child coming along, the Highland Park school district was the only place to live.

So, in November 1986, Richard and Nancy made their final move. The duplex on Shenandoah Avenue was just the thing, right in the heart of Park Cities with a front-yard view of the campus at Southern Methodist University. Typical of old University Park homes built with thrifty college professors in mind, the side-by-side upstairs-downstairs units were somewhat less than a dream home. The rooms were cramped—tiny, actually— the floors uncarpeted hardwood, and the house without central air and heat. The price for the rundown old duplex— $240,000—would have caused jaws to drop in dismay in many parts of the world, but in Park Cities the numbers seemed pretty much in line.

As with all their housing investments, Richard and Nancy went in on a shoestring. The duplex's owner carried $190,000 of the purchase price on a personal note—backed by Big Daddy's guarantee, of course—and the First of Park Cities chipped in $70,000 (likely the true loan value of the old house) on a second lien. The $20,000 over and above the purchase price went to renovate the duplex and accompanying servants' quarters. All told, the payments on the original and second-lien notes amounted to in excess of $3,000 per month, with $1,200 recoverable in rents on the servants' quarters and other half of the duplex. Added to the loans on the two duplexes for which the couple was already obligated, the Lyons now had monthly obligations that would frighten even the most ambitious of yuppies. They were, however, at long last official residents of Park Cities. On whatever scale the upper class uses to measure things, Richard and Nancy Lyon had finally arrived.

The move was just in time, almost coincidental with Allison's birth at Presbyterian Hospital. The baby girl was gorgeous, blessed with Richard's even-featured good looks and Nancy's lovely skin and eyes, and was plenty of reason for rejoicing in both the Lyon and Dillard homes. Nancy had a normal vaginal delivery and three-day hospital stay, then proudly remained at home for a month while friends and relatives came by for a look at the new addition. During this time Richard was particularly attentive to his wife. He took several half-days off from work, cooked meals, brought Nancy her favorite treats while she recovered.

The pregnancy leave was a short one, however. Since she had no plans to remain home with her new daughter on an extended basis, Nancy never considered breast-feeding as a steady diet for the baby. By just after Christmas, in fact, Allison was already weaned to a bottle, and Nancy was preparing to return to work. Since both parents would be plunging ahead with their careers—and since Big Daddy agreed to foot the bill for a portion of the domestic upkeep—Richard and Nancy interviewed a series of prospective nannies. They finally settled on Lynn Pease, and she reported for duty just after New Year's Day of 1987.

A soft-spoken, hardworking native of Oxport, Maine, Lynn had served as a Park Cities nanny since she'd been eighteen. Her twelve-year career had earned her references that were top-of-the-line. Though she suffered from multiple sclerosis, the disease hadn't reached a point that it interfered with her work. She was and is a naturally loving young woman, and eventually came to care for Allison Lyon and her sister, Anna—born two years later—as she would her own daughters.

Lynn's employment in the Lyon home was to continue, with a few brief interruptions, for the better part of three years, and there were a couple of things about her work that bear mention here. So close did she become to the Lyon children, and so much an integral part of the Lyon existence was she during the time that both Richard and Nancy worked at their jobs, that she became as family. Both Richard and Nancy discussed many things with Lynn that one wouldn't normally talk over with a domestic employee. Lynn listened closely to everything she was told, and she has an excellent memory.

Another thing notable about Lynn's employment with the Lyons had to do with her living arrangements. It is customary when hiring a nanny that the employer provide living quarters, but Lynn couldn't live with the Lyons because the servants' space was rented out. So she bunked in the garage apartment at Big Daddy and Sue's Rheims Place home, and during her time with the Lyons became as close to Nancy's parents as she was to Richard and Nancy. Eventually, Lynn's unservantlike integration in the Lyon and Dillard affairs, along with her closeness to Big Daddy and Sue, would contribute greatly to Richard's downfall.

Her new baby's care now mainly in the hands of a nanny, Nancy went back to work at Tramell Crow Partners in early 1987. Though she'd enjoyed her maternity leave, she couldn't wait to return to the job. Nancy feared that if she stayed away from the office at the Westchester subdivision for too long, she would lose control; it had taken time for her to wrest employee allegiance from David Bagwell, and she feared loss of the progress she'd made within the organization. At the time she returned to work her conflicts with Bagwell were minor, just the typical friction between a strong-willed young woman and a man from whom she'd taken over the reins, but who now held a position with the company superior to hers. It wouldn't be long, though, before her rift with David Bagwell would develop into something serious.

13

Lest David Bagwell be forever tarred with the villain's brush in his parting of the ways with Tramell Crow and, ultimately, his role in Richard Lyon's defense to murder charges, let it be known that the partners in Tramell Crow have historically been in somewhat of a locked-in position. It is true as stated earlier that Crow's empire was built on the theory that every good performer should be in for a piece of the action and that, on paper at least, many of Crow's partners have become millionaires. But to picture the company's founder in a cotton-trimmed red suit and flowing white beard, his mouth drawn up in a bow as he slides down the chimney with goodies for one and all, would be somewhat unrealistic. Mr. Tramell Crow didn't just get off the boat from the Old Country with his belongings tied in a bandana hung from a pole over his shoulder. No, indeed.

The total worth of a Tramell Crow partner's ownership is deposited in an equity account along with the total worth of all the other partners, and there it remains. Once a Crow employee attains an equity position, raises in salary cease, the company's sales pitch being that the partner's three-thousand-a-month salary is more than supplemented by his healthy interest in the equity account. However, since the Crow partner is "encouraged" to own a home in Park Cities, Bent Tree, or another of North Dallas' super-affluent subdivisions, thus maintaining the company's image, and additionally receives the "suggestion" that it would be "beneficial" for the partner to belong to the most exclusive country clubs and take a certain number of meals in the to-be-seen-in restaurants, the partner's salary doesn't go very far.

To make up for the deficit between the partner's salary and his cost of living—which is considerable—the partner may borrow rather freely against his equity. The loans are made at preferred interest rates by the company, and since the advance is truly a loan, supported by all the necessary documents, the partner doesn't declare the money received on his income tax return. The net result is that just about every Crow partner lives up to his equity and owes the company an amount equal roughly to the worth of his ownership. Additionally, the company takes no FIT withholding from the loan and pays no Social Security benefit. Suffer the tax collector.

"It's pretty slick for old Tramell," our real estate vet tells us, now on his fourth bourbon and water and signaling the waitress for more. "There's no real equity for anybody but Crow because all these so-called partners don't have any way to get their money but to borrow it. Works two ways. The partners that are pulling their weight all owe the company too much for them to leave. Eliminates competition for Tramell, you know? And the guys that aren't pulling their loads, well, all of a sudden they're looking for a job, and then old Tramell swallows their share of the equity account to pay off their loans." He snorts as he knocks off the rest of his drink, offers the empty to the waitress, and receives a full glass in return. "They can call it a partnership if they want to, but those guys are just a bunch of high-living slaves, if you want to know the truth about it."

There is the occasional partner, of course, whose share of the profits outstrips his debt to the Crow company, and as partner-in-charge of all residential development, David Bagwell was one of those. It is the Crow partner who actually has money coming who eventually becomes disgruntled, because his equity is in name only. If he ever leaves the company, the company simply refuses to buy him out and he remains a partner forever. Moreover, since he has no way to cash in, his equity may as well not exist at all. As David Bagwell prepared to leave the company and go into development on his own, he knew the Crow system very well.

Since Nancy Lyon was a relatively new Tramell Crow partner, and since she had Big Daddy's assets on which to fall back, it was unnecessary for her to borrow against her equity. She hadn't been—and actually never was—exposed to the downside of the Crow partnership system. Therefore, when sums of money began to disappear from the Westchester subdivision accounts in the form of transfers into David Bagwell's name, she had no choice other than to accept his explanation that the money amounted to draws against his equity in the partnership. Nancy was never comfortable with the situation, but Bagwell was, after all, her boss. She chose to keep her mouth shut and tend to business.

Also somewhat uncomfortable with the transfer of funds was Kathleen Cunningham, who worked directly for Bagwell as his assistant at the Tramell Crow main offices. Kathleen, a pretty brunette with a willowy model's figure, was even in less of a position to question Bagwell because, unlike Nancy, Kathleen wasn't a partner. Furthermore, she respected David Bagwell and liked working for him, and though he could be aggressive in getting his way at times, she considered him a serious, hardworking executive. Bagwell's direct superior in the company was after all Michael Crow, one of Tramell's sons, and, Kathleen reasoned, if there was anything improper about the money transfers, surely Michael Crow would have put a stop to the practice.

Though they talked many times over the phone, Kathleen in the North Dallas office and Nancy at the Westchester subdivision out in Grand Prairie, the two young women met in person only one time. The occasion was a meeting at the Grand Prairie Zoning and Planning offices that Kathleen attended as Bagwell's representative, and while the two exchanged pleasantries and were cordial enough, they certainly had no reason to discuss their boss-in-common. Throughout David Bagwell's final months with Tramell Crow, Kathleen Cunningham and Nancy Lyon were the only Crow employees who were aware of the money transfers, and neither had knowledge that the other knew of Bagwell's activities.

Though what Nancy perceived to be David Bagwell's overdomination was a thorn in her side at work, and though she considered her boss a Jekyll-and-Hyde type who might need counseling, she had enough going on in her own life during 1987 and 1988 so that when she was away from the office, she gave him barely a thought. She spent most of her evenings with Allison—Richard was well into his high-flying tenure with Ken Hughes Industries and was often out of town—but still had time for evening and weekend projects for the Historical Society and the Junior League. Then, during the summer of 1987, when Allison was barely six months old, something happened that frightened Nancy. She became pregnant again.

Besides the potential health hazards of a pregnancy so soon after having Allison, Nancy feared the effect another maternity leave might have on the Lyon family finances. Her concern wasn't misplaced, either. With the additional load that the Park Cities duplex put on their monthly obligations, the couple needed every dime of their joint incomes just to make ends meet, and the expense of having another child right away would be more than they could bear. Though going to Big Daddy for help never seemed to concern Richard all that much, Nancy absolutely hated asking her father for money.

Nonetheless, she had no choice but to enter prenatal care once again. To insure that she got plenty of rest, she called on Lynn Pease to work overtime two or three nights a week so that the nanny could care for Allison. Nancy also went on a strict maternity diet and began the same pelvic-strengthening exercises she'd learned in childbirth classes before delivering Allison. As time went on, she got over her initial concerns and let her mothering instincts take over. Finances be damned; if Nancy was to bring a baby into the world she was going to do everything possible to make the child feel loved and wanted.

However, this baby wasn't to be. When Nancy was four months pregnant, during one of her regular checkups the doctor heard no fetal heartbeat. After the various additional tests revealed no life within Nancy's womb, she went to Presbyterian Hospital, where doctors aborted the child.

The incident crushed her, understandably so, and unlike the period following Allison's birth, this time Richard wasn't very helpful. Nancy thought her husband's attitude over the failed pregnancy cold and uncaring, and confided as much to friends and family. It was the first time outsiders knew of any trouble between the Lyons, but it was hardly the last.

The abortion and accompanying trauma also caused Nancy to consider her own mortality for the first time in her life. She was now thirty-three years old. Not only did she have herself and Richard to worry about, she now had Allison as well, and the thought of what might become of her baby daughter should she suddenly become motherless cost Nancy quite a bit of sleep.

Finally she made a decision. She consulted with Big Daddy, who referred her to an expert on the subject, and then she took out a life insurance policy. It contained cash value and annuity clauses, both attractive features to the Lyons since, try as they might, they didn't seem able to put anything aside for a rainy day. The policy's face value was a half-million dollars each on Richard's and Nancy's lives, with the survivor of the two as beneficiary, and with Allison as the recipient of the money should anything happen to both of her parents. Richard and Nancy both took physicals and qualified with flying colors. As they signed the company forms at the kitchen table in the downstairs rear of the Park Cities duplex, Richard joked that he was now worth more dead than alive. The premiums were more than they could really afford, but Nancy was determined not to let the policy lapse. To pay for something as important as life insurance, she would even go to Big Daddy for help if she had to.

A half-million dollars is a nice round figure for life insurance coverage, and was also the amount of damages requested by the plaintiff in the Dallas County lawsuit entitled *Tramell Crow Partners* v. *David Bagwell,* filed in the spring of 1989. The suit came into being a few months after Bagwell left the company and went into the residential construction and development business on his own, and was brought largely as a result of matters Nancy Lyon called to Tramell Crow's attention.

Once Bagwell had resigned and was no longer Nancy's boss, one of her first orders of business was to audit the subdivision's books to determine exactly how much Bagwell had placed in his own accounts. Since the money transfers had come in bits and pieces, Nancy didn't have an inkling as to the total. Moreover, she hadn't really had her mind on business of late. She was pregnant once more.

But when she did finally get down and examine the Westchester books, Nancy felt a chill. The total was staggering, and it immediately occurred to her that since she was in charge of the subdivision, someone might accuse *her* of taking the money. She first thought about talking the problem over with Richard, then changed her mind. It wasn't her husband's decision to make; it was Nancy's and Nancy's alone. She then called Tramell Crow's main offices and made an appointment with the Big Man himself.

It may have been David Bagwell's idea that because of his interest in the partnership equity account, he was entitled to the money from the Westchester development, but Tramell Crow certainly didn't agree. He immediately called for an in-house investigation of the matter, and the first employee questioned was Bagwell's former assistant, Kathleen Cunningham. Though obviously nervous and upset, Kathleen didn't hesitate. She said that she'd noticed the transfers herself, but because Bagwell had been her boss, she hadn't felt it her place to bring the matter up to anyone. Kathleen's story did corroborate what Nancy was saying, though, and that was enough for Tramell Crow. Within days, Crow attorneys were hot on the trail. After months of preparation the company sued David Bagwell, alleging fraud and misappropriation of funds. Both Nancy Lyon and Kathleen Cunningham were named in the suit as plaintiff's witnesses. It is interesting to note that Crow made no attempt to press criminal charges, which gives some credence to the theory that Bagwell may have been entitled to the money to begin with as compensation for his partnership equity.

Now, in addition to her duties as partner-in-charge of the Westchester development, Nancy found herself at the disposal of a gang of company lawyers. There were depositions to give, written statements to prepare, and a seemingly endless string of witness-rehearsal sessions. Her involvement in the Crow-Bagwell lawsuit was a real eye-opener for her; she learned very quickly that the facts in a lawsuit were not nearly as important as the manner in which the case was presented in the courtroom. She told Richard that she felt at times as though the Crow lawyers were putting words in her mouth, and she was having real bouts with her conscience over the entire matter. Additionally, she was having physical problems. As she gained weight by leaps and bounds due to her pregnancy, she found it harder and harder to work. The fall and winter of 1988 were not pleasant times for Nancy Lyon. So involved did she become in her work and in preparation for trial of the lawsuit, she didn't take maternity leave until she was a week from term, in early January 1989.

Anna Lyon bubbled and cooed into the world at Presbyterian Hospital. The vaginal delivery was normal and without complications. Mother and daughter alike did fine, and for a brief period there was once again time for rejoicing in the Lyon and Dillard homes. Big Daddy seemed even more enchanted by his two granddaughters than the children's parents; the veteran of hard-nosed corporate wars had become a doting and devoted grandfather.

Torn between her duty as a mother and her obligation to the Tramell Crow Companies, Nancy cut short her maternity leave and was back on the job when Anna was only two weeks old. Anna was to spend her first year of life more in Lynn Pease's care than that of her natural parents; Richard was traveling a great deal while Nancy spent ten-to-twelve-hour days at the office, both in running the subdivision and preparing herself to testify against David Bagwell. The trial of the lawsuit was scheduled for early the following year.

★ ★ ★

Mark October 16, 1989, as the date that Nancy Lyon's feeling of dislike and distrust for David Bagwell turned into fear. October 16 was the day that Nancy Lyon in Grand Prairie and Kathleen Cunningham in Tramell Crow's North Dallas offices received identical letters. The letters were in plain business envelopes—a later examination wouldn't turn up a single fingerprint on the envelopes' surfaces—and came hand-delivered via messenger service. Both letters were typed on plain twenty-pound bond copy paper, and the messages were identical: "Stay out of the Bagwell case or suffer the wrath of God."

At first Nancy thought that someone was playing a joke on her. There had been a few remarks around the office, made in jest, about the lawsuit and Nancy's upcoming testimony. David Bagwell hadn't been an altogether popular man among the employees at Westchester, and there were some who were secretly tickled to death over his current difficulties. Certain that the letter was a prank, Nancy asked around, but after her questioning of the other employees she realized that no one in the office knew anything about the threat's origin. She looked helplessly at the piece of paper in her hand as a chill spread through her body.

Whether or not David Bagwell had anything to do with the threats, Nancy clearly believed that the ominous letters were her former boss's doing. Both she and Kathleen turned the envelopes, along with their contents, over to their superiors with Tramell Crow, who conducted their own investigation without turning up anything concrete to tie Bagwell to the delivery of the letters. The messenger service had received the order anonymously. David Bagwell himself has made no public comment one way or the other, though he said after Nancy's death that he had nothing but respect for her. Since the lawsuit was eventually settled without going to trial, the only testimony regarding the threats to Nancy and Kathleen came while Richard faced murder charges. Like many things having to do with the death of Nancy Lyon, the origin of the strange letters remains shrouded in mystery.

For Nancy's part, the threat only magnified the problems she already had in her personal life. In recent months she'd had things on her mind that shoved David Bagwell, the threatening letter, and the Crow Companies' lawsuit far into the background. The events leading up to her death had already begun, and would soon develop into a fast, furious, and lethal parade.

The years immediately following Nancy's marriage to Richard didn't go well for Bill Jr. at all. During the seventies, the real estate market had been such that dealers in land made money hand over fist regardless of whether they were prudent in business or not, but the first half of the eighties brought an unforeseen and inexplicable downturn. Suddenly the solid-for-centuries advice for young men to invest what they could in land no longer held water. By 1985 no one in the real estate game was making money. Everyone bled.

The survivors were those who had socked money away during the gold rush, but Bill Jr. didn't fit in that category. As one after another of his ventures went sour, he had to turn again and again to Big Daddy for help. But Big Daddy's reserves, once thought bottomless by the elder Dillard son, had eroded as well. Loans defaulted. Process servers bearing lawsuit notices came by.

For a number of years Bill Jr. had been in the denial stage of his addiction, and as his financial picture worsened, he drank more and more. Deep in his cups almost every night, he became resentful, belligerent, and nasty. More than once over dinner—following a string of pre-meal toddies, of course—he berated those around him to the point that he lost many friends. On the night before his baby brother died, Bill Jr. very nearly lost the support of his entire family.

Tom Dillard's hopeless battle with brain cancer ended in 1985. Of all the Dillard kids, he was the best liked by his peers. He was a considerate and loving son to his mother and father, and during the final year of his life he maintained his cheery attitude in spite of his condition. Radiation treatment slowed the tumor's growth, bringing temporary dreams of victory, but the radiation eventually failed, and equally as futile was the chemotherapy. Finally it was apparent that Tom had lost the battle. Eventually he drifted into a coma. All hope lost, the Dillards gathered at Big Daddy's house and waited for Tom to die.

Susan and her husband drove down from Wichita Falls, and Nancy and Richard came directly to the Rheims Place house after work. Mary Helen, Bill Jr.'s wife, was already there, sitting alongside Sue. She'd already called Bill Jr.'s office and left word that he was to come to his father's immediately. Throughout the evening, Nancy, Mary Helen, and Sue took turns trying to reach Bill Jr. Their efforts were in vain.

It was midnight when he finally arrived, drunk as a lord. He was staggering. His fly was open and there were urine stains on the front of his pants. When he entered the house and looked groggily around at the rest of his family, both Mary Helen and Sue burst into tears. Big Daddy glared at his elder son, then lowered his head and left the room.

Not even his brother's death slowed Bill Jr.'s addiction, and during the years immediately following Tom's death, Bill Jr.'s behavior became even more erratic. Friends approached Nancy in confidence and wondered why Mary Helen didn't file for divorce. Nancy was often ashamed of her brother during the height of his drinking, and wondered herself why Mary Helen continued to put up with her husband. Mary Helen, though, had a deeper understanding of addiction than all of the Dillard clan combined. She secretly attended Al-Anon meetings and prayed that one day the man she had loved and married would come to himself. The turning point for Bill Jr. came in the early spring of 1989.

The addict is always the last to recognize rock bottom, and Bill Jr. was no exception to the pattern. He felt that everyone around him was exaggerating his behavior; often he'd been so drunk the night before that he didn't remember the things he'd done that alienated even those who cared the most for him. During the early months of 1989 he had a number of blackouts. More than once he woke in the morning with no recollection of where he'd been the night before, and without the slightest idea how he'd driven home. One May morning his car was parked in his own front yard. At long last his drinking and compulsive drug use began to frighten him.

Finally, shaky but sober, he approached Big Daddy. He told his father that he couldn't stop drinking on his own, and that if he didn't get help he would lose his family, his sanity, and likely his life. Big Daddy listened with a glimmer of hope for his son; this wasn't the first time that Bill Jr. had vowed to change, but on this occasion he seemed sincere. Finally Big Daddy offered Bill Jr. a choice: he could get help or be forever cut off from his wife, his friends, his sisters, his mother and dad. Bill Jr. bowed his head. He told his father that if he could be free from drink and drugs, he was willing to try anything.

The discerning addict has a number of choices, depending on available funds, though a lifetime of defeat in the battle with drugs and alcohol has left most penniless. Indigent drunks are thus dependent on Alcoholics Anonymous, which supports itself on dollar-here, quarter-there donations from its members, and continues to have the highest rate of recovery among all of the cures. Charter Hospital services middle-class Dallas area jug and cocaine heads for a fee of around $10,000; for the money, the desperate addict receives a bed, meals, and round-the-clock orderly service, and in addition to the identical program that Alcoholics Anonymous provides at no charge receives withdrawal-assistance drugs. The practice of substituting one drug for another has come under criticism.

Just why the free A.A. sessions show the most success is an interesting study. One wealthy resident of Fort Worth, off the bottle for going on nine years, thinks he has the answer. "I've tried 'em all," he says. "You go someplace and pay through the nose, you've got trouble going in. All the drunks in these high-dollar places, they think just because they're paying all this money, somebody's going to do something magic to make 'em quit. It doesn't work that way. People going to A.A., they're really wanting help. If you don't have the desire, no amount of cash is going to save you."

When money is no object, the addict's options broaden. Just as there are "in" places to live, and "in" places to vacation, there are "in" places to dry out as well. Park Citizens whose fingers tremble at the sight of a bottle of Chivas or Johnny Walker Black are familiar with the pecking order: Betty Ford Clinic is all right for those hoping to meet a movie personality or rock star on the mend, but in recent years is considered rather gauche; Timberlawn has been "in" for years but, since it's right there in Dallas, poses optimum risk of discovery. So, for wealthy addicts wanting comfortable surroundings, contact with the crème de la crème among the drunken set, and the utmost in discretion, there's only one place to take the cure. Period. Sierra Tucson is the cutting edge.

Sierra Tucson's name belies the true nature of the institution. So do the surroundings, a breathtaking stretch of Arizona desert with a rugged, canyon-gashed mountain range as a stunning backdrop. The low-slung, Indian-style adobe building, fronted by a circular drive with a huge cactus sprouting from its center island, looks more like an upscale dude ranch than an addiction-recovery center. Even the address, on Lago del Oro Parkway a half-hour drive from downtown Tucson, reeks of exclusivity.

Within the Sierra Tucson compound, patients live the good life. Each resident, shortly after arrival, meets with his or her own personal dietician to plan individually customized meals that not only provide the proper vitamin and calorie intake, but are tailored to the patient's taste buds as well. Inside the building are both group and intimate dining facilities, along with a workout room featuring treadmills, stair-climbers, and the most up-to-date weight-lifting equipment known to man. There is a heated pool and bubbling hot tub. The nearest liquor store is forty miles away.

The mountain air is crisp and invigorating. Group therapy sessions take place in natural amphitheaters on rugged hillsides. The institution has its own riding stable; for those who wish to participate, there are morning and evening horseback trots over meadow and mountain. His attitude better than it had been in years, his jaw set in determination, Bill Jr. checked into Sierra Tucson during the middle of April.

Family participation is part and parcel of addict recovery. If the alcoholic or drug user's treatment is to have any chance of success, the support and understanding of loved ones is a must. Once the addict is on the road back, wives, children, parents, and siblings must know not only the possibility of future relapses, but how to deal with them. Ranting at or lecturing the addict only causes more problems; sternly pouring the liquor down the drain only makes the alcoholic drink in secret. Also important is a basic knowledge of the factors that contribute to the addiction to begin with—and the factors are varied and numerous, some physical, others mental—and methods for dealing with the family's own frustrations. To aid in recovery, Alcoholics Anonymous holds separate Al-Anon meetings for families of members. Sierra Tucson does things differently, inviting the loved ones up for a few days of rest, relaxation, and individual counseling while the addict prepares to return to the world where the troubles began.

The Sierra Tucson family gathering that launched Nancy Lyon on her journey to meet the Grim Reaper took place over a five-day period encompassing Memorial Day of 1989. Big Daddy and Sue accompanied Mary Helen to Tucson to be with her husband. Nancy and Richard came separately, and brought the new baby along. Anna was five months old. Allison stayed in Dallas under Lynn Pease's care. Susan Dillard Hendrickson and her husband, Billy, were the last to come, Billy's orthodontics practice having caused a late departure from Wichita Falls. On arrival at the institution, the entire clan hugged and encouraged

Bill Jr., and all agreed that he looked marvelous. His eyes were clear, his complexion good. Time in the workout room had trimmed and firmed his body.

Their first night together, the group went into Tucson and had dinner. Relaxed and gaining confidence, Bill Jr. gave his family a blow-by-blow description of his treatment. He seemed excited over his recovery chances, even though he realized that the acid test was going to come once he returned to Dallas and tried to function away from the sterile environment at Sierra Tucson. Big Daddy and Mary Helen asked many questions.

Nancy was silent during the meal. She'd been thinking of many things of late. She had done her own private research on addiction and codependency, and she had some ideas. The following day she would bring up her thoughts during counseling sessions.

"If I understand this correctly," Nancy said, "things we bring up in these sessions, if we get them out in the open, talking these things over is going to help him understand his problem."

"Almost, but not entirely right," the counselor said. "The recovery process involves not only the patient, but those closest to him. Addiction affects the entire family unit, not just the one individual. So it's not really proper to say that our sessions will help Bill alone; the entire family unit has to recover along with him."

The counselor spoke in an even, pleasant tone. It is part of the psychologist's function to be a sounding board, a sympathetic ear, a calm presence in the face of all emotional outbursts. The couple now in for their private session were well dressed and obviously well educated. The young man who sat beside the woman on the counselor's sofa was dark and handsome and wore a thin, perfectly trimmed mustache. He seemed uncomfortable, perhaps even a bit skeptical about the whole proceeding. His attitude wasn't unusual. The pretty, dark-haired young woman showed more concern; she would be directly related to the patient while the man would be an in-law. The counselor confirmed the relationship with a quick glance at the file. The lady was the patient's sister, the man the lady's husband. Visible through the window behind the counselor's desk, desert terrain rolled off into the distance to warm the feet of rugged, snow-capped mountains. The counselor bent forward over the low coffee table and waited for the young woman to speak.

"Well, if it's for the whole family," Nancy said, "shouldn't they all be here?"

The counselor touched manicured fingertips together and regarded Nancy. "All in good time. The private sessions, often one feels more comfortable discussing certain things away from others. There'll be a group session later on, sort of a buzz session. Whatever you want to bring up then is up to you. Now, too. You don't have to discuss anything in this session unless you want."

Nancy lowered her gaze, then shot a quick, nervous, sideways glance toward Richard. "I want," she said.

The counselor rested chin on interlocked fingers, not saying anything. It was time to let the subject do the talking, let her innermost feelings pour out.

"It's so hard," Nancy said. "Is it always this hard?"

"Do you feel that it's difficult?" The counselor answered the question with a question, being careful to suggest nothing that might alter the subject's train of thought.

"The hardest thing I've ever done," Nancy said. She looked to her husband. "Oh, Richard . . ."

Richard nervously cleared his throat. It occurred to the counselor that Nancy's husband might be a problem. He didn't seem supportive at all. The counselor leaned back and waited.

Nancy wet her lips and regarded the carpet. "When we were teenagers, Bill and I." She looked up. "When we were kids, you know?"

"Something happened when you were children?" the counselor said.

"For a while. A few years." Nancy gently closed her eyes. "Physical things."

The counselor listened calmly, watching the husband more than the woman. Richard's eyes widened slightly. This is trouble, the counselor thought, he doesn't know anything about this. Incest among older brother and younger sister was a whole lot more common than most people realized, and nothing new in addiction counseling. The shock of bringing it out in the open was hard to deal with for those unaccustomed to such things. "How did you feel about that then?" the counselor said.

"You mean, what was happening between Bill and me?"

"Yes."

Nancy wrung her hands in her lap. "I'm not sure. Helpless, I suppose."

"You felt helpless?"

"Helpless. Confused. I wasn't sure if it was wrong or not. My . . . mother. She caught us at it."

The counselor didn't want to get into the pain of discovery by the parents, not just yet. The acts themselves and the subject's reaction were much more vital to recovery. "Tell about feeling helpless, Nancy," the counselor said.

Richard riveted his gaze on the scene outside the window and kept it there, his square jaw thrust slightly forward. His lips tightened into a rigid line.

"Sometimes I'd . . ." Nancy paused, firmed her posture. "Sometimes I'd pretend it wasn't happening. A few times I read a book while Bill was . . . at me." Now she wouldn't look at Richard at all; she kept her gaze on a point somewhere between the counselor's chin and the top of the coffee table.

The counselor blinked. "And when your mother found out . . . ?"

"I was eleven and Bill was thirteen. She was horrified. They sent him away to school, up in New Hampshire."

"And how did you feel about that?"

"About Bill going away?"

"Yes."

"I think I was glad at first. Then, as we grew older and he stayed away, all the time except for holidays, I started to feel guilty."

The counselor crossed one leg over the other. "And now?"

"Angry. Angry that no one told me it was wrong for me to . . ." Nancy reached for Richard's hand. He allowed her to pull his hand into her lap, but his fingers were rigid.

It's going to be very difficult for them unless the husband shows more understanding, the counselor thought.

* * *

For Nancy, after the anguish of bringing up the issue at a private counseling session in front of an unsuspecting Richard, approaching the subject with the entire Dillard clan gathered in one room was a whole lot easier. Her convictions told her that until the whole family had dealt with the problem and brought it out in the open, Bill Jr. had no chance of recovery. Furthermore, her own feelings of inadequacy, her hesitancy in sex, all of these things she felt would never be over until the entire Dillard family faced up to the long-ago problem. In the group counseling session Nancy talked about the incest with her brother without a moment's hesitation. She said that the Sierra Tucson psychologist had recommended that she go into private incest counseling.

Sue Dillard's jaw dropped in shock. Mary Helen looked as though she'd just been kicked between the eyes. Bill Jr. paled slightly and regarded the floor. Susan Hendrickson and her husband exchanged stunned looks.

Big Daddy remained stoic. He leaned back and clasped his hands behind his head. "Now, that wasn't any big deal."

Nancy was devastated. "No big deal? Daddy, *no big deal?*"

"You kids were playing doctor is all, it happens all the time. It doesn't have anything to do with what we're here for, Nancy." Big Daddy would deny to the bitter end that the problem was all that serious.

"It has everything to do with it." Nancy swept her family with a determined gaze. "If what Bill's going through here has any chance at all, we've all got to face up to it. It was incest, Daddy. We all need help."

The entire group fell silent. Richard seemed even more morose than the rest, fixing his gaze on the ceiling as if both shocked and embarrassed. Big Daddy folded his arms. "It wasn't any big deal, Nancy," he said more softly.

She then dropped the subject. It was apparent that if the problem was going to come to a resolution, she and Bill Jr. would have to work it out between the two of them.

Denial, psychologists say, is the absolute roadblock to cure. Whatever the contact between Nancy and her brother as youngsters—Bill Jr. was later to acknowledge in public that there was intimate touching between the two, though he would deny that there was intercourse; notes that expert witnesses and Big Daddy himself identified in court as being in Nancy's handwriting, however, would tell a much different story—it is clear that her *perception* of what had transpired had an enormous effect on her overall outlook. Nancy had done a great deal of study on the matter, and she felt that bringing it up at the family session in Sierra Tucson was vital.

Psychologists list a number of often contradictory traits as typical of adult incest survivors. Sexually, the female survivor might become totally promiscuous, or she might withdraw into herself and become frigid. Driving ambition is often observed, caused, psychologists say, by a burning desire to overcome what the victims perceive to be terrible shortcomings in themselves. Alcoholism and drug addiction are common, particularly among the aggressors in sibling incestuous relationships. Physicians believe that the addict has a physical craving as well, to go along with a deep-seated sense of guilt and inadequacy. In extreme cases incest victims have been known to mutilate themselves, usually with razors or knives.

In the case of Nancy Dillard Lyon, one other trait common to adult incest survivors bears mention here. It is the single most dangerous symptom, the tendency psychologists strive hardest to combat during counseling. Incest survivors, it seems, have a propensity for suicide.

On the way back to Dallas, Nancy and Richard didn't get along at all. She'd just been through an experience that would have upset the most stoic of women, yet the one person in the world whose comfort and support she needed failed to offer any. The whole idea of the incestuous relationship disgusted Richard, and he told Nancy as much. How could she have done those things with her own brother? According to Richard there had to be something terribly wrong with Nancy, Bill Jr., and the entire Dillard family.

Richard's antagonism drove Nancy deeper and deeper into a shell from which she was never completely to emerge. Once back home she entered therapy, attending counseling sessions at night in addition to the twelve hours a day she put in at the office. That Richard refused to participate in the sessions—and even expressed disgust that she was in incest counseling at all—horrified her. The couple had many nasty fights over the matter, both over the dinner table and in the bedroom as well. Nancy became frigid, shrinking away at the slightest touch from her husband, and her resistance to sex drove Richard up the wall. More than once Nancy accused him of being a sex addict; Richard countered by openly questioning her sanity. The Lyons' constant fighting affected the kids; with the sixth sense that makes children aware of rifts between their parents, Allison and Anna became quarrelsome and difficult to control.

So distant did Richard and Nancy become in the following weeks and months that, whereas he'd previously hurried home from business trips in order to be with his family, he now made excuses to spend more nights on the road. To keep her mind off the widening chasm between herself and her husband, Nancy immersed herself in her counseling sessions and work.

Left to its own devices, the problem between the two might have worked itself out. Time heals many things. Eventually Richard might well have gotten used to the idea that, regardless of what had happened to Nancy as a child, she was still his wife and needed his support and love. For her part, Nancy might have forgiven Richard's lack of understanding, and the two might have grown close once again and gone on as before. But an unforeseen factor was about to enter in and become yet another ingredient in the deadly recipe that would end Nancy's life. Very soon Richard was to begin an affair.

Trying to explain Debi Denise Woods' appeal to men is very much like attempting to justify one's fascination with a beautiful song. The melody haunts and the lyrics tantalize. There is no one portion of the tune that stands out, no single compelling line among the lyrics which will go down in eternity. Each note and word is a part of the whole, and the whole is unforgettable.

The legs are good and supple, with a muscular tautness to calf and thigh, and work tirelessly even in the sitting position; the knees constantly cross, uncross, and recross again in perpetual fluid motion. The dainty suspended foot jiggles and twitches. A pair of NBA-sized hands would encircle the waist with thumbs overlapping, possibly to the first knuckles. Denise's own hands are small and active; she speaks with many gestures. The chest is unremarkable and even boyish, the arms slender, the neck photogenically firm. The chin is determined. The mouth is enchanting, small and drawn, turning up at the corners only slightly when she smiles. The eyes are azure velvet. The hair is cornsilk blond, cut short, and flips efficiently as she tosses her head. The voice is soft, its tone comforting. The speech is both with-it and educated, a little gee-whiz combined with a large helping of chic. She sometimes wears small-lensed glasses. On entering a crowded room she draws no god-almighty-lookee-there glances, but men who have gotten to know her have traveled many miles to cherish her company.

Denise is a bit of a chameleon. In her contracting business—at which she is very good—she is reserved and professional. At social functions she fits in well, both at formal charity fund-raisers and more casual upper-class happenings, but neither would she be ill at ease guzzling longnecks in the back of a pickup with bare feet hanging out over the open tailgate. She has never wanted for escorts.

She grew up as Debi in the upper-middle-class Dallas suburb of Richardson, and on attaining adulthood switched to her more literarily mature middle name. She's bright and articulate; her grades at the University of Texas in Austin were good, but could have been better had she had a less active social life. She likes being in business on her own, and has no problem with being part of a minority group. Her status as a woman entitles her to preferred bidding on public contracts, and preferred assistance from the Small Business Administration. She takes advantage of both. Her father is himself a successful general contractor, and advises his daughter well.

She has been in demand among the Dallas trust-fund crowd; her escorts and lovers have included Texas marquee names. She is little impressed by fame, only slightly more so by fortune. She is accustomed to life among the upper class, and expects the men in her life to treat her well. With very few exceptions, they do. When Richard Lyon met Denise she was twenty-six years old. Like many torrid relationships, it all began with a disagreement.

"Look, none of those things people are saying—" Denise says, "I'm just not like that, a home wrecker or anything. I've been in therapy over this. Some days I think I know the truth, others I think it's all a lie."

"You mean, whether he did it or not?" the interviewer says.

"That, sometimes. Yeah, mainly. Sometimes it's just, whether we really had anything. For someone not sure about that, I've really laid it all on the line, huh? I can't even live in my hometown, with all the newspapers hounding me."

"Austin's not that far away," the interviewer says.

She firmly shakes her head; the blond hair flips in emphasis, then settles down on her forehead. "In miles maybe. At least here my phone doesn't ring off the wall, and when it does ring I'm not afraid to answer it."

It is just after dusk. The downtown Austin restaurant is Central Texas trendy, rustically carved wooden planks serving as pillars, an old wagon wheel on the wall. Hanging baskets around the perimeter of the room hold thorny ferns and upright cactus. The lights are dim, a single candle flickering in the center of the table. The waiters and waitresses are college kids mostly, some working part-time after class, others having dropped out for a semester or so to save up a bankroll and have another go at getting a degree. Some will go back to school, others will not. Denise has salad and tender, succulent baked halibut. She drinks scotch and water in dainty sips. The interviewer pigs out on prime rib and has plain soda with a twist. He wants liquor, but after thirteen years without a drink knows he still can't handle it.

"You still see him, don't you?" the interviewer says.

"Richard?"

"Yes."

Denise stares vacantly into flickering candlelight. "He calls. Yeah, I go down there some. It's not the most pleasant trip." She wears a plain tan dress with thigh-length skirt, and very little makeup. Her eyes appear tired, with worry lines at the corners beyond her years.

"Not the best company, either."

Denise lays utensils aside. Her eyes are misty. "Man. All those poor women with little kids dressed in rags. Every time I leave there, I'm so down it takes days for me to recover."

"Not a pleasant subject for you, Denise," the interviewer says. "I don't guess I've got anything pleasant to ask you. You said earlier you were having doubts about whether he did it. Any particular reason? All during the trial you were tough on his side."

"Oh, I still am. It's just . . . once a guy's convicted, you know? I can't imagine a guy that went to Harvard, if he was going to poison somebody, that he'd be that stupid."

"There was some testimony, about buying the poison."

"The mysterious blonde?" Denise takes on a slightly huffy tone. "That's all a lot of bullshit. I'll tell you it wasn't me."

"And all the time you were . . . with him and all, you didn't have any inkling that he was, might be, planning anything?"

"Look. Once and for all, okay? He was devastated when she died, and I was with him a lot. The guy's an engineer, not a drama major. He couldn't have been faking it."

The interviewer studies the table. "Then you don't have regrets?"

"Regrets? Sure I have. I'm sorry she died. I'm sorry the whole thing between me and Richard started to begin with, in the long run. But I don't feel to blame for it. I thought that Nancy was crazy all along, and that's something I haven't changed my opinion on."

"You knew her, then?"

The brief head shake, the slight flip of the hair. "Only saw her one time in my life, and then she didn't know who I was and we didn't speak. But the whole time they were separated, anytime we were ready to go out and she found out about it, she'd call up Richard and say she was sick, and off he'd run to her."

"And it never bothered you that he was married?"

"Are you kidding? Of course it bothered me. Look, haven't you ever been attracted to someone? I mean, like, really attracted?"

"Obsessed?"

"Call it that if you want to," Denise says. "But whatever, once Richard and I got together, neither one of us could have stopped what was happening any more than we could fly. And as for Nancy, Richard didn't kill her. I'm sure of it."

"You think it was one of the other suspects?"

"You mean, like Bill Jr.?" Denise says.

"Or the other one. Bagwell," the interviewer says.

"No. That's never been my theory. Nancy took that poison

herself, is what I've always thought. I told you I thought she was crazy, you know?"

Richard was spoiling for a fight when he went to Houston the week following the Sierra Tucson trip, and there was more to his mood than his problems with Nancy. In addition to the troubles he was having at home, Richard's employer was in serious financial straits, the result being that his own job was in jeopardy.

It was now 1989, and the boom period of the seventies and early eighties was ancient history. High-flying Hughes Industries was now navigating on severely clipped wings, two of its primary lenders having failed and two more having shut off credit to the company due to delinquent loan payments. Dallas had glutted itself with high-rise office buildings, many of which had suffered foreclosure, and even if the interim financing had been available to Hughes to do the jobs, large construction projects in the company's home base city were nil. Desperate for work, Hughes Industries along with other Dallas contracting firms began to look outside the Dallas territory.

The renovation of Houston's Pavilion Mall—with Saks Fifth Avenue as the cornerstone store—was a job at which, only a few years earlier, Hughes would have turned up his nose. Remodelings are specialist's work and not really designed for a general building contractor, but the toughness of the times made taking the contract a necessity. Richard was the superintendent on the job, and during the project spent most of his weekdays in Houston. The remodeling was nearly complete, but he still had quite a bit to do. The mall's owners, now that they had spiffy new corridors and overhead deco, needed someone to insure that the individual retail spaces were finished on time. Due to the lack of work in Dallas—and also because they were desperate for money—Hughes Industries put Richard on loan to the mall. The mall's owners paid him directly, and for the duration of the project he reported directly to them.

That the same motive—lack of work in Dallas—had caused Denise Woods and her partner to travel to Houston to work at the Pavilion Mall is somewhat ironic but true. Denise's partner at the time was a man named George Sheban—the two shared living quarters as well as interest in the business—and the two of them had contracted to do interior preparation on Sam's Cafe, one of the prime Pavilion Mall locations, whose owner was the actress Mariel Hemingway. So if there had been no economic crunch in Dallas at the time, Denise and Richard might never have met, and Nancy might still be alive. Fate moves in treacherous ways.

To portray Denise Woods in a hard hat with a loop belt strung with hammers and chisels around her waist, or possibly in a welding mask à la Jennifer Beals in *Flashdance,* would be stretching it. The fact is that, at least in her partnership with George Sheban, Denise's participation in the actual deal-making or supervision of the construction crews was minimal. Her main contribution to the success of the business had to do with her gender; any company fifty percent owned by a woman is entitled to federal preference as a minority contractor and all the advantages thereto. It was Denise's first experience in business on her own, and she was to make the most of it. She was an astute observer and a fast learner, and she was to use the Houston experience wisely in her future business dealings.

Richard's first encounter with Denise, during the week following the trip to Sierra Tucson, had to do with a serious problem. She was far behind schedule in her work, and if the restaurant wasn't ready to open on time, the mall's owners were to suffer rental penalties. It was up to Richard to either get Denise into high gear to finish the work, or off the job and replaced with a contractor who would. Denise and her partner had an hour-long meeting with Richard in a booth at Sam's during the afternoon business lull. Since it was a weekday, customer traffic in the mall was sparse. Richard sat on one side of the booth while Denise and George Sheban, side by side, were across from him. All three drank iced tea.

Just what went through Richard's mind in that first meeting with the azure-eyed, flip-haired blonde is known only to him, but it is clear that he felt an immediate and strong attraction. Whatever his reaction to her charms, the meeting ended without a resolution; Denise's company retained their contract and the work continued at a snail's pace. During the ensuing months Richard was to face a lot of heat over Denise's work on Sam's Cafe. He was to receive weekly instructions from the owners to give Denise and her partner a lesson in hardball. If Sam's was to desert its lease because of the delays, the owners said, the next call Denise would receive would be from the mall's attorneys. Richard's weekly recommendation to the owners was always the same: Denise was doing her best, many of the delays were not her fault, and the owners should let her go on. The cafe's opening was indeed delayed, but Sam's Cafe kept the leasing agreement and Denise Woods received full payment on her contract. Richard's true motive in allowing her to continue on the job is anybody's guess.

Richard confesses that even though he and Denise were adversaries to begin with, from the day of that first encounter he couldn't get her off his mind. For Denise's part, she viewed Richard originally as only a business acquaintance; she knew that he was married. Not only that, she was into her own relationship at the time. So the afternoon meeting at Sam's Cafe, as opposed to the picture the prosecution would attempt to paint at trial, didn't hurl Richard and Denise spontaneously into each other's arms. It was a beginning, though.

Richard wasn't the only one worried about Hughes Industries' finances. During the company's final turbulent months the list grew to include creditors, owners of projects the company was in the process of building, and, ultimately, employees who fell victim to bouncing paychecks in Hughes' death-rattle closing weeks.

Carol Poor was more loyal than most, sticking firmly by the company until her need to eat overcame her desire to help Hughes Industries over the hump. That's when she sought and found employment with a downtown Dallas law firm. While with Hughes Industries, Carol acted as Richard's secretary and assistant, and during the months when he spent virtually all of his time in Houston, Carol in effect acted as Richard. She fielded his calls, answered his correspondence, and—somewhat unwillingly, but effectively, due to Carol's genteel and cooperative nature—became Richard's and Nancy's go-between. Carol is a pretty brunette, a fervently religious young woman who was willing to do what she could not only to help Nancy and Richard with their

marital problems, but to aid Nancy in her confusion over her adolescent incest. During Nancy's final year of life she took Carol
into her confidence and told her many things that she told no
one else, and that included her family. Nancy and Carol often
prayed together.

"I didn't have any use for that Denise," Carol says. "I let Richard have it more than once over her."

"Do you think it was her personally," the interviewer says, "or
just her relationship with Richard?"

"Both. Anyone carrying on with a married man."

"He was separated," the interviewer says.

"Not when it began," Carol says rather curtly. There is a plate
of lemon chicken on the table before her; Carol's preference is
Chinese. The interviewer wonders briefly how many different
kinds of food he's going to sample before his research is over. It
is mid-afternoon; the restaurant is an inexpensive place located
in an East Dallas strip shopping center. The table's centerpiece
is a Chinese lantern with a light bulb glowing inside.

"When did Nancy begin calling you?" the interviewer says.

"We spoke to each other the whole time I worked there. When
she'd call for Richard, you know. It was right after that Sierra
Tucson trip, though, when we started getting on a personal
level."

"What do you think caused her to confide in you?"

Carol shrugs. "She knew that I was interested, that I really
cared. Richard wasn't helping her any, even before his affair
started. I think Nancy hoped I could talk some sense into him."

"And did you try?"

"As much as I could. Richard became pretty distant during
that period. All he seemed interested in was getting his hands on
that woman. I think now he's come to his senses, though it's
likely too late for him. I've got a letter where he's telling me, 'If
this isn't hell it's the next thing to it.' He's into prayer in prison.
I'm praying for him."

"Did Nancy talk to you about her counseling?"

"All the time. There was a lot more to that incest business
than what they brought up at trial, at least according to her,"
Carol says.

"Did the counseling seem to help her?" The interviewer toys with his own plate of Moo Goo Gai Pan. On a scale of one to ten, Chinese food is around number nine on his list.

"I don't think the counseling did much for her. She wrote down a lot of things, a lot of things that troubled her. She needed Richard badly at that time, but he just wasn't there for her."

"And in spite of all that, you don't think he killed her?"

Carol is firm here. "I know he didn't."

The interviewer is puzzled. "He was having an affair. Without her inheritance he had nothing, and there was the half-million in life insurance."

Carol wrinkles her nose. "Bull. She changed the beneficiary on the policy to the kids a long time before she died."

"But Richard didn't know that. Lynn Pease, you know, the nanny? She testified that after Nancy died, she's the one that told Richard that the kids got the life insurance money, because Lynn witnessed Nancy's signature on the policy change. Richard put a letter into evidence where Nancy notified him of the change in beneficiary, but the letter was typewritten and Lynn testified that Nancy couldn't even type. The prosecution's position was that Richard phonied up that letter along with the other writings."

Carol firmly folds her arms. "Nancy told me she'd changed the policy. And all those writings of hers that Richard submitted in court? Nancy wrote every bit of that, I don't care what any experts said. Richard didn't profit a dime by Nancy's death, and knew all along that he didn't get the insurance money. Lynn, the nanny? She didn't know near as much as she said she did. I think Richard pointing Lynn out as a suspect in the poisoning made her mad, and that's why she said those things."

The interviewer frowns. "Carol, Nancy told you about changing the life insurance policy?"

"That's what I said. I don't know why Richard's lawyer didn't put me on the stand. I was ready to testify all along."

The interviewer is silent, wondering about the defense's motives in not using Carol as a witness, but then he understands. Her testimony about what Nancy told her would have been hearsay, which makes it even more ironic that Nancy's statements to Dr. Bagheri were admissible in court while what she had told

Carol wouldn't have been allowed. The interviewer sighs. "What's your theory, Carol? One of the other suspects? Bagwell maybe? Bill Jr.?"

Carol's expression softens. "I wouldn't begin to accuse anyone, I'm not even acquainted with those other people. What I do know is, I'm just sure as we're sitting here that Richard didn't do it."

"In all your talks with Nancy," the interviewer says, "all your prayer sessions together, she never said anything that made you think she was afraid she was going to die?"

Carol appears thoughtful. "Not that she was going to die, exactly. But there were things in her incest counseling. She told me more than once that there was discussion in those sessions about incest victims committing suicide. And I'll tell you something else. Nancy was so worried about her marriage breaking up, so obsessed with Richard, I don't think it's impossible that if she was sure she was going to lose him, she might have killed herself. It's not impossible at all."

Relations between Richard and Nancy were miserable during the summer after the Sierra Tucson trip. Nancy's determination to continue her incest counseling was a constant thorn in Richard's side, but certainly wasn't the only bone of contention between the couple. They argued often about everything from money—the real estate crash had put them in a position where the rents from their duplexes didn't cover the amount of the monthly notes, and the couple was constantly in a bind and having to borrow from Big Daddy to get by—to sex, which for them was nonexistent, and they often slept in separate rooms. It was during this time that Nancy first experienced frequent illnesses. She missed quite a bit of work during the period, and went in late often due to feeling under the weather.

Richard says that her suspicions drove him up a wall. She constantly accused him of sex addiction, and of sleeping around (even though his affair with Denise Woods wasn't to begin until the fall, he complains). There was one incident that summer, however, related by Richard from the witness stand at his trial, which shows that Nancy's fears regarding his sexual appetite weren't totally unfounded.

"She used my car one day," Richard said, "and for some unknown reason took it on herself to search the trunk. What she found in there blew her mind. There were some *Playboy* magazines and a sex aid in there, and when I got home, there she stood with those things. I tried explaining to her that since we weren't sleeping together, I had to get relief somewhere, but she just started in about the sex-addiction thing. It wasn't a pleasant scene."

This testimony brought a few guarded snickers, both from the prosecution table and the defense side in the courtroom. The sex aid mentioned was still in Richard's car when the police eventually searched the trunk after Nancy had died, and was in fact a soccer ball with holes punched into its surface at various strategic locations. Whatever his other activities at the time, Richard was indeed desperate for love.

Richard's sexual frustration finally came to an end on a warm September night in downtown Houston when, after months of verbal foreplay, he and Denise went to bed together. Since she was at the time living with George Sheban, her business partner, it was a somewhat risky venture for her as well.

After another in the seemingly endless string of afternoons haranguing over Denise's failure to stay on schedule with the Sam's Cafe contract, she offered to take Richard to dinner as a sort of peace offering. They chose a secluded Italian restaurant in downtown Houston close to Richard's hotel, the Remington, and in addition to linguini with clam sauce consumed two bottles of wine and more than a few scotches with water. The lights were dim, the candlelight flickering, the conversation intimate. Before either was aware of what was happening, they passionately kissed.

Since Richard was well known at the Remington and couldn't afford to be seen there with a woman, he rented a room for the night at the more upscale Ritz Carlton. He later confided to close friends—and finally announced to a packed courtroom and the nation at large—that the sexual experience with Denise that night was the most wiltingly satisfying of his life, before or since. Denise bristles at any discussion of her bedroom life with Richard, but acknowledges that she was as taken with him as he was with her. Whatever. The evening charted a new course in Richard's destiny. In addition to fueling his reckless passion for Denise, and forever driving a wedge between him and Nancy—if the events of the previous months hadn't already placed an insurmountable barrier between the two—the amorous encounter put the erotic career of the soccer ball indefinitely on hold.

Once Richard had given in to his yearning for Denise, he pulled out the stops. His affair was a secret for a very short time; once the Pavilion Mall project was complete, Denise returned to live full-time in Dallas. So did Richard, reporting to work at the floundering Hughes Industries by day and using every possible excuse—they were numerous: night work, charity projects, fictitious board meetings at the St. Phillip's School—to be away from home in the evening to be with his lover. To say that Richard was less than discreet about his affair is putting it mildly; he openly escorted the lithe, azure-eyed blonde to the best restaurants and nightclubs along the Greenville Avenue strip and Addison's Belt Line Road, and often didn't return to his Shenandoah Avenue duplex until three or four in the morning. Evenings on the town weren't nearly enough to satisfy his need, real or imagined, to be with Denise; during the following months he concocted fictitious business trips and took Denise along with him to New Orleans, New York, and on a journey to Los Angeles that included a couple of days' stop-off for Colorado skiing.

North Dallas in general and Park Cities in particular are small, small towns within a big city. As in all upscale yuppie areas whose residents have plenty of extra money to spend, philandering is common among Park Citizens. The participants' names are generally known to all, except, of course, for the cuckold spouses. The players believe—erroneously in many cases—that there is safety in numbers; the I-won't-tell-on-you-if-you-won't-tell-on-me attitude is prevalent. But comeuppance works the same way among the philanderers as in a network of drug dealers; one caught, all caught, the apprehended cleansing their souls by ratting on the rest of the gang. Nancy heard about Richard's affair less than a month after it had begun.

Nancy was crushed. Now, in addition to dealing with her incest recovery and the even more devastating problem of a husband who showed no compassion for what she was going through, she was the subject of nasty gossip. In the S&S Tearoom (the "in" Park Cities ladies' lunching establishment) and in the trendy hair salons in Highland Park Shopping Village, tongues were a-wagging. Nancy knew the system and knew it very well.

At first she didn't confront Richard. Typically, Nancy felt guilty and was certain that she'd driven her husband into another woman's arms. She still had her hangups about sex, but was determined to do anything within her power to save her marriage. Hesitantly but willingly, she once again invited Richard into her bed. Tragically, she immediately became pregnant again.

To what degree her turmoil over incest counseling, coupled with her anxiety over Richard's affair—not to mention the threatening letter received at her office over the Bagwell case—contributed to Nancy's second miscarriage will never be known, but likely all three were factors. In early November 1989, Nancy once again entered Presbyterian Hospital for an emergency D&C, the official reason being listed as fetal demise. No matter what she tried, no matter which way she turned, things simply refused to get better for her.

★ ★ ★

The upkeep on three duplexes, the extravagant affair with Denise, and the general cost of living in Park Cities put a terrible strain on Richard's (and Nancy's) income. Moreover, another in the series of disasters leading up to her death occurred in mid-October when Hughes Industries finally gave up the ghost and sought the protection of the bankruptcy courts. Richard was out of a job. Since his life-style had never permitted him to stockpile any cash reserve, and since he now had to rely solely on his wife's salary to pay the monthly bills, to support his extramarital activities he was forced to go to work on the credit cards.

Richard was later to portray himself in the courtroom as a man satisfied with the simple pleasures, and Denise was to state defensively that "Richard was the most unmaterialistic dude I've ever run across," but the record from September to December of 1989 bears out neither assertion. In Richard's trips with Denise, the couple traveled first-class and stayed in the best hotels. During a trip to New Mexico he charged a $4,500 watch as a present for Denise, and on other occasions showered her with numerous smaller—but still pricey—gifts. Denise liked golf, so Richard charged an expensive set of woods and irons along with a Proline leather bag for himself so that he could join her on the course. He also bought an Alfa Romeo on credit. Before the year was out, Richard's debt to American Express was to exceed $25,000.

Nancy became frantic over Richard's erratic spending, almost as frantic as she was crushed over his affair. She finally confronted him with the rumors she'd heard that he was seeing a flashy blonde. Richard denied all. Nancy persisted. He clammed up and left the house in a huff. Totally at a loss over what to do, she went to Big Daddy and tearfully spilled the beans.

Since business lunches among male Park Citizens are every bit as gossipy as the women's noonday meals, Big Daddy had already heard that Richard was running around. His discussion with Nancy was the first he had heard about Richard's spending sprees, however, and the idea that his son-in-law was blowing exorbitant amounts on another woman while his little girl was left to pay the bills infuriated him. He quickly told Nancy exactly what to do. The following week while Richard was off skiing in Taos with Denise, Nancy closed the bank accounts and canceled the credit cards. The shutting off of the funds successfully curtailed Richard's activities for a while, but not for long.

His access to money gone, Richard went in remorse to Nancy and said he'd do anything she wanted him to if she would only forgive him. But instead of relenting as he obviously expected, she set up a meeting between him and his incensed father-in-law. Big Daddy was every bit as firm with Richard as he'd earlier been with Bill Jr.; if Richard wanted help, he had to agree to take the cure. Under threat of becoming penniless, Richard had to go along, and in mid-November became the second member of the Dillard clan in less than a year to take the trek to Sierra Tucson. There he enrolled not only in the sexual addiction program, but also in treatment for alcohol dependency. Uncertain whether Richard's problem was sex or booze, Big Daddy wanted to cover all bases.

Richard's stay in the refreshing mountain air at Sierra Tucson lasted exactly two weeks, after which he went over the hill and sought the even more comforting climate of Denise Woods' arms. He met her in Aspen, and the two of them went skiing. On this occasion he had plenty of funds to make the trip a memorable one; the money he took on the Aspen trip was Big Daddy's advance for the Sierra Tucson treatment. When Big Daddy discovered, months later, where his money had gone, he was less than thrilled.

In spite of the unscheduled detour from treatment at Sierra Tucson, and in spite of his knowledge that Richard was having an affair, Big Daddy found his son-in-law yet another job. It was never clear to trial spectators (or, apparently, the jury) what point the defense was trying to get across, but Richard's lawyer spent a great deal of time cross-examining Big Daddy about the various positions he'd gotten for Richard and the various letters of recommendation he'd written. Whatever his reasons for getting Richard jobs in the past, Big Daddy's motive after the Sierra Tucson fiasco is abundantly clear. Richard's debt was astronomical and mounting by leaps and bounds. Further, Big Daddy was Richard's principal creditor, and one of his checks to his father-in-law had already bounced. So if Big Daddy didn't find work for

Richard, it was likely that Big Daddy would never see his money. Whatever his earlier reasons for helping out, Big Daddy now had a bonus incentive to spur him on.

The breakfast-meeting partner on this occasion was a tenacious forty-five-ish Dallas businessman named Stan Wetsel, who himself had deep roots in the city's twentieth-century history. His father, J. C. Wetsel, was one of SMU's first bona fide all-American football players, and Stan himself attended the university on a baseball scholarship. Stan Wetsel had earlier prospered in the landscaping and nursery business, but like many Dallas contractors, the eighties had been a nasty experience for him. Unlike many other casualties, though, Wetsel was a fighter. Down but far from out, he had recently formed a company called Architectural Site Services in an effort to regain his balance and get moving again. The new company was doing very well for a fledgling venture, and an out-of-work landscape architect with a Harvard degree was right up Wetsel's alley. Big Daddy set up an appointment for Richard, and Wetsel added Richard to his staff the very next week.

New employment for Richard should have been a bright spot for him and Nancy; not only did steady work give him less opportunity to stray from the straight and narrow, there was now an income in the family in addition to what she brought home. But there was a drawback to the employment with Architectural Site Services that is crystal clear to twenty-twenty hindsight. There had been little if any economic recovery in Dallas—and would be no upturn, in fact, for three more years; therefore it was necessary for ASS to look for work just as Hughes Industries had done. The only attractive contracts in all of Texas at the time were being performed in Houston, so trips to the Bayou City were once again to be part of Richard's routine. And just as his travels to Houston with Hughes Industries had begun his affair with Denise, Richard's trips to the bayou while in ASS's employment were to bring even more woe to those close to him.

Richard's new job did help the Lyons financially, but also gave him more opportunity to be away from home in the evenings and, therefore, more opportunity to tryst with Denise Woods.

During the final month of 1989 and the first month of 1990, he did so often, in spite of the fact that he'd assured Nancy that his affair with Denise had ended. For her part, Denise kept her secret rendezvous with Richard a closely guarded secret, and for a very good reason. She had her own quite active social life, and didn't want news of her trysts with a married man to leak out and muddy other waters for her.

In December 1989, the Rolling Stones came to Dallas to blow the roof off of Texas Stadium, and Denise's date for the rock concert provided her with a couple of extra tickets, which she slipped to Richard. Even though Nancy wouldn't have given two cents to watch Mick Jagger cavort and gyrate, Richard insisted that his wife accompany him to the blowout. When the performance was over, the two walked hand in hand through the parking lot toward their car with the domed Texas Stadium roof looming ominously overhead. Suddenly they were face to face with a young man who had his arm around the shoulders of a saucy, flip-haired blonde.

Richard stiffened noticeably. The two women, wife and lover, were face to face for just an instant, then Denise and her date excused themselves and detoured around the Lyons to continue on their way.

Nancy watched the other couple's retreating backsides, then turned coldly to Richard. "That's her, isn't it?"

Under the circumstances, Richard's parting with Nancy was likely inevitable, but the straw that finally brought the camel to its knobby knees fell in late January when he told her he was going on a business trip to New Mexico. Nancy was suspicious because New Mexico wasn't in Richard's normal travel itinerary, so called the hotel where he was supposed to be staying to find that he wasn't registered.

Incensed, she called MasterCard (Richard had regained use of his credit cards by this time) and traced him through airline tickets and hotel charges to Crested Butte, where he and Denise were skiing once more. Richard's handsome Lebanese features twisted in dismay when, while he was in bed beside his lover, Nancy called him in his supposedly secret hideaway. Nancy had

had enough, she said, and ordered her husband to move out immediately. This time Richard had no choice. On a late-January morning of 1990 he loaded what belongings he could into his Alfa Romeo, kissed his tearful little girls goodbye at the curb, and drove away.

The story could have ended that way, with Richard leaving home to be permanently with his lover, Nancy filing for divorce, and the Lyons living uncongenially apart for the rest of their days. But as Richard drove away on that January morning, the final nightmare for Nancy Lyon lay just around the corner.

Ellen Rose doesn't resemble anyone's idea of a seller of poisons. She is a slender and studious young woman who views the world through harlequin glasses, and who takes her employment with General Laboratory Supply very seriously. General Lab Supply is a chemical wholesaler located in the northeast Houston suburb of Pasadena, and doesn't rely on poison as its main source of income. The poisons the company does happen to sell are normally incidental to its other sources of income.

"It doesn't take a permit to sell it, and it doesn't take a permit to buy," Ellen says. "There's no law governing poison, and anyone who walks in here can buy the stuff, cash, charge, or otherwise." Since the government seems to regulate everything else under the sun, why don't they keep an eye on the poison business? "I don't know," Ellen says. "I just work here."

At first she had no memory of the swarthy, handsome young man who entered General Lab Supply's offices on January 24, 1990, and had to research her records to locate the name of Richard Lyon on an invoice of that date for one hundred grams of lithium hydroxide, an innocuous general-purpose substance sold often in the company's normal course of business. Ellen's own meticulous notation on the invoice mentioned that Richard had paid by personal check in the amount of $21.90, but she had no independent memory of the transaction. After all, she waits on hundreds of customers. How could anyone expect her to remember just one of the many?

Ellen Rose also frowningly failed to recall Richard's visit to General Laboratory Supply only two weeks later, on February 8, an occasion on which he purchased one pound of triple-distilled mercury and paid with greenback dollars. She did, however, have a copy of that invoice as well, and caused some raised eyebrows among Dallas homicide detectives when she pointed out that Richard gave his address at that time as 2323 Bryan Street in Dallas, which, strangely enough, is Big Daddy's office location. Richard did provide a local Houston telephone number on the invoice, which was the number of his job site.

There were numerous other times during the year that Richard stopped by or phoned in orders to General Laboratory Supply, none of which Ellen Rose could remember offhand, but for all of which she could locate the company records in the computer. By August, for example—the eighth, to be exact—Richard had his own General Lab Supply catalog, and on that date furnished not only the names of the products he wanted, but the products' catalog order numbers as well. The August 8 invoice caused the homicide detectives to scratch their noses thoughtfully, because in addition to barium carbonate, cyanogen bromide, and lead nitrate, Richard also purchased five grams of sodium nitroferrocyanide. Aha, the detectives thought, *poison*. That Richard had thoughtfully left a trail by paying with his own personal check apparently didn't seem strange to the police, who were further disappointed to learn that the suspected substance on the invoice was merely another in a long list of red herrings that appeared during the investigation. Sodium nitroferrocyanide, it turned out, is merely a nontoxic substance used in the treatment of heart patients. Ellen Rose likely could have pointed out to the detectives that, Hey, fellas, the barium carbonate, that's the poison in the order, but the detectives were looking for arsenic and the significance of the barium carbonate wouldn't come out until much later.

During none of the other visits from Richard did he buy any arsenic according to company records. After a lengthy interview with Ellen Rose, in fact, the detectives decided that the General Laboratory Supply lead—which Nancy's family had supplied from records of Richard Lyon's checking account—was a complete blind alley. Nonetheless, they did present Ellen with an array of pictures—some of the snapshots were of plainclothes detectives, others were mug shots of prisoners, and one was of Richard Lyon—for her perusal. After a careful examination of the photo lineup, Ellen ruefully shook her head. She was sorry, but she couldn't identify anyone. The detectives sighed in disappointment, thanked her for her time, and left. The police interview with Ellen took place in mid-February of 1991, some six weeks after Nancy's death.

Ten months later at trial, after the investigation had unearthed further information to indicate that Richard in fact *had* ordered arsenic from General Laboratory Supply, Ellen Rose sat primly on the witness stand and pointed in the direction of the defense table. She specifically identified Richard as the man who'd been in her office on numerous occasions, and as the man who'd placed the various orders she'd pulled from company records. Her powers of recall at that time were astonishing, and likely were a tribute to the Dallas Police Department's intensive memory-enhancement campaign.

Mary Ann and Bruce Will didn't pay a whole lot of attention to their new upstairs neighbor for quite some time. The Springbrook Lane condo neighborhood in Richardson was quite transient to begin with, many of the residents being move-in, move-out Texas Instrument employees and subject to transfer at any time. Besides, a nice-looking thirtyish single man moving in with a minimum of possessions was certainly nothing to write home about; the big-city divorce rate pumps fresh bachelor material into the system constantly. The eye-catching young blonde who visited the new tenant on an almost daily basis didn't particularly stir the Wills' interest, either; behind nearly every broken marriage there is a willing new partner ready to step in and comfort the lonely. So, as long as he didn't throw loud all-night parties or play his stereo at a volume that vibrated his floor and their ceiling, the new neighbor was A-OK as far as the Wills were concerned. Hello, how you doing, and that was that.

Mary Ann Will is much more outgoing than her husband; when Bruce comes in from work he's generally in for the evening. Except for weekends, the man upstairs was usually gone, but Mary Ann did manage to have a few conversations with both him and his girlfriend. She was impressed with the man's intelligence, particularly when she learned that he was a Harvard graduate, and also liked his politeness and impeccable manners. She wasn't that impressed with the girlfriend, however, and thought that the blonde talked too much. Otherwise, though, she was nice enough. Mary Ann also found out that the man had been recently separated (I told you so, she later told her husband) and that he traveled quite often since he worked for a contracting firm that had business in Houston.

Mary Ann also noticed that the man brought a lot of experimental paraphernalia and chemicals home, and that he had set up an easel in his apartment and was a remarkable painter. The man seemed to have few acquaintances other than the girlfriend; at least no one else stopped by on a regular basis, and when the girlfriend was over, the two went upstairs and kept mostly to themselves. The few times that Mary Ann visited, she felt that the man had a lot on his mind. Later, in fact, she would recall that her new neighbor had seemed quite preoccupied.

One incident a few months after Richard moved into the Springbrook Lane condo gives some insight into Nancy's frame of mind while the Lyons were separated. On the sun-washed Easter Sunday of 1990, around two o'clock in the afternoon, there was a loud knock on Bruce and Mary Ann Will's door. Mary Ann answered to find a pretty but slightly wild-eyed brunette on the porch. The visitor was dressed for church and wore a bonnet. Her car sat out at the curb with its motor running, and in the car were two little girls in bright lacy Easter dresses.

"Do you know where Richard is?" the brunette asked—or, more precisely, demanded, as Mary Ann Will was later to recall.

Mary Ann was confused, and said so. Though she'd seen him and his girlfriend come and go, she didn't know her upstairs neighbor's name. At first she thought that the woman was referring to Mary Ann's own husband, and told her visitor that her husband's name was Bruce.

"The guy up there," Nancy said, pointing upstairs, "is my husband. He's run away and left me with these kids, and doesn't even have the decency to visit his own children on Easter. Well, if he doesn't want to visit us, I've brought the children over to see him."

Mary Ann was polite, though she was a bit nervous at the confrontation, and told Nancy that she hadn't seen Richard in over a week. Nancy spoke in a high, tense voice, and to Mary Ann seemed totally irrational. In fact, she was later to tell police that she couldn't imagine why Nancy would burden a total stranger with her marital problems, and also that she couldn't remember seeing a more distraught person in her life.

Richard's conduct during the period in which he occupied the condo was anything but consistent. Not only was it a harrowing experience for Nancy, it was an emotional roller coaster for Denise Woods as well. Denise confesses to being hopelessly in love with Richard by the time he vacated the Shenandoah Avenue duplex, and that not only was theirs a wild and intense sexual relationship, she more or less looked on Richard as her mentor in her contracting business. And face it, Richard Lyon knew a lot about construction. It was on his advice that Denise took on several of her contracts during the year.

She had feelings of guilt over her affair with a married man from the beginning, but once Richard moved out, Denise felt the relationship somewhat cleansed. No longer did she feel any need to keep her love for Richard a secret, and she began to speak openly to friends about it. Denise also wrote and mailed a long letter to Nancy, outlining her feelings for Richard, and also telling Nancy a little white lie. Denise said in the letter that she had never dated Richard until after the separation. Nancy never replied.

Richard's reaction to having two attractive women in love with him at the same time was, inarguably, somewhat less than mature; he seemed to delight in playing one against the other. Though it had been Nancy who ordered him to move in the first place, he hadn't been living in the condo for a week before she was begging him to come home. Richard declined, but took distinct advantage of her invitation. Just as he'd often lied to Nancy about his whereabouts in order to carry on with Denise, he now fibbed to Denise, concocting fictitious business trips when in reality he was at the Shenandoah Avenue duplex, spending the night in Nancy's bed. In fact, Richard boasted to some that he had sex with his wife more times during their separation than in the entire preceding year while they lived together. When Denise learned during the murder investigation that Richard had been sleeping with his wife during the separation, the news was a shock to her.

Richard also took vicious pleasure in telling Nancy all about his and Denise's bedroom activities. According to what Nancy told her sister, Richard went into great detail describing the things Denise had done that he found erotically pleasing, and then asked that Nancy do the same. Harried out of her wits, and willing to do anything that she felt might bring her marriage back together, Nancy often complied. When she did, Richard threw it all back in her face in the form of degrading insults at every opportunity.

Throughout the final year of her life, Richard played Nancy's emotions like a yo-yo. Often he would be tender and caring. Then, suddenly and without warning, he would hatefully tell her that she was too fat, and that the only reason he'd married her to begin with was because of her money. Further, Nancy could never be a sexual match for Denise. Nancy responded to this form of abuse by crash-dieting down to a twig of a woman, performing whatever sex acts seemed to please Richard—although she considered some of them disgusting and degrading—and even changing her hair to blond in order to match Denise's. Richard reacted to the dye job by laughing in Nancy's face and telling her that she was playing the fool. No matter what she tried in order to please him, her strategy backfired, and if she was indeed nearly out of her mind during the period, her lack of total sanity is certainly understandable. During 1990 both Nancy and Denise traveled pathways strewn with thorns.

There are different points of view concerning the reasons for Nancy's departure from Tramell Crow Partners. She took a leave from the company within two weeks after Richard moved out, and the reason given family and friends was that she wanted to spend more time at home with Allison and Anna. Many close to the company disagree; they say Nancy became so distraught over her personal problems that she was no longer doing the job, and that Crow higher-ups forced her to quit until she could get her affairs in order. Whatever the truth of the matter, Nancy was out of a job, and Richard's income was now called upon to support two separate households in addition to his generous spending where Denise was concerned. His money wouldn't begin to stretch that far, of course, and before the year was out Big Daddy would come to the rescue many times.

Both the telephone and the electricity at the Shenandoah duplex were disconnected during the period, and Nancy often found herself without money to buy food. Although Richard had never minded asking Big Daddy for help, Nancy simply had too much pride. She lived without electricity for three days before Big Daddy happened to drop in on her and, seeing the problem, went directly to the utility company and had her service placed in his own name. Furious, he tried to contact Richard to read his errant son-in-law the riot act, but Richard and Denise were out of town.

So desperate did Nancy become for money that she contacted Tramell Crow and attempted to collect her partnership equity, all to no avail. Company policy. Nancy had become a partner, was still a partner, and would remain so until she died.

Big Daddy finally took the financial pressure off by undertaking Nancy's total support. He paid her bills and provided her with a weekly income. When he ran across the premiums due on Nancy's half-million-dollar life insurance policy, though, he drew the line. He told her that he wouldn't pay for the life insurance unless she switched the beneficiary from Richard to the girls. Gratefully, Nancy complied. Whether or not she ever notified Richard of the change is a point of contention.

There was one confrontation during the year that still gives Denise Woods sleepless nights. She was in a Blockbuster Video store with Richard when, out of the blue, Big Daddy approached. The older man was breathing fire.

First Big Daddy glared at Richard, then at Denise. Finally he sputtered angrily to Richard, "Is this your . . . your *fiancée*?" And spun on his heel and marched out of the video store. If looks could kill, Denise thought, she never would have survived the meeting.

Both novel and motion picture have heralded the killer bee during its inch-by-inch migration up from Mexico, and its name conjures images of horrified citizens flailing helplessly at the critters, screaming in agony, and dying in droves. Though San Antonio is about as far north as anyone has thus far spotted the abnormally aggressive hybrid flying sting-merchant, scientists from coast to coast and up into Canada religiously track the killer bee's progress through North America.

In-the-know Texans chuckle at the furor because, reputation or no, the killer bee has yet to actually kill anyone. Smiles fade from weather-bronzed faces, however, at the mere mention of the killer bee's lesser-known traveling companion, the fire ant. The fire ant is no laughing matter. The killer bee, in comparison to its little red buddy, is nothing but a pansy.

The fire ant has far outstripped the killer bee in its steady northward journey, having already infested Texas, New Mexico, Oklahoma, and parts of southern Kansas. The individual insects are barely larger than the head of a pin, but each fire ant sting raises a welt that comes to a boil-like head and burns and itches for weeks. The population of each bed numbers into the tens of thousands, and humans need be wary of where they step; fire ants attack in hordes and sting hundreds of times within seconds. The tiny insect is hostile, dangerous, and even potentially deadly.

Normal pesticides are useless against the fire ant because it exhibits not only an aggressive nature, but a strangely effective survival instinct as well. At the first hint of danger to the bed, the worker ants rally around the queen, pick her majesty up bodily, and transport her to safety. Thus while a poisoned bed quickly becomes dormant, an even stronger colony will spring to life just yards away on unpolluted ground.

Given its lofty status among the universally loathed creatures of the world, the fire ant is likely unconcerned over its involvement in the death of Nancy Dillard Lyon, and is probably equally unconcerned that it is probably the only insect in history to be investigated by homicide detectives. But investigated the fire ant was, and thoroughly so.

Nancy first noticed the dangerous ant bed in the backyard of the Shenandoah Avenue duplex in early summer during her separation (or semi-separation, since he spent about as much time at home as he did in his Richardson condo) from Richard. The fire ants had taken up shop in a hard-to-reach location; the center of the bed was underneath a sidewalk twenty steps outside the Lyon back door, and right beside a sand pile where Allison and Anna played. Nancy was horrified. Her immediate reaction was to scoop both little girls up, tote them inside, and forbid them to enter the backyard until Mommy said. Instructions to two toddlers were useless, of course, and Nancy had to lock the back door and keep it secured. On Richard's next visit, Nancy told him of the problem.

The battle against the backyard fire ants became one of the only things during Nancy's final months in which she and her husband totally cooperated. The insect invasion brought out the inventor in Richard, and in addition to working for Architectural Site Services and alternately sleeping with Nancy and bedding Denise Woods, he spent the rest of the summer scheming against the nasty critters. He tried dousing the bed with boiling water, but that only increased the fire ants' aggressiveness. Various ant and roach killers proved useless; the queen was so protected by the sidewalk roof over the bed that the ants didn't even bother relocating their quarters. As summer dragged by, the fire ants thrived.

Whatever differences there were between Richard and Nancy at the time, the two Harvard grads put their heads together in the fire ant war. Between the two of them they finally concocted a plan, and even set their campaign down in a series of elaborate drawings. They'd studied the creatures' habits and knew that whatever they used to kill the ants must be applied in a hurry, before the workers could move the queen. The Lyon plan of attack included an electric drill with a large bit attachment; they would use the drill to break through the sidewalk and instantly zap the bed with poison. They were sure the plan would work; the only thing of which Richard and Nancy were uncertain was which poison they should use. In selecting the proper lethal potion, they agreed that they should consult someone who knew.

Charles Couch is a big, sturdy bear of a man, and tracks time around the football season, recalling events as to point in time by whether or not the season was in swing when the event occurred. His love for the game isn't surprising; his son is a bang-up linebacker now on scholarship at Vanderbilt, and the son's visits to various college campuses for recruiting purposes would one day affect the trial of Richard Lyon. Astonishing but true.

That Charles Couch ever became involved in the case at all is somewhat curious. He isn't an exterminator, and his name appears on no known list of insect experts. What he did for a living during the summer of 1990 was about as far removed from the ant extermination business as it could possibly be; Couch was proprietor of a firm called Chemical Engineering, Inc., a manufacturer of industrial soaps, and as a sideline he engaged in carpet recycling. He didn't know Richard Lyon, Nancy Dillard Lyon, and Denise Woods from Adam, Eve, and the serpent.

Couch is dead certain that the phone call he received came in late July. Why is he so positive? Why, the Dallas Cowboys were in training camp at Thousand Oaks, California, at the time.

What connection Couch made between the call and the Cowboys isn't clear; perhaps his phone rang while he was going over the rookie scouting report. Nonetheless, he did receive the call.

Just where the woman on the phone got Couch's name—or why she thought that Couch might be a fire ant consultant—isn't known, either. Also somewhat hazy is the reason for Couch's instant cooperation; he didn't disavow knowledge of fire ants, and he didn't tell the woman to consult the Yellow Pages. What he did, in fact, was enter the fire ant war as if he were the Green Berets.

According to Couch, the woman told him that she lived in a duplex near SMU, that she had fire ants in her backyard, and that she needed a formula for a no-baloney poison to kill the nasty things. In this instance the lady had certainly dialed the right number. Had one of Couch's Chemical Engineering employees taken the call, the uninformed employee might've told her that if she didn't want to buy some industrial soap or recycle some carpet, she should take her business elsewhere. But Couch agreed to drop everything and, without any compensation whatsoever, get right on the lady's problem.

That very night Couch went to the science library at SMU. He certainly knew the way. Football again; the SMU Mustangs had heavily recruited Couch's son. And in a couple of hours' research Couch came up with the answer. Normal insecticides used for roaches and whatnot have no effect on fire ants, because while the garden-variety poisons easily penetrate the roach's soft underbody, the fire ant is a hardshell creature and resists everything that doesn't pack a real Sunday wallop. By the time he left the college library, he had concocted a formula he was certain would be foolproof. The formula, of course, included arsenic trioxide as one of its pivotal ingredients.

20

Nancy endured Richard's comings and goings for slightly better than half a year. She felt during the time that she had reversed roles with Denise Woods; though she and Richard were still married, she felt as if she'd become the other woman. And in a manner of speaking, she had. Richard made no bones about extolling Denise's sexual prowess to Nancy, but where Denise was concerned, the fact that Richard still slept with his wife on occasion was a deep, dark secret.

Nancy went ahead with her incest counseling and devoted most of her time to Allison and Anna. She was hoping against hope that Richard would come to his senses and return home for good, but after six months of him bouncing back and forth between home and his rented condo, Nancy made up her mind that reconciliation was never going to happen. Finally, emotionally drained, she wrote Richard a long, tearful letter and mailed it to his Springbrook Lane condo address. In it she reaffirmed her love for him, but stated that it would be harmful to both her and the girls to continue this way. She told Richard that if Denise was what he wanted, so be it. Nancy wanted a divorce.

It is likely that Nancy was attempting some reverse psychology in the hope that Richard would come back to her, but her strategy backfired once again. By this time Richard was under heavy pressure from Denise to put up or shut up. In fact, she had temporarily ended the relationship, telling him that if he ever chose to proceed with his divorce and make an honest woman of her, he should give her a call. She had begun seeing other men, and a headline story on the society pages featuring Denise and her escort, jetset restaurateur Shannon Wynne, at a gala opening of Dallas' Northpark location for Barney's New York, drove Richard into a frenzy. Therefore, Nancy's letter played right into his hands. He replied that he wanted a divorce as well, and immediately made arrangements for him and Nancy to see a mediator.

The divorce mediator is a creation of Texas law, though a number of states have now begun the same practice. It is the function of the mediator to bring warring couples together on property settlement prior to filing of the divorce petition, and the idea behind mediation is to save the court time. If the couple has already agreed on a division of debt and assets, the divorce proceeding itself becomes quite simple. The couple can then file their own petition and thus save on legal fees. In the Lyons' case, Richard selected the mediator.

So badly did Nancy want heartache out of the way and to get on with her life, she was determined not to let material things delay the proceedings. She meekly agreed to a down-the-middle split of everything; if she couldn't have Richard, money and property meant nothing to her. The eventual property settlement drawn up by the mediator, and originally approved by both Nancy and Richard, illustrates the point. While Nancy was allowing emotion to rule her decisions, it is clear that Richard was not. He had honed directly in on the financial issues.

The truth of the matter was that Richard and Nancy Lyon were, in their own right, penniless. There was no net worth to divide. All three of their duplexes—the two M-Street locations where they'd previously lived plus the Shenandoah Avenue house they now called home—were mortgaged to the hilt, and would likely not bring enough to settle the debt against the property. Further—largely due to his erratic spending on trips with and presents for Denise Woods—Richard and Nancy were up to their eyeballs in debt to the credit card companies. The only assets of value were Nancy's profit-sharing interest in Tramell Crow Companies (which she was unlikely to see), and her trust funds that Big Daddy had set up for her. Under Texas law, gifts from relatives are separate property and not subject to division under divorce proceedings; nonetheless, Nancy agreed to give Richard one-half of the whole nine yards.

The divorce might have proceeded according to Richard's plan, and he and Denise might have lived (arguably) happily ever after, but just before the agreement was finalized, Nancy took a step that her estranged husband hadn't anticipated. She showed the mediator's settlement agreement to Big Daddy, and, understandably, he hit the ceiling. If his daughter didn't understand the Texas community vs. separate-property laws, Big Daddy certainly did.

He knew Mary Henrich through her participation in the Masters Swim Club, and also knew her reputation as a stand-up, knock-'em-dead women's divorce attorney. Within twenty-four hours after he viewed the settlement agreement, he had retained Ms. Henrich in Nancy's behalf. Mary Henrich immediately put Richard on notice that she was now Nancy's attorney, and that any contact he had with his wife was to be through her lawyer. To the courthouse Mary went and filed the petition, and the anticipated mediator's property settlement was forevermore out the window.

Thus Nancy Lyon, largely through Big Daddy's prompting, stood on her hind legs and began to fight. It was shortly after her lawyer rejected the settlement and informed Richard that she'd see him in court that Nancy first became nauseous. During the short time left to her, she would experience strange illnesses over and over again.

One of the first things Nancy did when she and Richard separated, and she left her job with Tramell Crow Companies, was to fire Lynn Pease, the nanny. No small consideration was Lynn's salary, which Nancy could no longer afford. Additionally, there had been a conflict brewing between Nancy and Lynn for quite some time.

Though Nancy publicly said that she liked Lynn and considered her a hardworking and genteel person, she secretly thought Lynn a threat to her influence over the two little girls. Since they'd been more often in the nanny's care than in their natural parents', it's not surprising that Allison and Anna had come to look on Lynn as more of an authority figure than their mom.

For Lynn's part, she had grown quite fond of Richard, but thought Nancy a bit standoffish. The young man from rural Connecticut had never been accustomed to having servants when he was a child, and often laughed and joked with Lynn and treated her as an equal. Nancy, however, looked on things from a different perspective; the barrier between upper-class persons and their domestic help was, after all, ingrained in her genes. Once Richard moved out, Lynn felt that Nancy talked down to her and looked on her as a servant; that she would no longer be working for Nancy didn't particularly bother Lynn. Her separation from the children, though, was a horse of a different color.

During the years that Lynn had worked in the Lyon home, she had come to love the little girls as if they were her own children. She took the Lyon kids with her everywhere; the girls loved her old beat-up car and called it the Zoomobile. In fact, even though she had access to one of the Lyons' luxury cars while keeping the children, Lynn drove her own old wreck most of the time because it pleased Allison and Anna.

Though dismissed from her duties at the Lyon home, Lynn quickly found a job; she went to work for Big Daddy and Sue. Therefore, even though she was no longer working for Nancy, Lynn had the opportunity to drop by two or three times a week, primarily to check on Allison and Anna. Sometimes Nancy would let Lynn take the kids for a ride, sometimes Nancy wouldn't. She often took advantage of Lynn's drop-in visits by using her former nanny as an unpaid baby-sitter. So, during the year of Nancy's terrible loneliness, Lynn was a constant visitor to the Shenandoah duplex, and what Lynn observed during Nancy's final year of life would not bode well for the defense at Richard's trial.

It was Lynn, for example, who called on Nancy the morning after the mysterious wine and gelatin capsules turned up on the duplex's front stoop. When no one answered Lynn's knock on the door, she let herself in and went upstairs. The pills were in their plastic container on a low hallway table, and it frightened Lynn that capsules of origin and content unknown were in easy reach of the children. She placed the container with the pills up on a high shelf, and entered the bedroom.

Nancy, pale as death, was huddled underneath the covers on top of the down mattress. She was retching uncontrollably and was barely able to move; Lynn had to help her former employer sit up in bed. Nancy told Lynn in a weak voice about the wine, and said she believed that it was the contents of the wine bottle that had made her sick. Later in the day, when Nancy felt better, and after she had talked matters over with Mary Henrich, Nancy asked Lynn to carry the wine and pills out and lock them in the trunk of the Zoomobile. She told her former nanny that if anything were to happen to her, she should turn the evidence over to the authorities.

It was also Lynn who happened to stop by the Shenandoah duplex on the day that Nancy signed the rider on her life insurance policy, eliminating Richard as beneficiary and adding Allison and Anna in his place as recipients of the insurance proceeds. It was convenient for Nancy on that day that Lynn had come to visit; she had Lynn witness her signature on the rider. A conversation between Richard and Lynn within days after Nancy's death, and the conversation's admission into evidence at Richard's trial, would be a devastating blow to the defense. Lynn says that she told Richard not to count on Nancy's life insurance money because his dead wife had changed the beneficiary; Richard's reply was, according to Lynn, "If she was going to do that, she would have told me about it."

There were several other suspicious incidents which occurred as Lynn came and went from the duplex—one that comes immediately to mind is the story about Richard giving Nancy a doctored Coke in a darkened movie theater, an event that Nancy related to Lynn in great detail—and her meticulous testimony at trial was one of the major prosecution tools which did Richard in. There was one occurrence, however, also witnessed by Lynn, the story of which the jury never heard.

So much did hearsay testimony influence the outcome of Richard's trial, it is important to point out the legal difference between the evidence that would have helped his case and testimony which drove the nails into his coffin. As previously outlined, neither the wine and pills nor the Coke in the movie could have been admissible had not the doctor testified that Nancy had told him those things on her deathbed. Once Dr. Bagheri had related the stories from the witness stand, then Lynn's and Mary Henrich's testimony also became admissible as corroborative backup. Not so with the tale about the flowers.

A colorful and fragrant flower display appeared mysteriously on the dining table at the Shenandoah duplex during one of Richard's visits. There was an envelope attached to the spray by a twist tie, bearing the return address of the flower shop, and the penned inscription on the envelope read merely, "To Nancy Lyon." When Richard spotted the floral arrangement, both Nancy and Lynn Pease were in the room with him. Nancy told him that the flowers had come by delivery service the previous day, and that the arrangement was a gift from St. Phillip's School.

Naturally, Richard couldn't resist opening the envelope and having a peek. The card inside was a sympathy note to Nancy, telling her how regretful it was that her husband had mistreated her so. Though he only had Nancy's word as to the origin of the message, he had no reason to doubt her. St. Phillip's School is an institution for problem children, and one of the "in" charities to which Park Citizens donate, and Richard was on the school's board. He took pride in his position with the school, largely because it was one of the only things he'd accomplished on his own with no help from Big Daddy. That the St. Phillip's staff would take it on themselves to side with Nancy in the marital rift was a severe blow to Richard's ego, and understandably so.

By the time Nancy died, the flowers and note had long since disappeared from the Shenandoah duplex, but the investigations conducted both by the police and Richard's defense team turned up some startling things pertaining to the floral arrangement. While the staff at St. Phillip's School disavowed all knowledge of the flowers or who had sent them, Nancy's credit card records showed that she herself had purchased an identical floral arrangement, from the same shop, on the day before Richard spied the flowers on the dining table. If two plus two equals four, Nancy had sent the flowers to herself and then concocted the story that the school was responsible, her presumed goal being to have exactly the effect on Richard that it did.

Lacking the physical evidence—the flowers themselves, the vase in which they sat, or the note and envelope—the defense at trial was unable to get the story of the flowers into the record. Lynn responded in cross-examination that she did see the flowers, but since any statements made by Nancy regarding the origin of the floral arrangement would have been hearsay, the fact that flowers were on the table was as far as the defense's cross-examination was able to go. The jury never heard the allegation that the flowers came from St. Phillip's School, and likewise never heard about the subsequent finding that Nancy had bought the arrangement herself. In other words, though her statements to Dr. Bagheri became admissible as an exception to the hearsay rule, her declaration to Richard regarding the origin of the flowers did not.

Why is this important? Well, if Nancy had the flowers delivered, and then led others to believe that the arrangement came from St. Phillip's School, why couldn't the same hold true with the mysterious pills and wine? She was unarguably distraught during the period, and did many irrational things. Why isn't it possible that she created the wine and capsule incident in order to garner sympathy? Furthermore, if the wine and pills were Nancy's own doing, this provides a plausible explanation for her refusal to comply with her attorney's request that she bring the wine and capsules to the lawyer's office; if she had provided the wine and pills herself, Nancy would have feared discovery. If nothing else, the tale of the mysterious floral arrangement provides ample food for thought. The event certainly doesn't prove that Richard *didn't* poison Nancy—just as the circumstantial case presented by the state doesn't prove without question that he did—but in the courtroom, reasonable doubt is the name of the game.

If Richard thought that the filing of his divorce petition would
bring Denise Woods racing back into his arms, he had another
think coming. Denise had become twice shy. Once the petition
was filed, she did consent to see Richard on occasion—and to
have intermittent sex with him—but she was seeing other men as
well. She once might have been willing to have Richard as the
only man in her life, but his increasingly erratic behavior after
the divorce proceedings were filed gave her considerable pause.

Once it became apparent that Richard was in for a court battle
over money, his attitude toward his estranged wife did an about-
face. He began to cater to Nancy's every whim, all at Denise's
expense. He constantly showed up hours late for dates with
Denise, or stood her up altogether, and his excuse was always
that he was doing things for Nancy. He once left Denise's side on
learning that Nancy had taken the children to Massachusetts,
and on that occasion he flew all the way to Martha's Vineyard
and begged Nancy to come home. Another time, Denise learned
that Richard had taken Nancy on a skiing trip to Colorado; when

he returned, he told Denise that he and Nancy hadn't gotten along at all, and that he'd decided on the trip that he would file for divorce. (Richard's story here simply isn't true; the divorce proceedings had already begun, and Richard begged Nancy to go on the trip with him. While in Colorado, he tried once again to talk Nancy out of her decision to battle him in court over assets. According to what Nancy told friends, she became violently ill on the trip, vomiting continuously all night while Richard sat calmly by her bedside and read a book.)

Richard's attempts at appeasing Nancy were to no avail, particularly now that she was receiving guidance from Big Daddy. The preliminary hearing was a month after the divorce was filed, and Mary Henrich had Denise served with a subpoena to testify as a respondent. She tearfully complied, and Henrich reduced Denise to virtual mincemeat on the witness stand. Thereafter, Richard and Denise saw each other infrequently, and then only in secret. During the fall of 1990, Denise made up her mind that her relationship with Richard was never going to be permanent.

What Denise believed was the final straw between her and Richard came in early November, when she had to go in for cervical surgery. Only days earlier Richard had told her that he wasn't in love with her—which didn't particularly shock her—and his actions during her surgery and recovery certainly drove home his point. He dropped her off at the hospital for her operation, but never visited her or called to see how she was feeling. Denise wasn't to see Richard again, in fact, until Nancy had only weeks left to live.

Richard insists that he moved back into the duplex with Nancy in November, but Big Daddy and the rest of the Dillard family say that he lived apart from her until after New Year's Day. The record is clear that Richard didn't give up his Springbrook Lane condo until February, two weeks after Nancy died, but the conflicting accounts as to where he actually lived during November and December are probably Nancy's fault. In mid-November she gave in to her inner feelings and agreed to take Richard back, but after the furor that Big Daddy had raised over the divorce proceedings—not to mention his retention of Mary Henrich as her attorney—she was likely reluctant to tell her father that there was to be no divorce after all. In fact, Nancy didn't tell Big Daddy that the Lyon divorce petition was being withdrawn until just before Christmas.

It was also mid-November when Nancy began to be constantly sick. In fact, she never seemed to be completely well again. She had violent nausea and vomited over and over. After Thanksgiving dinner at Big Daddy's house, she went to bed and didn't get up for three days. During this period Richard spent almost every night at the Shenandoah duplex.

About a week before Christmas, the Lyons announced to one and all that they were reconciling. Those close to Nancy had mixed emotions; although most of them were fed up with Richard over his treatment of Nancy, they were happy for her that her marital breakup was at an end. Some decided that the separation had caused her ill health, and hoped now that things were better for her, they would once again see the Nancy they had always known.

During Christmas week Stan Wetsel had a dinner party at his home for all Architectural Site Services employees and staff. Wetsel's wife had seating placards, and when the first course was served all were present save Mr. and Mrs. Richard Lyon. There was no word from them until the party was over. Just as everyone was leaving for home, Richard appeared at the Wetsels' door. He seemed nervous and upset, and offered apologies to the Wetsels that he had given them no notice that the Lyons wouldn't be coming. Nancy Lyon, it seemed, had suddenly taken ill.

It was also during Christmas week, December 20, to be exact, when Denise gave a party at her Richardson apartment. Richard came late, had a few drinks, and smoked a couple of joints. The festivities carried on until the wee hours, after which Denise spent the night with Richard at his Springbrook condo. He told her on this occasion that he hadn't meant what he said in November, and that he was in love with her, and that once his divorce was final he could be with her always. Like Big Daddy, Denise wasn't clued in that the Lyons had dropped their divorce proceedings. Also, Richard neglected to tell her that his decision to drop by her party was a last-minute thing, and that he and Nancy had originally scheduled something else. The reason Richard was free for the evening was that Nancy was once again sick.

With Christmas only a few days away, Richard and Nancy decided to go to Connecticut and visit Allan and Rosemary Lyon. They decided to make the journey on December 26, and notified Richard's folks as to when they were coming. While Allan and Rosemary expressed happiness, via long distance, that the couple had patched up their differences, Rosemary was actually disappointed. She'd felt all along that marriage into the Dillard family wasn't the best thing for her son.

On Christmas Eve, Richard and Nancy had Carol Poor over for lunch. Since Carol had acted as Richard's faithful assistant during the final dark days of Hughes Industries, and also had acted as a go-between during the Lyons' breakup, Richard and Nancy wanted her to know that the marriage was on once more. Nancy cooked the meal, and Carol enjoyed herself. She remembers Nancy being all smiles during the visit, and that the couple seemed happy together gave Carol a warm glow inside.

But if Nancy was in high spirits at noon on Christmas Eve, by nightfall her condition had changed considerably. That evening she and Richard attended Christmas services at Trinity Episcopal Church in far North Dallas. In happier times they had been regularly attending members at Trinity Episcopal, and had once kept the small children in the nursery during Sunday school on a weekly basis. Bill Jr. and Mary Helen also claimed Trinity Episcopal as their church of choice, and at Christmas Eve services the two couples sat together. The other churchgoers were glad to see Richard and Nancy, wished them well, and expressed hope that the Lyons would once again become regular worshipers with them. Richard shook hands with all well-wishers and offered friendly greeting, but Nancy had very little to say. Later, Trinity Episcopal members would recall that on the final Christmas Eve of her life, Nancy Lyon was deathly pale and made numerous trips into the ladies' rest room. Once inside, she would lock herself into a stall, and from within would come the unmistakable sound of loud and uncontrolled retching.

Christmas Day was indeed merry for Allison and Anna. The two little girls were up at the crack of dawn, eyes bright and wide, and by sunup had Santa presents open and wadded wrapping paper scattered all over the Lyon living room.

In early afternoon the family went to Big Daddy's house; it was the final gathering of the Dillard clan Nancy was ever to attend. Mary Helen and Bill Jr. brought their kids over, and Susan and Billy Hendrickson drove down from Wichita Falls. Bill Jr. was sober and clear of eye, as he had been for over a year. There were more presents to open and more visiting to do; the Lyon girls made their second grand haul of the day. Big Daddy went out of his way to make Richard feel welcome; the senior Dillard knew by now that the divorce plans were off, and whatever turmoil he may have felt, he was ready to welcome his errant son-in-law back into the fold. After nightfall the entire group traveled the two blocks to Armstrong Parkway and gazed at the dazzling Christmas lights. Nancy had viewed the Highland Park yuletide display every year since she'd been a little girl, and the sight of the lighted Santas and sparkling tree branches had always excited her. On this evening, though, she seemed withdrawn.

Richard and Nancy spent a large part of the day after Christmas in packing for their evening flight to Connecticut. At least Nancy spent the day in preparation for the trip. Richard found some time to slip away.

In mid-afternoon, he showed up on Denise Woods' doorstep. He had a present for her. As opposed to the whimsical gifts he'd given her in the past—the $4,500 watch, the $1,000 necklace, various filmy underthings from Victoria's Secret—this present was more practical. It was a warm leather coat, which he had charged on his Visa. The price was $1,000.

Denise was thrilled. She snugged her hands deep into the coat pockets and modeled, doing a few pirouettes for Richard's benefit as the coat's hem swirled around shapely calves. Then Richard drew Denise down on the sofa beside him. He had some things to tell her.

He began by saying that he was leaving town with Nancy that evening, then quickly continued before Denise could throw his gift back in his face. His trip with his wife, Richard said, had nothing to do with being intimate, had nothing to do with any plans for him and Nancy to get back together. A reconciliation, he said, was out of the question. He said he was only going to be a comfort to Nancy, someone for her to lean on. She had been sick so often of late, Richard said, that the doctors had decided she had a rare and life-threatening blood disease. The reason for the trip back East was so that Nancy could get treatment at Mount Sinai Hospital. His burden off his chest, Richard kissed Denise and told her that he'd be back with her as soon as possible. He loved Denise, he said, and once this trip was over, Nancy would never stand between them again.

The trip to Connecticut was uneventful for the most part. Rosemary Lyon fixed scrumptious Lebanese meals for the visiting couple, and twice Richard's parents took Nancy and Richard on a tour of their son's childhood haunts around Mansfield-Willimantic. For the most part, though, the Lyons, parents and son and daughter-in-law, relaxed and visited. Both Allan and Rosemary Lyon recall that during the visit, Nancy didn't seem to feel really well.

Allan and Rosemary bade goodbye to their son and daughter-in-law on New Year's Eve. It was the last time they were to see Nancy alive; when they next saw Richard it would be to grieve alongside their son at Presbyterian Hospital.

On the way to catch their return flight, Richard and Nancy spent the night in New York City. They did New Year's Eve in Manhattan among the jostling crowds in Times Square, only blocks from the hotel where they'd stayed with Big Daddy and Sue while students at Harvard. To the couple from Texas the Big Apple seemed magic, and held memories for them. It was the same city where, not so long ago, they'd met at midnight, made love in secret, and had known feelings available only to the young. One can only hope that Nancy's last New Year's Eve on earth was a happy one. On January 2, as a jetliner bore the couple to DFW Airport, Nancy's remaining time dwindled to seven precious days.

It is sad that Nancy spent her last full day of consciousness worried about herpes. She'd developed genital lesions, and on January 7 visited the doctor. The physician ran tests and did a culture; then he prescribed Zovirax, one capsule every four hours. Nancy's culture would turn out negative; in retrospect, the doctor feels that she must have had a yeast infection.

Nancy filled her prescription on her way home, and began to take the Zovirax religiously. She'd had so much medicine of late. One more pill to swallow, she supposed, wouldn't matter. After her death the bottle containing the Zovirax capsules would never be found.

The following afternoon, the eighth of January, Allison and Anna played as quietly as possible. Their father had gone to Houston that morning—as far as the children knew, Houston might be on the moon—and Mother was in charge. Around one, Mother had gone to bed and had never gotten up again. Occasionally the girls would creep to the door of her room and look in on her; for the entire afternoon Nancy coughed and moaned in pain. What, oh, what, the children thought, could be wrong with Mommy? Allison and Anna decided that they would both be quiet as church mice. If they weren't too noisy, Mommy would surely get well.

23

After his meeting with Detective Ortega two days after Nancy died, Big Daddy didn't feel really confident that he'd taken a positive step. His impression was that the policeman had paid only lip service and was sticking by the hospital report that Nancy had died from septic shock. That afternoon Big Daddy expressed his concern to Bill Jr. Father and son agreed to be patient for the time being, but also agreed that if nothing was done in the foreseeable future, the authorities hadn't heard the last of the matter. Not by a long shot.

The Dillard family did take Ortega's advice to heart not to alert Richard that he was under suspicion. During the following two months, the Dillards bent over backward to make him believe that, as the bereaved widower, he had Nancy's family's utmost sympathy. Richard sat beside Sue at Nancy's funeral, and at the conclusion of the service mother and husband hugged each other and shed tears together. For Sue Dillard, with the turmoil brewing inside her, clasping the man she believed to be

Nancy's murderer to her bosom must have been a terrible ordeal.

The funeral brought a packed house, and a two-column story in *Park Cities People,* the town crier of the upper-class community. Nancy's friends from college days came from coast to coast, and former Dillard neighbors flew in from New York. The procession to the burial site closed off intersections for blocks on end, and consisted mainly of Caddys and Mercedes bearing business tycoons, society matrons, and ladies from the Junior League. Rena Henderson of St. Simons Island, Georgia, Nancy's classmate at Hollins, penned the following memorial read tearfully at Nancy's graveside: "Let it be of comfort to all of us that Nancy was a giver by choice. We are the recipients of her giving. We are assured through Christ that Nancy lives on, now without suffering. It is we who suffer now, without her earthly presence." Richard stood near the casket, head bowed, flanked by Allan and Rosemary, with the Dillard clan on both sides of and behind the trio. As Richard shed tears, the Dillards exchanged furtive glances.

Detective Don Ortega's personal opinion regarding the cause of Nancy's death didn't really matter; without a medical examiner's finding of foul play, the police were powerless to launch an investigation. In Dallas County, Texas, the medical examiner's office is notorious for taking its time.

The responsibility thrust on the M.E. by Texas law is awesome indeed; not only are forensics personnel to determine the cause of death, they are charged with the decision as to whether death came about from natural or accidental causes, was self-inflicted, or the result of foul play. In most instances this determination isn't difficult; if Jose is dead in an alley with a bullet through his head, there are no close-range powder burns around the wound, and Jose isn't clutching a pistol, then somebody shot the guy. In a case such as Nancy Lyon's, however, the gray area in the decision-making process is as wide as the Mississippi, and then some.

The building that houses Dallas County's Southwest Institute of Forensic Sciences—an uptown moniker for the medical examiner, crime lab, and toxology staff, either individually or any combination thereof, and often referred to by prosecutors in questioning expert witnesses merely as "swifs," thus confusing jurors as to whether "swifs" is the expert witness's name, some sort of buzz word known only to insiders, or possibly even a derogatory term applied to the defendant—is located on a horseshoe-shaped street directly behind Parkland Hospital by design. Parkland is the county hospital, and as such becomes the first stop-off for the carloads of murder victims trucked in from indigent parts of the city; once the Parkland staff determines that the person without a head is deceased, it is a hop, skip, and jump over to SWIFS for autopsy. For the remains of Nancy Dillard Lyon, the distance traveled from Presbyterian Hospital to SWIFS on the day before the funeral was about eighteen miles. Though she'd lived in Dallas County for most of her life, it was quite possibly her first visit to the neighborhood.

The esteem in which the deceased was held was obvious from the outset; Dr. Jeffrey J. Barnard, the county's chief medical examiner, personally conducted the autopsy at ten-thirty on the morning of January 15. Dr. Barnard dutifully weighed the body— the swelling caused by the catheter's puncturing of the vena cava had ballooned Nancy to 142 pounds—then removed her various organs and weighed them as well. He then inspected Nancy's insides piece by piece; he found her overall condition unremarkable and roughly normal. Her liver was covered by a smooth, glistening capsule; if Dr. Barnard found the condition of the liver unusual, he made no comment.

Analysis of internal fluids, fingernail clippings, hair (trimmed by Bill Jr. at the hospital), and toenails showed that arsenic had penetrated all parts of Nancy's body. The poison was in her liver, kidneys, urine, and blood. That the concentration in her hair and toenail roots was much higher than in the mid and distal areas indicated that she had received quantities of arsenic at earlier times, and one large jolt just days before she died. That there was five times the concentration of arsenic in her fingernails than in her hair and toes was somewhat of a mystery, and was also a revelation that Richard's defense would make much of.

Given Nancy's symptoms—the nausea, diarrhea, and uncontrolled projectile vomiting—the determination that she died from arsenic poisoning was relatively simple. Further given, however, that the M.E.'s office had access to no evidence other than the arsenic in Nancy's system, it would appear just as reasonable that she took the poison herself, either accidentally or on purpose, as did the eventual M.E.'s finding, eleven weeks later, that someone slipped her a Mickey. When questioned as to the process used in determining that Nancy was murdered, the medical examiner's staff is rather vague, giving answers ranging from "Well, it seemed likely," to "We had family telling us that someone hated her." Just how much outside pressure, either from the police, the district attorney's office, or the Dillards themselves, had to do with the finding of murder is a deep, dark secret. There was pressure applied, though, pressure aplenty. Whatever the justification, the medical examiner's opinion in Case No. 0158-91-0072JB, Lyon, Nancy, gives a ruling of Homicide. As far as the police were concerned, not until the opinion was signed and delivered did Richard become fair game.

During the weeks immediately following Nancy's death, Richard did little to endear himself to his dead wife's family and friends. On the day after the funeral, Alice Eiseman decided to pay him a visit at the Shenandoah duplex. Ms. Eiseman, a Highland Park native, had been Nancy's roommate at Harvard, and still lives in the Boston area. She'd flown in for the funeral and wanted to express her personal condolences to Richard before leaving town. What she found on arriving at the duplex troubled her greatly.

When Alice dropped in, Richard was in the process of moving every scrap of Nancy's belongings out of the upstairs bedroom. Allison and Anna were in the nursery across the hall, and during Alice's visit the little girls cried constantly for their mother. Richard ignored the children except for a single outburst. When the girls' wailing became so loud that it interfered with his conversation with Alice, he shouted across the hall, "She's not coming back and you may as well get used to it."

To further rub salt into the Dillard wounds, Richard wasted no time in taking up where he'd left off with Denise Woods and wasn't particularly discreet about it. In fact, he called her on the very day Nancy died to say his wife was dead. Two days later he came by a construction site where Denise's crew was doing work, and the two hugged and held each other for all to see. Within a week after Nancy's death, Denise was Richard's constant companion.

Nine days after Nancy's funeral, Richard packed Denise onto a jetliner, and the couple flew to the Pacific resort city of Puerto Vallarta, Mexico. There they checked into the very private and quite exclusive Garza Blanca Beach Club, a rambling elegant structure nestled between rugged mountainside and snow-white beach, and overlooking crystal blue Banderas Bay. They lingered for several days, enjoying tennis, natural waterfalls, tropical flowers, native palms, and spectacular views, all at a daily on-season rate of two hundred seventy-five dollars. If it is true, as Denise has often stated, that Richard was "the least materialistic dude I've ever run across," one must wonder to what sort of free-spending Good-time Charleys she had previously been accustomed.

Richard's open carrying on with Denise heaped coals on the fire, and Big Daddy grew more and more impatient with the Dallas Police Department's investigation—or lack of same—with each passing day. With his daughter not yet cold in her grave, and the man he believed to be her killer dressing in new mod clothes, wheeling around town in a sports car, and appearing in public places and high-profile resorts with a flashy blonde on his arm, Big Daddy simply couldn't rest. He called Detective Ortega on an almost daily basis, and when Ortega either failed to return calls or, when Big Daddy was able to get the detective on the line, simply said there were no new developments in the case, he switched his attention to another jurisdiction. If the Dallas police weren't interested in Nancy, then the University Park cops damn well ought to be.

Like Dallas' main police headquarters, the University Park station sits in the same location as it has for many decades, but there the similarity ends. University Park law enforcement works out of a red brick colonial-style building on University Boulevard set in among homes the size of small English castles, and standing directly across the street from four glistening city tennis courts. Perfectly clipped and trimmed St. Augustine lawns front the police building, and with the pristine surroundings goes a certain responsibility to the community. Unlike overworked Dallas detectives, when Park Citizens speak, University Park cops hop to.

Dillard pressure on the University Park force came to rest on the broad shoulders of Captain Mike Brock, and Brock had a problem. He knew that the Dallas police were working on Nancy's case and was reluctant to step on any interdepartmental toes, but at the same time he had a responsibility to keep the citizenry off his back. He contacted Detective Ortega and discussed the case, then, with Ortega's approval, called Richard on the phone and had the decedent's husband in for an interview. The meeting in Brock's office was the first law enforcement contact with Richard Lyon.

The meeting was less than informative. Richard was polite and cordial, and seemed genuinely willing to help, but added nothing that law enforcement didn't already know. The suspect simply repeated the same story he had told at the hospital; he was out of town on the day Nancy got sick, did everything he could to help her, and didn't have the foggiest idea what had killed her. He did ask Captain Brock if the police had any idea what had caused Nancy's death, and minus the still forthcoming medical examiner's report, Brock was restricted to the hospital's version. Officially, Nancy had died from septic shock, and for the time being at least, that was that.

After Richard had left, Brock made the proper notes and dutifully notified Big Daddy of the results of the meeting. From Big Daddy's point of view, the University Park cops hadn't accomplished a thing, and Richard was still laughing heartily in justice's face. Big Daddy wasn't through, though. He had many other rats to kill.

Big Daddy wasn't the only Dillard turning every stone to put the authorities on Richard's trail; if Big Daddy was incensed, Bill Jr. was even more so. Nancy's death had been a terrible blow to him. Just as he'd been getting his life together and could see the end of the tunnel in his battle with drugs and alcohol, and just as Nancy was coming to grips with the long-ago problem involving brother and sister, she had to die. The situation was terribly unfair. Bill Jr.'s chance to help his baby sister live down childhood mistakes, mistakes that had turned both of their lives upside down, was gone forever. Bill Jr. was more determined than anyone to bring the man whom he believed to be her killer to justice.

Once the family had made their suspicions known to the police, from a legal standpoint there was nothing to do but wait, but Bill Jr. wasn't willing to let things go at that. He made it a point to let everyone in earshot know the family belief that Richard had poisoned Nancy.

For example, it was only a day after the funeral when Denise Woods received a call from a man she knew, Jim Lozare, an officer with Chicago Title Company. (Her connections within the same circles in which the Dillards move are phenomenal; she seems to know everyone who either is or has been connected to Bill Jr.) Lozare point-blank asked Denise if she was "laying low" for fear of the investigation into Richard's poisoning of Nancy. She knew that Lozare was involved in some real estate ventures with Bill Jr., and knew exactly from whence his suspicions had come. Only three days after Nancy's death, Bill Jr. was spreading the word.

It would take several weeks of inactivity on the part of the police for Bill Jr. to decide that merely spreading the word wasn't sufficient. By this time Captain Brock had interviewed Richard, all to no avail, and the police's apparent lack of interest in the case had convinced Bill Jr. and his father that additional steps were necessary. Frustrated by the police's failure to act, the Dillards now decided to go directly to the district attorney. In the D.A.'s office Bill Jr. felt that he had connections.

Actually, the connection to the D.A. wasn't directly Bill Jr.'s; if he'd learned nothing else through his association with his father, Bill Jr. knew how to operate through channels. The connection was through a business associate, a University Park man named Hank Judin. Judin lived next door to Reed Prospere, a slender, slow-talking Mississippi transplant who is himself a defense attorney, and who got his start practicing law by prosecuting cases for the Dallas County D.A. Bill Jr. met with Prospere one evening, and Prospere agreed to go with Bill Jr. to the district attorney, or, more specifically, to Prospere's old buddy from his own days as a prosecutor, a superchief assistant D.A. named Mike Gillette. Less than twenty-four hours after Bill Jr. first talked to Prospere, he found himself seated across from Mike Gillette at his office in the Crowley Courts Building. For a time the Dillard contact with the D.A.'s office was every bit as frustrating as the talks with the police had been.

The Dallas County district attorney's office has had an image problem over the past few years, and for its troubles has only itself to blame. Things certainly weren't always like this. The district attorney's staff was once the darling of the community.

For most of the four decades preceding the eighties, a legendary maverick named Henry Wade ruled the Dallas County justice system with a free and heavy hand. A skillful politician with a knack for pushing just the right button at just the right time, Wade rode into office in the forties on a wave of public indignation over mobster rule. Unlike the prior regime—which included a sheriff, Smoot Schmidt, who spent as much time in illegal gambling houses as he did in running the sheriff's department—Wade lived up to his campaign promises; in short order he ridded the county of a series of murderous characters, and sent the most high-profile of the shady-siders, a high-stakes gambler named Benny Binnion, packing off to the more relaxed climate of Las Vegas. Binnion's Horseshoe survives today as one of the more visible casinos of downtown Vegas, and Benny swore until the day he died that he had Henry Wade to thank for the Binnion move to Nevada, and for making Benny an honest and wealthy man.

Wade served a total of eight terms as district attorney, and in the entire thirty-two years received next to no criticism from the media. A splendid orator and a square-shouldered, jut-jawed presence, Henry Wade knew exactly how to please the populace. Election year was sure to bring a crackdown on hot-check artists along with a high-profile indictment or two, and the romance between Dallas and its district attorney seemed never-ending. Wade was even immune to the ugly mark placed on Dallas by the Kennedy assassination; the D.A. put his old friend Jack Ruby on the hot seat and asked for the death penalty without batting an eye. It is a tribute to Wade's influence with the media that, while the results of the Ruby trial itself are known far and wide, the fact that the conviction was later reversed by the appellate courts is knowledge shared by only a few.

Wade lived by the theory that the *public perception* of law enforcement was of much greater importance politically than the *reality* of same, so while Dallas prosecutors cut backroom deals with murderers, rapists, and whatnot, which in effect placed a revolving door on the entrance to the penitentiary, woe be it to the lawbreaker who opted for public trial. During the sixties, for example, Wade declared open warfare on marijuana-smoking hippies, all to the background chorus of "Go, Henry, go," heard from the fundamentalist pulpits of the area, and long-haired love children of the time caught in the act of flushing joints down the toilet found themselves facing prison terms of as high as *1,500 years*. The staggering sentences were somewhat of a sham against the public—Texas law at the time permitted unlimited consecutive sentencing, so that each joint in the hippy's possession became a separate sentence in itself, yet statutes governing parole dictated that any sentence over sixty years was the same in respect to time actually served—but the whopping number of years handed out made for great headlines and public acclaim for the district attorney.

When Wade finally retired in 1980, his annointed successor became an automatic shoo-in at election time. John Vance held all the credentials: a long and distinguished career as a prosecutor and a stint on the bench as criminal district judge. Personalities, however, are what give charisma to public office, and Vance was an abrupt change from his predecessor. Whereas Wade employed an open-door policy to the media, Vance shunned attention to himself; whereas Wade responded to questions from reporters with tidbits of homespun humor and mesmerizing anecdotes, Vance read from prepared statements whose length and lack of witticisms caused reporters to doze before the D.A.'s point was driven home. Slowly but surely, the romance with the press that Henry Wade had nurtured over a three-decade period began to fizzle.

That the district attorney's office, constantly involved in drama of the courtroom variety, had its reputation indelibly scarred by a movie maker is probably fitting. Errol Morris's early-eighties documentary entitled *The Thin Blue Line* placed the integrity of Dallas County's police and prosecutors under harsh scrutiny. The subject of the film was the case of Randall Dale Adams, a dope-sniffing drifter convicted and sentenced to death for the slaying of a Dallas policeman during a routine traffic stop. The conduct of the prosecutors in the Adams case, it turned out, was somewhat less than impeccable.

Morris's documentary turned up facts that were both shocking and explicit. Not only was Adams not the shooter in the policeman's death, it turned out that the convicted man was in a cocaine stupor in a motel room during the murder, and wasn't even present at the scene. Witnesses who could have cleared the defendant were suddenly unavailable at trial, and though prosecutors at the time expressed wide-eyed dismay over the witnesses' disappearance, Morris's documentary offered proof that they were in fact holed up in an Oak Cliff motel room and in constant telephone contact with the district attorney's office. Largely due to public outcry over Morris's film, appellate courts reversed Adams' conviction in short order and remanded for retrial or dismissal of charges.

District Attorney Vance—who wasn't even in office during Adams' original trial but bore the brunt of its consequences—had an easy out in the case of *Texas* v. *Randall Dale Adams* that, inexplicably, he didn't use. Doug Mulder, the lead prosecutor, had left the D.A.'s office for a lucrative private practice, and would have made the perfect foil; Vance needed merely to point the finger in Mulder's direction, drop charges against Adams, and state publicly that the current administration's bib was clean as a whistle. Why Vance made the decision to bow his neck, ignore the facts, and proceed with a second prosecution in the Adams case remains a mystery.

That prosecutors finally acknowledged a total lack of evidence against Adams and made an eleventh-hour decision to drop the charges doesn't matter; for months on end, the papers and TV news editions were filled with photos and written accounts of a shackled and obviously bewildered Randall Dale Adams, led by stone-faced sheriff's deputies, as he shuffled in and out of court for one hearing after another, and graphic profiles of Dallas County assistant D.A.'s as they dodged questions, conducted closed-door meetings, and issued one terse no-comment after another. Adams' personal appearances on *Donahue, The Tonight Show,* and *Good Morning, America* once charges were dropped didn't help matters, either; not only was the D.A.'s credence in serious jeopardy, newspeople miffed over their treatment by D.A.'s during the Adams case—and at the same time ecstatic over the increased newspaper sales and higher Nielsen ratings—had developed a nose for blood.

The second helping of district attorney stew served up to the media came in the form of another faulty prosecution unearthed, that of a woman named Joyce Ann Brown. Her case itself wasn't that significant—an armed robbery conviction obtained by faulty eyewitness identification and some police shenanigans designed to hide the truth—but since Ms. Brown was both black and female, she made the perfect marketable object of abuse by the system. Once again presses and cameras rolled. District Attorney Vance showed more respect for his own hide in this instance; once the transgressions of police and prosecutors in the Brown case had become public knowledge, Vance dropped the charges in short, short order. Nonetheless, the D.A.'s image was soiled once more.

After the Adams and Brown cases, the district attorney's relationship to the press changed drastically. Once the scene of cordial news conferences and amicable friendships between prosecutors and media personnel, the majestic and impressive Frank Crowley Courts Building became a frustrating place for reporters to work. Crime-beat newspeople now had to rely on eavesdropping, public court records, and general courthouse gossip to find out anything at all; prosecutors stalked to and from court with tightly zippered lips, sweeping past knots of hopeful media reps with nary a word. As Bill Dillard, Jr., accompanied Reed Prospere to the Crowley Building for his initial meeting concerning his sister's death, the D.A.'s relationship to the media was, in a word, strained.

Both Bill Jr. and Big Daddy were wrong when they thought that a conference with Mike Gillette would put a bee under the police department's fanny in its investigation into Nancy's death. Their assumption was a natural one; Gillette is, after all, one of the D.A.'s superchief prosecutors. A short but sturdy man, pugnacious both in his trial demeanor and his stonewalling of media questions, Gillette is, next to First Assistant Norman Kinne, the most visible of the superchiefs. Like most of the public, though, the Dillards had a misconception of what the superchiefs are all about.

The term has nothing to do with railroads, of course. The pecking order in the D.A.'s staff goes something like this: Hirees begin in county traffic court and work their way up from there into misdemeanor prosecutions. It is in misdemeanor court that the weeding-out process begins, since most young lawyers are after the bucks to be had in private practice and view the D.A.'s staff as a springboard. Those who stick around on the county payroll through a year or so of drunk driving and petty shoplifting prosecutions eventually graduate to the third chair of one of the fourteen county felony courts, there to plea-bargain slam-dunk murders, rapes, robberies, and major thefts, taking only those defendants to trial whose records are such that the state makes no offer, and the defense attorney and client alike hope against hope for a jury of fools. It is from the first-chair felony court positions that the bulk of the prosecutors go for the money and gravitate to the defense side; above the felony courts, chances for promotion in the D.A.'s office narrow considerably.

Among the limited opportunities available are specialty divisions—white-collar, organized crime, appellate division, etc.—which require an expertise in a certain facet of the criminal statutes, and those prosecutors who go into the specialty fields are generally committed to a career with the county, moderate pay, generous retirement benefits, and a lifelong guarantee of anonymity. One may only receive fame on the D.A.'s staff by becoming a superchief, a hand-picked half dozen of trial specialists. The headlines go to the superchiefs by specific design.

There are two criteria to determine whether or not a case is worthy of superchief assignment, and two criteria only, the requirements being that the case has received maximum media coverage, and is one the county feels it simply must win at all costs. Plea bargains in superchief cases are rare; there is a desire to put both the defendant and the evidence on public display. It is arguable whether prosecutors seeking such lofty status must display an exceptional skill at their trade; it is imperative, however, that superchiefs be articulate and present a good appearance both in the courtroom and in front of the television cameras. The thick of tongue and the weak of chin need not apply.

When Bill Jr. originally met with Mike Gillette to outline the family belief that Richard had murdered Nancy, and to express dismay at the lack of police activity in the matter, the Lyon investigation simply hadn't gained superchief status as yet. The case was a likely candidate, to be sure—a wealthy Highland Park victim, the victim's family name famous in the business community, a hint of infidelity as a possible motive—but other than family suspicion, there was nothing to indicate that Richard could be convicted of blowing his nose. Out of respect for Reed Prospere, his old friend from the D.A.'s staff now defected to private practice, Gillette listened attentively and agreed to look into the matter, but the fact was that he had more pressing business on his mind. On the front burner in Gillette's list of priorities was a very important billboard-defacement case. The knowledge that a misdemeanor sign-painting violation would take precedence over Nancy Lyon's possible murder would have sent Big Daddy into indeterminate orbit, but at the time Gillette first reviewed the Lyon case, that was precisely the situation.

Actually, the billboard-disfigurement case included an intentional windshield wiper–breaking incident, and eventually evolved into a felony leg-breaking charge along with a rape indictment, but originally the sign-painting was all the D.A. had to go on. The perpetrator was a charismatic black man named John

Wiley Price, who coincidentally was the duly elected county commissioner from the Oak Cliff and South Dallas black districts, and who, not so coincidentally, was the number one critic of the county justice system in general and the district attorney's office in particular. Price's criticisms, for the most part, had to do with the systematic exclusion of blacks from juries—which had been a practice in Dallas County for decades—and the tendency for the D.A.'s to go easy on whites while prosecuting black defendants to the limits of the law. Be his methods right or wrong, it is abundantly clear that John Wiley Price is no one's Uncle Tom.

Price's run-ins with the law began when, while waging a war against the preponderance of alcoholic-beverage ads in black areas, he grabbed a brush and bucket of whitewash and proceeded to Tom Sawyer every billboard he could find in South Dallas containing a beer or whiskey advertisement. The defacement of the signs was a misdemeanor; Price pled guilty, paid a fine, and accepted probation to the chorus of "Right on, brother," heard from black businessmen and clergy throughout the area. Next, while leading a demonstration in front of Channel 8 news headquarters, the commissioner encountered a lady determined to drive her car through the picket lines, at which point he broke off the lady's windshield wiper. This resulted in a misdemeanor criminal mischief charge that Price carried to trial, was found guilty, and now faced a revocation of his probation for the sign disfigurement as well as sixty days in jail. Price appealed, remained free on bond, defiantly wagged his finger in the D.A.'s face, and went on with his campaign.

Just weeks after his criminal mischief conviction, Price led a demonstration in downtown Dallas during which a burly 220-pound construction laborer took exception to John Wiley's disruptance of a work crew, and made a valiant attempt to separate the commissioner from his head. Price, a black belt in karate, put the man on the ground in short order, and in doing so broke the construction worker's leg. Now the charges had evolved into something serious: felony assault. To top things off, one of Price's former campaign workers had filed a rape complaint, stating that the commissioner had assaulted her in his office during the election. That the young lady had waited almost two years to decide that the commissioner forced her into sex against her will is strange; some have even accused the D.A.'s office of prompting the girl to file the charges. Nonetheless, a rape charge it was; the case was Mike Gillette's assignment, and an investigation into a possible wife poisoning was something the superchief prosecutor simply didn't have the time for.

If Gillette thought he was going to get away with providing mere lip service to the Dillards' claims, however, he was every bit as mistaken as the police department. After two weeks had passed with no activity from the D.A.'s office, Bill Jr. appeared at the Crowley Building along with Reed Prospere a second time. In this meeting with Gillette, Bill Jr. wouldn't take no for an answer. The Dillards wanted action. Gillette, up to his ears in the pursuit of John Wiley Price, realized that he would have no peace until some sort of action commenced in the Lyon case, so Gillette opted to pitch out; he heaved a lateral down the hallway into the hands of another superchief prosecutor named Jerri Sims. And with Jerri in charge, the Dillard persistence was finally to bear some significant fruit.

To say that Richard Lyon, a married man with a wandering eye, was finally brought down by two gorgeous blondes is an accurate statement, but somewhat misleading. There were two beautiful blondes involved, it is true, but only one of these lovelies craved Richard's body. The other was in steadfast pursuit of his hide.

If a casting director were to sashay through the Dallas County district attorney's office in search of an extra for a prosecutor's role, he'd likely bypass Jerri Sims. She'd pop into the director's mind, though, the next time he needed a flaxen-haired western beauty complete with an accent straight off the range. Jerri, in fact, is the epitome of looks that deceive.

The hair is awesome, the color of spun gold, falling in fluffy waves to a point halfway down the backs of Jerri's thighs. The body is slim and athletic, the result of thrice-weekly jogging and weight training, the posture erect, the bearing confident. The face is almost elfin, the lips eager to turn up in an infectious

Tinker Bell grin. In casual conversation she shows the beguiling innocence of a farm girl—which she was—while in the court-room her questions are concise and to the point with no wasted phrases. That she became a lawyer at all was in defiance of the odds.

Jerri was born in Fort Worth, where she lived until the ripe old age of two, and that was the extent of her city life until she'd graduated college. Her folks eventually settled on a farm near the West Texas town of Wellman. Wellman isn't even a speck on most maps, and claims Brownfield, barely a wide place in the road in its own right, as its nearest metropolitan neighbor. One school houses grades one through twelve in Wellman, and the lo-cal six-man football team plays its games without grandstands as townspeople, horses, and dogs roam the sidelines and greet hometown touchdowns with cheers accompanied by joyous barks and neighs. Jerri's named for her father, though he spells his with a "y." Her mother is Wilma Sims.

"It's country," Jerri says, leaning back in her office, her wealth of hair hanging down behind her chair back. "Real, real country, I guess, but it's home."

"Youall had FFA, I suppose," the interviewer says. "Future Farmers of America."

Her nose wrinkles in a grin. "Sure, I was the queen. Home-coming queen, too, one year. Only times we ever got to Dallas was on FFA trips, to the state fair, and sometimes for Cowboy games. I was third in my class, but I guess that's not much in Wellman. I might've been first, but I hated math to beat all." She pronounces it "may-yath," and one pictures Laurie, her bare toes wriggling in cornfield dirt as Curly rides up singing, "Oh, what a beautiful mornin'."

Music? Willie an' Waylon, right?

"I never liked country music till I moved to Dallas, which is sort of funny, I guess. But Brownfield, that was just a few miles, had this station, KKVB, that played pop. The Eagles and the Doors. The Bee Gees, that's what we had for hayride music."

"Third in your class and then on to college?" the interviewer says.

Jerri thinks about this one, turning her head to gaze out her window across the elevated portion of Stemmons Freeway as it bends into the Austin interchange. "I didn't really want to go, but Mama insisted. Texas Tech. In my neck of the woods, everybody that went to college either picked Tech or West Texas, in Canyon." It's a figure of speech; in Jerri's neck of the "woods," one may drive for miles and never lay eyes on a tree. The Tinker Bell grin lights up the room. "I did pretty well once I got to college, though."

Good grades?

"Three-point-five"—a fleeting look of pride melting into one of her infrequent frowns—"but I wasn't really getting anywhere. Started as a psychology major, but, you know, a lot of that is bull. I wound up majoring in speech therapy."

Sorority?

A pleasant laugh. "I was too independent for all that stuff."

"So you took the LSAT and went on to law school," the interviewer says.

She shakes her head; the hair waves back and forth. "I got married first."

"Oh? Boy from college, or someone from Wellman?"

"Neither. A banker from Houston. See, I worked part-time for Avis at the airport. He was passin' through, sort of." One pictures Jerri in a TV commercial, hand raised in the honest-injun sign, still second but trying harder. "We moved to Houston, and I didn't take the law school test until the next spring. That fall I enrolled at University of Houston Law School."

"So hubby worked while you went to school."

"Till we got divorced."

"Sorry to hear that."

"One of those things. It's the reason I moved to Dallas, though, as soon as I passed the bar exam."

"And you went to work for the D.A. here?"

"Not right away," Jerri says. "I was in family practice for a while, but that bored me to death. I interviewed with Judge Vance"—though he's been off the bench for a decade, District Attorney Vance is still "Judge" to his assistants—"but then he sort of hemmed and hawed. I had a job with the Tarrant County prosecutor before he finally called me. Might have made Tarrant

County mad when I reneged." Jerri says this with confidence; she'd be a welcome addition to any D.A.'s staff, and knows it. An astute and inquisitive legal scholar, Jerri will likely run for judge in the not too far distant future. She'll probably win.

"And now you're one of the superchiefs. Tell me, Jerri—"

"Uh-*huh.*"

"—an attractive single woman, does it scare men off that you maybe could put them in jail?"

"It's the hardest part of it," Jerri says reflectively. "That's why most law enforcement people, if they have any social life at all, it's with each other. My boyfriend, *was* my boyfriend until not long ago, he's a homicide detective I met on a case I prosecuted." It doesn't bother her that one romance has fizzled; a woman with Jerri's looks and smarts will never lack for suitors. She presently enjoys her Valley Ranch home, just down the road from the Dallas Cowboys' football practice field, which she shares with a cocker spaniel named Monroe and a Samoyed named Sam.

The interviewer adjusts his yellow legal pad in his lap and turns over a page. "Now, in Richard's prosecution . . ."

Jerri is suddenly concerned. "Now, I already told you, I can't talk about the case while it's on appeal. The judge's gag order is still—"

"Not the case itself, Jerri, I know you can't talk about that. I'm really wanting to talk about attitudes, like, how you would have felt if you'd lost. Would you have taken it personally?"

A determined blink. "You bet."

"More so than with other cases?"

She reflects on this, elegant lashes lowering, and then raising once more, the wheels of her mind practically clicking audibly as she prepares to translate thought into spoken word. "Look," she finally says. "There's always conflict in trial. The other side's trying to win, I'm trying to win, okay? But a lot of these defendants you can work up sympathy for, they've had a tough life. But not this guy. He's had every advantage. God, what I wouldn't give to have gone to Harvard."

"But surely there are worse crimes than what he's been convicted of," the interviewer says.

Jerri's brows shoot upward. "Are there?"

"Rape, murder in a robbery . . ."

"All committed by unbalanced people. He's not a bit crazy. He was after the money. Nancy loved him, and because of that she overlooked all these—these signs, and trusted the guy. He used her love and trust to turn around and murder her. There's no worse crime on the face of the earth, if you're asking me."

Jerri Sims listened carefully to what the Dillards had to say and took extensive notes. She could see problems. It would be difficult to convict Richard even with stacks of physical evidence—and even if the stories Nancy had told about the wine and pills and the Coke in the movie could be brought out in court in spite of the hearsay rule, which Jerri seriously doubted—because jurors live in an orderly world. Every juror would question Nancy's motives; if she suspected that the guy was trying to poison her, why on earth would she let him move back into the house? As she listened to Bill Jr. and Big Daddy recite the circumstances, Jerri was already considering her arguments. Somehow, some way, she would have to make jurors see the total chaos that had boiled in Nancy's mind.

25

Exactly how much the Dillard meeting with the district attorney influenced the sudden kindling of police department interest in the case is up for grabs. But within days of the second conference at the Crowley Building, homicide detectives got on the stick. Though still lacking a medical examiner's ruling, Detective Ortega and his partner, Detective Kathy Harding, went to Big Daddy's Rheims Place mansion on February 24, six weeks after Nancy had died. If Richard had indeed murdered Nancy, he'd had ample time to cover his tracks.

The detectives met with Big Daddy, Sue, and Mary Helen in the Dillards' majestic living room, a far cry from the surroundings to which Ortega and Harding were accustomed. Ortega had already heard Big Daddy's story, but now the detectives listened to Mary Helen's version of the tale, and Bill Jr.'s wife had much to add. For one thing, she told Ortega and Harding about Richard's canceled checks made payable to Houston's General Laboratory Supply, and for the first time made Ortega feel that he had something solid to go on. So important did the information seem, in fact, that Ortega and Harding flew to Houston the following day and had an extensive discussion with Ellen Rose of General Lab.

The initial trip to Houston ended in frustration. Yes, Richard had made purchases, but no, none of the orders included arsenic. The only toxic substance that Richard had bought, in fact, was barium carbonate, which on February 25, 1991, meant exactly nothing to the investigation; not until the analysis of the wine and pills hidden in Lynn Pease's trunk came to light would Richard's original buy from General Lab mean anything at all. One pill, one single capsule located near the bottom of the clear plastic container found on Nancy's doorstep, was packed with barium carbonate, but as Ortega stood in Houston on February 25, the single tainted capsule remained undiscovered. Ms. Rose of General Lab couldn't even identify Richard's picture in a photo lineup, for goodness' sake. As Ortega rode the Southwest Airlines jet from Houston back to Dallas, he felt that he'd wasted his day.

The following morning, Ortega went over everything he had, and drew a total zero. Barring a sudden discovery of a poison buy, the General Laboratory lead was virtually useless. Nancy's revelations to members of her family meant nothing without backup evidence, and her revelations might not be admissible in court. After much thought Ortega decided it was time to take the bull by the horns and interview Richard Lyon in person. A face-to-face encounter would make up Ortega's mind as to whether or not the Dillards were barking up the wrong tree, and could put the entire matter to bed.

Anyone who is literate enough —and, hopefully, sufficiently intrigued—to have read this far, and who hasn't spent the past thirty years or so in a vacuum, can likely recite the Miranda warning by heart. Screenwriters and authors of police thrillers have the words down to a T, but pulp and movie fiction blow the importance of Miranda in the overall scheme of things out of proportion. Policemen do not beat their fists into bloody pulps against the wall while the criminal, freed because no one read him his rights, saunters out of the jailhouse while grinning and shooting the finger, and haven't in decades. Just as prosecutors have learned ways to steer around the hearsay rule, policemen know legal gymnastics that render the Miranda warning totally useless as an escape hatch for the accused. Those contemplating a life of crime should pay particular heed to the following.

The Supreme Court of the United States has ruled that no one, regardless of the amount of intimidation employed by law enforcement, has a right to a Miranda warning unless that person is under arrest. Policemen know this, and also understand the state of mind common to all suspects in a criminal case. All suspects believe they can convince the cops that they're after the wrong person. So, keeping this in mind, detectives no longer clap the suspect in irons, place him under a spotlight, and grill him through the night while blowing cigarette smoke in his face. The modern cop apologetically tells the suspect that he, the cop, is sure that the suspect is innocent, and that if the suspect will drop by the station for a "visit," the investigation will likely end right then and there. "Do I need a lawyer?" the suspect says. "What for?" the policeman says. "This little chat we're going to have would bore a lawyer to tears." Gets 'em every time. On February 27, 1991, Richard Lyon wasn't under arrest, and therefore wasn't entitled to a Miranda warning.

A great deal depends on surprise in the questioning of suspects, so Ortega didn't call Richard to say that he was coming. Richard answered the doorbell at the Shenandoah duplex around nine-thirty in the morning on February 27, and blinked in surprise as he read the detective's ID shoved in his face. Richard was groggy with sleep, having just returned from a business trip. Ortega tersely introduced himself, told Richard that he was investigating Nancy's death, and asked if Richard would come downtown with him to answer a few questions.

Ortega, with twenty years' experience in murder investigations, feels that he can determine whether or not a suspect is hiding something just by the suspect's reaction to certain things, but many would question the detective's theory. After all, anyone awakened by a policeman on their doorstep is apt to be somewhat nervous. One would expect Richard, on learning for the

Where life began: the home on Normandy Avenue where the Dillard children grew up. It was here that Sue discovered Nancy and Bill Jr.'s relationship. In later years, Big Daddy and Sue relocated to their present Rheims Place mansion. PHOTO BY MARTHA GRAY

Where life ended: Presbyterian Hospital (among its more famous patients—J. R. Ewing and Nancy Dillard Lyon).
PHOTO BY DANIEL GRAY

Nancy in happier times, with daughters Allison and Anna. (From police evidence files.) PHOTO BY PAT STOWERS

The duplex on Shenandoah. Richard and Nancy lived in the lefthand two stories; Nancy found the wine and pills behind the low brick wall on the left. PHOTO BY MARTHA GRAY

Nancy rubbing elbows: (*from left*) Michael Crow, Barbara Bush, Nancy, Tramell Crow. An inscription beneath the photograph reads, "To Nancy Lyon—I so loved our talk. Warmly, Barbara Bush." (From police evidence files.) PHOTO BY PAT STOWERS

Between his arrest and trial, Richard gained weight, shaved his mustache, and shortened his hair, taking on a more clean-cut appearance.
PHOTO BY *THE DALLAS MORNING NEWS* / JUDY WALGREN

BELOW: Guthrie, Richard, and drill: Guthrie's repeated triggering of the drill kept the jurors and spectators jumping. PHOTO BY *THE DALLAS MORNING NEWS* / CATHARINE KRUEGER

Richard in custody on the day of his arrest. Detective Don Ortega, warrant in hand, escorts the suspect through the basement entry to the Lew Sterrett Justice Center. PHOTO BY *PARK CITIES PEOPLE*

A former track star and virtuoso of federal defense work, Dan Guthrie had never before defended a murder case. He almost won. PHOTO BY DANIEL GRAY

BELOW: Judge John Creuzot. A maverick Democrat in a hotbed of Republicans, his presence assured Richard a fair trial. PHOTO BY PAT STOWERS

Prosecutor Jerri Sims: "There's no worse crime in this world, if you're asking me." PHOTO BY PAT STOWERS

Charles Couch. It was his testimony regarding Nancy's arsenic purchases which sealed the fate of the defense.
PHOTO COURTESY OF RITA GREEN

Nurse Kim Grayson. She quietly avoided Richard and left Presbyterian's ICU to take delivery of the wine and pills from Bill Jr. and Lynn Pease.
PHOTO BY DANIEL GRAY

David Green (*left*) and John Reamer. Private eye Jim Bearden interrupted their business plans with a court order for them to give testimony on Richard's trial. PHOTO BY DANIEL GRAY

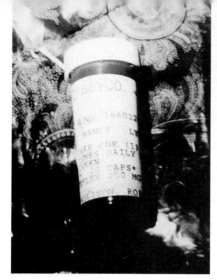

ABOVE LEFT: Perhaps the most damaging physical evidence of all: Nancy's Keflex prescription, found by the new tenant at Richard's Springbrook condo. One of the capsules contained sodium nitroferrocyanide.

ABOVE RIGHT: The plastic container of pills, now shown along with the wine bottle. The wine contained no foreign substance, but for a while it had law enforcement in a dilemma. PHOTOS BY PAT STOWERS

Backyard of the Shenandoah duplex, where the fire ants burrowed underneath the sidewalk. PHOTO BY MARTHA GRAY

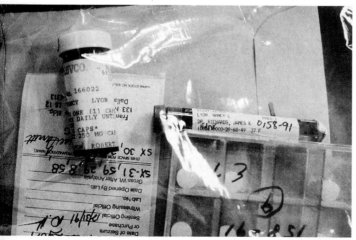

Parts of the evidential noose: (*lower right*) the plastic container of pills found on Nancy's doorstep; (*upper right*) Nancy's tainted blood sample; (*upper left*) one of Nancy's many prescriptions. PHOTO BY PAT STOWERS

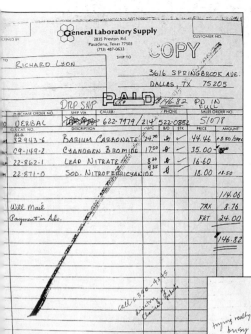

LEFT: A receipt from one of Richard's many purchases at Houston's General Laboratory Supply. The barium carbonate is toxic and is the substance that filled one of the capsules which Nancy found on her porch. This was a cash purchase, unknown to police until Richard's fatal interview with Detective Don Ortega.

BELOW: Nancy's "sick sex" incest counseling notes. The portion in the lower left, beginning with "fear of Bill . . . ," is the section the prosecution contends Richard wrote himself in order to throw suspicion on Bill Jr. PHOTOS BY PAT STOWERS

Sierra Tucson, where Bill Jr. underwent addiction recovery treatment, where Richard reported for treatment, and where Richard first learned of Nancy's adolescent relationship with her brother. PHOTO BY PAT STOWERS

Nancy's mom. A tearful Sue Stubbs Dillard accepts solace from a friend shortly after Richard's conviction. PHOTO BY *THE DALLAS MORNING NEWS /* DAVID WOO

first time that the police were involved in the matter, to be curious. Why did the police want to question him, and why was the Dallas homicide unit interested in the matter at all? Nancy had died from septic shock, hadn't she? Richard asked none of these questions, however. He merely nodded dumbly, told Ortega to wait while he dressed, and accompanied the policeman downtown in an unmarked city car. Even before the questioning session, Ortega was certain that he had his man.

Once they arrived on the third floor of the dismal old downtown police building, Ortega sat at his desk with Richard in a straight-backed chair to the detective's right. Kathy Harding sat across from Ortega. Ortega produced a legal pad for taking notes. Richard nervously crossed his legs.

"I'm not sure what this is all about," Richard said.

"You're not?" Ortega interviews suspects in a monotone; if anyone shows emotion during such sessions it will be the suspect. Ortega has big round eyes that give his face a peaceful expression, as if nothing in this world could upset him.

Richard clasped his hands in his lap. "I know it's about Nancy. How she died, I guess."

"What did she die from?" Ortega said.

"I don't know exactly," Richard said. "Septic shock, whatever that is, is what the doctors told me."

"She was poisoned," Ortega said, then doodled on his pad to allow the statement to sink in. That the police were still without the medical examiner's report was, of course, something Richard had no way of knowing. This was his opportunity to ask how the police knew that Nancy's death wasn't accidental, but Richard merely regarded the floor.

"Mr. Lyon," Ortega finally said. "To save time. While we're talking here, do you mind if Kathy Harding goes and searches your house and car?" Matter-of-factly, in an even tone of voice.

Richard hesitated. Inexperienced suspects always do in situations like this. Above all, suspects wish to appear innocent; any criminal attorney or convicted burglar would have told Richard at this point that if he allowed the cops to conduct a search without a warrant, he was a fool. At long last, Richard said, "Of course not," and tossed his car keys onto Ortega's desk.

Ortega scooped up the keys and turned them over to Kathy Harding, who left the office immediately. Then Ortega took pen in hand and regarded the suspect. "From the beginning, Mr. Lyon. Tell me everything you can remember about the day, and the night, you took your wife to the hospital."

Richard now told Ortega the identical story he'd related to the nurses in the hospital, and the same tale that he was to tell later on the witness stand. He'd gone to Houston on business that day—once again the tale included intricate details of the people he'd met in Houston, and with whom and where he'd eaten lunch, and a description of his ticket purchase at the airport using his credit card—and had returned home between five and six to find Nancy ill. He told Ortega about the morning coffee and how it had tasted terrible to him. He'd done everything he could to make Nancy feel better using home remedies, and had even had her doctor phone in a prescription to nearby Eckerd's Pharmacy, which Richard had personally filled. Around midnight, he said, when it became apparent that Nancy wasn't going to recover on her own, he'd taken her to the hospital. Richard's story has never changed, down to the minutest detail.

Ortega listened impassively and took notes. When Richard had finished speaking, Ortega said, "Mr. Lyon, if someone had wanted to kill Nancy, you got any idea who that someone might be?"

This question is designed to cause the suspect to stammer and sweat, but Richard had a surprise in store. He said quickly, "Well, there's her brother."

Now Ortega had difficulty keeping his own composure. "Oh?"

"Yeah," Richard said quickly. "Bill Dillard, Jr. The guy had incest with Nancy when they were kids."

Here Ortega nearly dropped his ballpoint. Understandably, the long-ago problem was something the Dillards hadn't discussed with the police or anyone else. Ortega lowered his head, made a note, and didn't say anything.

"The guy," Richard went on, "he's always in a bind for money. Nancy's inheritance goes to him." This wasn't entirely true, of course, as long as Big Daddy and Sue were still kicking, and on Big Daddy's death, Susan Dillard Hendrickson would be entitled to the same portion of Nancy's inheritance as Bill Jr. The statement, though, did give Detective Ortega pause. He wrote down Bill Jr.'s name.

"Anyone else?" Ortega said, almost as an afterthought.

"Well, yeah," Richard said.

Ortega lifted his eyebrows.

"This guy she worked with," Richard said, as if he'd suddenly found oil. "David Bagwell. Nancy was going to testify against him in a lawsuit, and she got a death threat at work. And, oh yeah, the guy's brother is a doctor and was on duty at Presbyterian while Nancy was dying. Have you ever heard of the Black Widow?"

Of course Ortega had heard of the Black Widow; it was his own homicide unit that had helped the Tulsa police investigate Sandra Bridewell in connection with her third husband's death, and also had looked into the death of Betsy Monroe Bagwell.

"Well, John Bagwell," Richard said, "David's brother. He's the guy whose wife was killed."

Ortega was hitting paydirt; he'd started the day with only one suspect, and now he had four. He wrote the Bagwell information down, then favored Richard with a heavy-lidded stare. "Mr. Lyon," Ortega said, "have you ever kept any poisons around the house?"

"Certainly," Richard said. "We've had fire ants. Amdryl, Amdro, commercial products. Damn fire ants are in the backyard, right where the children play."

Ortega was careful with the next question; it was something he'd been setting up all along. Casually he said, "Besides the fire ant poisons, have you ever bought any chemicals?"

And Richard said, very quickly, "No."

It was a lie. Ortega immediately dismissed the Black Widow, David Bagwell, Bill Jr., and anyone else other than Richard. The man was lying. Keeping his tone on an even keel, Ortega bored in. "Mr. Lyon," Ortega said, "have you ever bought any chemicals in Houston?"

Richard paused, swallowing. "Well, no. Not that I—"

"What about from General Laboratory Supply, Mr. Lyon?"

Richard gave a nervous laugh. "Oh. Oh, yeah."

Ortega laid his pen aside and folded his hands. "You're sure."

"Sure, I bought . . . mercury. To fix a battery I was building."

Ortega had trouble keeping his elation in check. None of the invoices he'd seen showed a mercury purchase. The detective picked up his pen and wrote something down. "Is that all you bought from them?"

Now Richard was trapped. He seemed lost in thought. "Well, I bought some arsenic acid down there."

Ortega nearly pressed a hole through his notepad. "And when was that?"

"October. November maybe."

"And for what purpose?"

"The fire ants."

Ortega was, understandably, confused. It wouldn't be until he had Ellen Rose go over General Laboratory Supply records once more that the answer would surface. The invoices Ortega had already seen, traced by using Richard's canceled checks, were all in the name of either Hughes Industries or Architectural Site Services. Richard had made other purchases in his own name and paid in cash. Ortega said merely, "Do you still have the arsenic acid at the house?"

By now Richard couldn't hide his nervousness; his gaze averted, he said, "I think . . . I think I threw it away so the kids wouldn't get into it."

"You threw it away. Did you throw anything else away?"

"Listen," Richard said. "Maybe I should call my attorney."

Ortega stared. "Mr. Lyon, were you having an affair?"

Richard swallowed. "Huh?"

"An affair. Our information is you were having an affair with a Miss Debi Denise Woods."

"What does that have to do with . . . ?"

"I didn't say it had anything to do with anything," the detective said. "I asked if you were having an affair."

"Nancy knew about that," Richard said.

Ortega nodded. "So she did."

"I don't think I should answer any more questions without an attorney present," Richard said.

Ortega leaned back and intertwined his fingers behind his

head, his round Hispanic face impassive. "Suit yourself, Mr. Lyon. But it's too late for this session. I'm through asking questions."

Richard glanced in panic at the door. "I'm free to go?"

Ortega waved a hand in the direction of the exit. "Sure you are. By the way, did you poison your wife?"

Richard's cheeks sagged, his facial muscles out of control. "Of course I didn't."

"Well, if you didn't," Ortega said, "there's a way to get us off your back."

Richard showed a questioning look.

"Polygraph," Ortega said. "Lie detector. You mind taking one before you leave?"

Richard's gaze shifted. "How long would it take?"

"Half hour. No more than that. You got time." The last was a statement, not a question. "Unless you're hiding something," Ortega added.

Richard was indignant. "Suits me. And no, I don't have anything to hide."

Ortega smiled. "I hope you don't, Mr. Lyon." He pointed a finger off to one side. "Polygraph guy's right down the hall, sir. Follow me."

Meanwhile, Detective Kathy Harding went over the Shenandoah duplex with a fine-tooth comb. She started with the small upstairs bedrooms, opening and rummaging through closets, stooping to peer underneath the beds, all the time catching glimpses of the dome atop SMU's Dallas Hall through the windows. She went downstairs, past the photos of Richard and the kids—all pictures of Nancy were gone—and did a thorough search of the living room. Then the attractive brown-haired police detective went to the back of the house into the small, outdated kitchen, knelt to look under the sink, stood on tiptoes to open the cabinets, and finally went through the back screen door into the yard. She paused to look around.

The connecting garage and servants' quarters were at the back of the yard with an entrance opening onto the alleyway, and Detective Harding decided that the garage was the next place to search. As she walked in that direction she passed a stone cherub on her right, and crossed the sidewalk under which, eight months earlier, Nancy had discovered the fire ant bed. The February wind bit with icy teeth; Kathy Harding hugged herself as she entered the garage. Her nose wrinkled slightly at the musty odor of stored paint, then she went to work. Her search of Richard's tool cabinets and underneath his work bench, plus a careful survey of every corner, nook, and cranny turned up the same thing she'd found in the house: exactly nothing. In the garage she did find a half-full green and red sack of Amdro, a common fire ant poison sold in feed stores and supermarkets. Though she doubted its value in the way of evidence, she took the Amdro with her.

Back in front of the house, she stood in the driveway and opened the trunk of Richard's Alfa Romeo. She'd found nothing of significance inside the car, just as she'd found nothing in the way of evidence in the house, but she did discover one thing in the trunk that gave her pause. The strange item was a soccer ball, which Detective Harding picked up and turned around in her hands. Someone had poked a number of holes in the ball's leather hide. The soccer ball, Detective Harding thought, was a puzzler.

After Richard had taken the polygraph exam, he got on the phone and found his own transportation home from police headquarters. He'd apparently decided that the less time he spent in Detective Ortega's company, the better off he was going to be. As Richard stood in the doorway leading to the third-floor hall, shifting his weight nervously from one foot to the other, the short, round-faced detective regarded the suspect with a stone-faced glare. Ortega then told Richard in no uncertain terms that he was the prime suspect in Nancy's murder, that he was free to go, but that he hadn't heard the last of the matter. As Richard walked away down the corridor, he was trembling all over.

When Richard had gone, Ortega went over his file. The incest stories he'd heard from Richard plus Richard's alleged suspicion of Bill Jr. and David Bagwell, all of these things Ortega decided were mere smoke screens. Aside from Ortega's certainty that

Richard was lying, he still hadn't been able to shake the suspect's story of what had occurred on the day that Nancy died. Richard's admission that he'd bought arsenic acid in Houston was the biggest break in the case thus far, and since Richard hadn't been entitled to any Miranda warning—which was the plan in having the suspect in for a talk to begin with—Ortega himself could testify in court to what Richard had told him. Still and all, it wasn't a great deal to go on.

Ortega needed more information and rapidly thumbed through the notes he'd made, both in his conversations with the Dillards and his just-finished chat with Richard. Somewhere, Ortega knew, he had Denise Woods' address and phone number. If anyone could shed light on a murder prompted by marital infidelity, that person would be the other woman.

26

If Richard had been nervous about going to the police station, Denise Woods was absolutely petrified. Ortega called the striking, azure-eyed blonde just moments after Richard had left the homicide division, and tersely demanded that she come in for an interview that afternoon. Up to that point, Denise had thought that the rumors regarding an investigation into Nancy's death were nothing but vicious gossip. After she'd hung up from speaking to Ortega, she sat speechless and stared at the phone for several moments. Her insides were cold.

By the time Denise had dressed, driven downtown, and located the Crimes Against Persons section at main police headquarters, it was nearly three in the afternoon. Denise had never seen the inside of a police station in her life; as she told the receptionist her business, her voice quavered. The receptionist directed Denise into the lobby waiting area and picked up the phone to buzz Ortega. Denise sank down in a waiting room chair. She felt as if she might faint.

She didn't have long to wait. As she sat staring at the far wall, a burly, square-jawed man in a flashy blue suit came out of the homicide office, flopped down in the chair beside her, and said, "You Denise?"

Denise recoiled as if slapped. "I'm Miss Woods," she said timidly.

"I'm Detective McNear," the man said, leaning back and crossing thick legs. "I guess you know this is about your boyfriend."

"My . . . ?"

"Your boyfriend. Mr. Richard Lyon, the guy that murdered his wife."

Denise was on the verge of tears. "Look, I don't know anything about this."

"Come on, we know he did it," McNear said. "There's no point in beating around the bush about it."

Denise swallowed hard. "You have evidence of that?" she said.

"We've got some," McNear said, nodding. "You bet. Well, follow me and let's get this over with."

He crooked a finger in her direction, then got up and led the way past the receptionist into the homicide section, making it very clear that as far as he was concerned, the "Ladies first" rule didn't apply. As she followed the broad back and swaggering shoulders down the hallway, it dawned on her that the guy was treating her as if she was a suspect herself. She practically gagged with fear.

McNear took Denise to a small interview room containing a bare wooden table with straight-back chairs on either side, told her to have a seat, went out and closed the door behind him with a bang. Denise sat and nervously drummed her fingers. McNear had put the fear of God into her, and she had no way of knowing that the burly cop was merely a warm-up act for what was to come.

Now it was Ortega's turn. The short detective entered the room at a brisk walk, his round-eyed gaze on Denise, his legal pad dangling at his hip. He sat across from her and readied a ballpoint. "You already know what this is about, don't you."

Denise hugged herself. "I'm sorry. But who are you?"

"Detective Ortega. You know what this is about?"

Denise was still petrified, but now was getting angry as well. "I don't think I do."

"Well, it's about your Mr. Richard Lyon killing his wife. Don't you know that?"

"I don't believe Richard killed anybody," Denise said. "This is all a bunch of bull."

"Yes, he did," Ortega said aggressively. "Nancy Lyon was poisoned slowly over a period of time. At the end it took just a teensy bit to push her over the edge."

Denise crossed her legs and testily rocked her foot. "I don't believe that."

"Doesn't matter if you believe it or not. First I want to ask you about—"

"What kind of poison?" Denise said.

"Arsenic. Cyanide. Strychnine. What does it matter? I'm asking the questions here." Ortega prepared to write. "First I want to know about this trip to Mexico you took with him."

Denise's anger melted instantly into shock. Up to that moment she'd thought that only she and Richard knew about the Puerto Vallarta trip; underestimating the Dillards' pipeline was a serious mistake. She said faintly, "Mexico?"

"Mexico," Ortega said. "Our information is that two weeks after his wife died, this guy took you to Puerto Vallarta. Anything to that?"

"What does that have to do with—?"

"Listen." Ortega laid his pen aside and pointed a finger. "You're about two inches away from being in a heap of trouble yourself. Me, I'm the one deciding what has to do with what. Now, did he take you to Mexico or not?"

Denise's gaze lowered, and she said meekly, "Yes."

"That's better. Where did youall stay down there?"

"Garza Blanca." Denise's vacant gaze was impassively on the wall above the detective's head.

Ortega's tone intensified as he said, "That's a helluva note, miss. The guy's wife not even cold in her grave and you're gallivanting off to Mexico with him."

Denise was suddenly hoarse. "I just went along as a friend."

"A friend? A *friend*? A man and woman going off together, and you're saying you're just a friend? Tell me something. You think that's normal?"

Denise shut her eyes tightly, turned away from Ortega, and folded her arms. "I'm not answering any more of your questions."

"Don't make it hard on yourself," Ortega said.

Denise was practically screaming. "You've already made it hard on me. And you can put me in jail or whatever, but I've got nothing more to say."

Ortega expelled a breath, then stared at Denise for the better part of thirty seconds. Finally he rose, extended a hand, palm out, and said, "Just a minute." Then he took a couple of steps, stopped, and said, "Don't move a muscle," and left the room.

Denise couldn't breathe. It was as if her lungs were frozen. Would they lock her up? In less than a minute, when a not unpleasant-looking woman entered the room, Denise decided that she was in fact going to jail. The woman must be her keeper. To Denise's surprise, the newcomer sat in Ortega's place and smiled across the table. "Denise, I'm Kathy Harding. You'll have to excuse these men around here, they're awfully rude sometimes."

When shown on television, the bad cop–good cop routine is often humorous. In real life the situation is anything but. Denise breathed a large sigh of relief. "I'm not hiding anything. Really I'm not," she said.

Suddenly Ortega reentered, pulled up a second chair, and sat next to the woman. Denise flinched.

"He's going to sit in," Harding said, "but I'll ask the questions, okay?"

Denise stared daggers at the male detective, then said to Harding, "All right, but I won't speak to him."

"Fine," Detective Harding said. "And, I'll tell you, this case is in the investigation stage. Nobody's accused anybody of anything yet."

"That's not what *he* told me." Denise pointed at Ortega.

Harding smiled. "Well, maybe he jumped the gun. Denise, do you use any poisons in your business?"

"No. What's all this talk about poison, anyway? Have you found some?"

"Nancy gave some things to her friends," Harding said, "which we believe are poisoned. Some wine and some pills."

"Why not have them tested?" Denise said.

"We're doing that." Harding glanced at Ortega, who sat impassively by, taking notes. "Denise, I know you've been close to Richard," she said. "Did you even know that he was sleeping with Nancy?"

"No. He hasn't in over a year."

Harding slowly shook her head in a just-between-us-girls attitude. "Not true, Denise. I hate to be the one to tell you. He came by her house, by *their* house, on Shenandoah pretty often, without telling her he was coming."

Denise was surprised and, though she tried not to show it, just a bit jealous. "He respected her," Denise said, "and they were into shared parenting."

"Oh, Denise," Harding said, sympathetically shaking her head. "Listen, let's change courses. Richard's already told us he bought arsenic in Houston. Did you ever see it?"

"The ants, he . . . no, I never saw it, but he bought it for fire ants. He threw it away when he was through, I think."

Harding examined her nails. "He threw it away. During the times you've been with Richard, have you ever known Nancy to be sick?"

Denise pursed her lips. She was sorry the woman was dead, but still bore a grudge. "Nancy was sick," Denise said, "when it was convenient for her to be sick. If she'd find out Richard and I were going out somewhere, she'd call him and whine that she was sick. Away he'd run to her, then when I'd see him again he'd tell me there was nothing wrong with her all along."

"*He* said."

Denise lifted her eyebrows. "I beg your pardon?"

"Richard told you there was nothing wrong with her, is that right?" Harding said.

"Well . . . yes."

"Denise," Harding said, "did you ever know Richard to lie?"

Denise was firm. "Only once. Only once in the whole time I've known him."

"Oh? When was that?" Harding's voice was soft and encouraging, a real change from Ortega's gruff male tenor.

"It was only so I wouldn't know the real reason he went on a trip with her, that was just after Christmas."

"And what did he tell you? What did he say that was a lie?"

"He told me, just that . . ." Denise paused to gather her thoughts. "Well, he told me the reason they went on this trip was because she had this rare disease, and she needed treatment at Mount Sinai Hospital in New York. But he was just covering his . . ."

Denise paused. The two cops were staring at each other, Ortega sitting forward with an attitude of urgency. Finally he spoke. "Will you sign a statement to that effect?"

Oh, my God, Denise thought, what have I told them? She pursed her lips together in determination. "No."

The detectives exchanged glances. Kathy Harding regarded Denise, the detective's gaze soft and caring. "Look, Denise. I've got to tell you," Harding said. "Richard's been here today, and he busted hell out of a polygraph test. We're going after Richard in a big way. Please, Denise, don't let him drag you down along with him."

Denise lowered her head and closed her eyes. At that moment she wished she'd never been born.

Denise refused to sign a statement and was never to give her consent, but the detectives knew full well that the signed statement didn't matter. If necessary, Jerri Sims could subpoena Denise and put her on the stand where, under oath, Denise would have to repeat the story of Richard's lie or suffer the consequences. The lie showed intent, and next to Richard's admission of the Houston arsenic buy, was the best information the police had yet uncovered. After Denise had gone home, the detectives talked things over. They had enough to proceed. More than enough, in fact.

The following day, Ortega did something that was uncharacteristic for him, and newsmen who know him are still in a quandary as to his motives. Ortega had never before confided in the media, not once in his two decades as a homicide cop. But for whatever reason, Ortega got together with Captain Mike Brock of the University Park Police, and the two of them called a news conference. With minicams grinding and newspeople scribbling furiously, Ortega stated that the death of Nancy Dillard Lyon was no accident. She'd been poisoned, Ortega said, slowly and systematically over a period of months. There was only one suspect as far as the police were concerned, Ortega said, and that man was Nancy's husband, Richard Lyon.

After the headlines appeared in both the *Dallas Morning News* and the *Times-Herald* the following day, Richard went into seclusion for a while. He called Stan Wetsel at Architectural Site Services and resigned, stating that his life was in too much turmoil for him to continue working. Wetsel, who'd read the papers along with the other three million metroplex residents, accepted Richard's resignation willingly, and no doubt with some relief. And Richard did have problems. Massive problems. His first order of business was to find a good lawyer.

Young Dan Guthrie could pick 'em up and lay 'em down. He was, as they say on the dusty West Texas plains, a runnin' fool. As a mere colt of a kid he went all the way to Minneapolis to blister a northern track with a 22.4-second 220-yard dash, then a national record for thirteen-year-olds. Ain't no way, grizzled West Texans thought, they can keep the Guthrie boy out of the Olympics, once he gets some seasonin' to him.

As a boy, Dan Guthrie was a nomad, a year here, two years there. His parents divorced early on, and Dan lived with his dad, a radio and TV announcer for small-town stations in Sweetwater, San Angelo, you name it. And wherever his father put down for a spell, Dan Guthrie would run and run. As a seventh-grader in Abilene, Guthrie's hero was his next-door neighbor, a champion high school sprinter named Carlton Stowers, who was to grow into a writer and win an Edgar award; Dan spent months and months doing his best to mimic Stowers' running style.

So talented a sprinter was the Guthrie lad that his parents agreed, when Dan was a ninth-grader, that the boy needed roots;

each time Guthrie transferred high schools, he would lose a year of his track eligibility. So Dan went up to Dallas to live with his mother, and spent his prep school years at Bryan Adams High. As a senior he recorded a 9.6 in the hundred-yard dash, which back in those days was movin' on. His high school record earned him a scholarship to Rice Institute in Houston, where as a freshman he was considered a shoo-in to one day be the Southwest Conference champion sprinter.

Dreams tend to fade, however, and Guthrie never lived up to his high school promise. His decline as a runner was no fault of his own; he suffers from a congenital defect known as spinal bifida, which causes hamstring muscles to pull easily. Guthrie's college track career was riddled with injuries.

Unable to run as he wanted, Guthrie moved fast in other ways. At Rice in the sixties he became a campus leader and a skillful fund-raiser for college projects; it was largely through his efforts that the university obtained money for a campus radio station. He also did nighttime duty as a disk jockey, spinning platters for Houston's KILT radio under the pseudonym of Jim Gregory. After the tragedy at Kent State University, Guthrie, along with a college sidekick named John Sortore—who today lives in New York City and serves as president of Drexel Burnham, a stock trader of some note—became a campus rover and searched for hidden bombs. By 1971, when Guthrie earned a bachelor's degree from Rice in economics and accounting, he had experience in several trades.

He went on to law school at the University of Texas in Austin, though he swears he never really wanted to be a lawyer, and passed his bar exam in 1974. Guthrie's lack of legal ambition is borne out by his next endeavor, which was an earnest campaign to secure the Dallas franchise for Mr. Gatti's pizza. After losing out to his competition by a nose, he looked for other business ventures but drew a total blank. Reluctantly Guthrie turned to the practice of law and went to work for Henry Wade at the D.A.'s office.

In the trial court arena, Dan Guthrie ran faster than ever before. Handsome and athletic, with a prominent chin, chiseled features, and a wealth of coal black hair combed just so to wave jauntily above his forehead, he is quick of wit and thinks well on his feet. Before he was thirty years old he was chief prosecutor in one of Dallas County's felony courts, and so fierce was his pursuit of lawbreakers that he headed up a special D.A.'s task force for the prosecution of habitual offenders. He represented the State of Texas in the first prosecution ever for welfare fraud.

An ambitious lawyer can only run so fast and so far as one of the D.A.'s staff, and by 1978 Guthrie had gone about as far as a county man as he felt he was ever going. In that year he took his talents down the street to the United States Attorney's office, where he specialized in the prosecution of white-collar crime. Other than meeting his second wife, also a staffer with the U.S. Attorney (an earlier marriage to his high school sweetheart had floundered), Guthrie doesn't have fond memories of his time as a federal man. Constantly at odds with the methods employed in the prosecution of federal cases, he finally resigned in anger over the granting of probation to a drug dealer in order to secure the man's testimony against what Guthrie believed to be a lesser offender. At that point he joined a firm that defended the same bankers, doctors, and drug defendants whom Guthrie had formerly prosecuted, and it was in private practice that he found his niche. There are no limits to the distance a defense attorney can run.

Even the most successful of men will acknowledge an element of luck in hitting it big, and Dan Guthrie couldn't have picked a better time to go into criminal defense work. It was the early eighties, the time when the FBI was just beginning to let the hammer down on banks and savings and loan institutions on behalf of the FDIC and FSLIC, and the men who'd built empires from Reagan's deregulation blunder were scrambling to stay out of jail. More than any other time in memory, white-collar criminal defendants had money to burn.

The biggest of the big among savings and loan prosecutions, an intricate and exhausting case known as the I-30 Condo Scam, took place in Dallas. The defendants were members of a group headed by a semi-literate painting contractor named Danny Faulkner, who took control of Empire Savings & Loan—located in the Dallas suburb of Mesquite—increased the institution's assets twenty-fold in one year by offering unrealistic interest rates on CD's and savings accounts, then loaned the money to groups involved in the purchase of land from Faulkner and his associates. There were land flips involved, some parcels sold as many as five times in a single day with the nighttime price four to five hundred percent of what the land had brought only that morning. Also involved were inflated appraisals, falsified loan documents, and, eventually, the collapse of Empire Savings & Loan. At the time the federal investigation into the I-30 condo dealings commenced, Danny Faulkner's personal worth was in excess of 100 million dollars.

Guthrie didn't represent Faulkner himself in the I-30 case, but was the lawyer for one of Faulkner's chief lieutenants, a former high school football coach named Kenneth Cansler, who himself had earned millions in the sale of the property. Guthrie did a good job for Cansler—his sentence of five years is considered peanuts in comparison with the thirty and forty years handed out to other defendants in the case—and for his trouble received a fee that is mind-boggling. The fee itself wasn't the main reward Guthrie reaped, however (Guthrie is, alas, himself somewhat of a gambler; he invested most of his I-30 fee in land, hoping to build a retirement nest egg, and, due to the collapse that continued through the eighties, instead guaranteed himself a lengthy career in the fervent practice of law); the publicity generated by the case placed the name of Dan Guthrie high on the list of Dallas' most prominent defense attorneys.

Shortly after close of the I-30 case, Guthrie disassociated from his partners and entered practice on his own, setting up prestigious offices across the street from the living end of all Dallas locations, the Crescent Towers. With Guthrie's reputation as a defender of businessmen accused of crimes, it isn't surprising that the civil firm to which Richard Lyon went for advice steered the business Guthrie's way. There is, however, an important thing to keep in mind regarding Richard's choice of lawyers. In early March 1991, as a visibly shaken Richard entered Guthrie's offices, the attorney's practice heretofore had been limited exclusively to white-collar federal cases. High-profile as he had rapidly

become, Guthrie had never before represented a client charged
with murder.

A crime is a crime, be the charges state or federal, but this
statement is a truth that bears scrutiny. Effective defense strategy
in the two arenas is entirely different, particularly in the procedure before the trial. This is especially true in cases that receive
a lot of media attention.

Veterans of courtroom battles believe that when a prospective
juror states that he or she has no preconceived opinion of the
case, in spite of the fact that the charges have been hashed and
rehashed in the newspapers and on television for the several
months preceding the trial, the prospective juror is usually lying.
Media coverage is almost always slanted for the prosecution—the
reason being that prosecutors are constant sources of information for reporters, but tend to clam up when questioned by the
media person who has previously favored the defense—and the
individual who isn't influenced by newspaper stories is rare indeed. That prospective jurors come to the courthouse with a tendency to convict certainly isn't the situation envisioned by the
framers of the Constitution, but is nonetheless a fact of life when
dealing with the justice system.

State charges are specific: either John killed Mary or he didn't;
either Pete was the robber in the grocery store heist or he wasn't.
In a state case, no matter how much information the prosecution
manages to leak to the newspapers in advance (and, generally,
the weaker the case against the defendant, the more information
the media will have), the district attorneys still have to bring hard
evidence into the courtroom. Seasoned defense lawyers in state
cases know this very well, so do not comment to the media beforehand and do their talking only after the starter's gun sounds.

Federal charges are general (or even nebulous, defense lawyers
say, to the point of being laughable), and U.S. attorneys actually
have to prove very little to get their cases before the jury. Since
the courtroom evidence presented in a federal case has little to
do with what has actually caused the prosecution to begin with,
the trial outcome often depends on which side has obtained the
most favorable media coverage. The best defense strategy in fed-

236 / A. W. Gray

eral cases is to give sufficient information to the media so that prospective jurors, when lying about whether they have preconceived notions concerning the case, will at least have heard both sides of the story. Since the attorneys understand that the judge's inevitable gag order in a federal case comes long after both sides have popped off to the newspapers anyway, good federal defense lawyers give many interviews.

Be the defense strategy in the Lyon case right or wrong, when Richard retained Dan Guthrie to defend him against charges of murdering his wife, Guthrie's first move was to call a press conference of his own. The same reporters and TV newspeople who only days earlier had listened to Detectives Ortega and Brock outline their case now trooped into Guthrie's quarters in a horde. In an elegantly furnished conference room Guthrie and his client, both dressed to the nines and barbered like actors in a courtroom drama, waited side by side. Each made a brief statement, then threw the session open to questions. The defense position was clear: Not only had Richard Lyon not poisoned Nancy, he was investigating the case on his own to uncover the real murderer, and currently had three suspects in mind. One was Nancy's brother, Bill Dillard, Jr., with whom Richard had learned his wife had had an incestuous relationship, and another was David Bagwell—whose brother John, in case the reporters didn't remember, had been involved in the notorious Black Widow investigation—from whom Nancy had received a threat while she worked for Tramell Crow. For good measure, Richard gave the media a third suspect, Lynn Pease, the Lyons' former nanny (Lynn's inclusion in the finger-pointing was likely spite; Lynn had been supplying a great deal of information to the detectives, and it was Lynn who was named eventually as the state's main informant on Richard's arrest warrant). While newspeople gripped pencils tightly enough to cut off circulation in their fingers and threw incredulous glances at one another, Guthrie promised that the case would reveal nothing short of a Perry Mason whodunit.

There was, by the way, one outsider in the media group jammed into Guthrie's conference room. *Hard Copy,* the nightly TV tabloid, had picked up on the stories of the previous police press conference, and had sent along a representative. Bulging at the seams with wealthy Texans as principal characters, and spiced with incest to add flavor, the story had all the ingredients necessary to send the tabloids into drooling fits. As Richard and Guthrie entertained reporters with the aplomb of a couple of seasoned talk-show hosts, the death of Nancy Dillard Lyon was about to become a national event. The circus was on.

28

Jerri Sims hit the ceiling as she watched the Richard and Dan Show on television the night after the news conference in Guthrie's office. The hidden accusation in the conference was clear: the police and district attorney were carrying on a vendetta against Richard and ignoring the existence of other suspects. As Richard's lawyer it was Guthrie's job to make his client appear as pure as the driven snow, of course, but seeing Richard confidently tell reporters of his innocence made Jerri's blood boil. She was in the midst of preparing an indictment against him for presentation to the grand jury, and she had some information about which the media—and, hopefully, Guthrie and his client—were not aware.

The first solid bit of evidence the police had turned up, other than the Dillard family suspicions and Richard's ill-advised statements to Detective Ortega, came from a general contractor named Thomas L. Saba. Saba makes his living doing make-ready work on vacated apartments. On January 20, 1991, he made a trip to 3616 Springbrook to check out the premises based on a move notice signed by the tenant, Richard Lyon, who was in the process of relocating back to the Shenandoah duplex. It is Saba's practice to do a personal inspection of premises prior to engaging work crews to paint, clean, and replace carpet where necessary.

Saba, a rawboned, all-business individual with a sharp eye and an amazing memory for details, was somewhat irritated to find quite a bit of clutter still lying around the condo; his information was that the tenant had already moved and that the coast was clear for the contractor to go to work. That wasn't the case at all, however, as Saba discovered as he went over the premises inch by inch.

There were clothes still on hangers in the closets, and in the bedroom were an easel, brushes, and watercolors. Leaning in a corner behind the bed was an over-and-under double-barreled shotgun; Saba carefully checked both barrels to be sure the gun wasn't loaded. There were screwdrivers, pliers, and wrenches lying about in every room, and Saba wrinkled his nose when he opened the refrigerator to find some spoiled food. On the kitchen counter were some potted ferns and cactus, and in the cabinet under the sink was a cardboard box containing three different brands of pesticides. Beside the box was a jar containing what appeared to be vitamin capsules. In rummaging through the kitchen drawers, Saba came across a plastic Baggie full of empty gelatin caps of the same general appearance as the filled capsules inside the jar. Back in the bedroom underneath a pile of dirty clothes was another Baggie of empty gelatin caps. Saba remembers wondering what the tenant was doing with so many empty capsules. He decided that the tenant in fact hadn't moved as yet, and finally left after making a notation on his schedule to check back on 3616 Springbrook at a later date.

On the day after his interview with Richard and Denise Woods, Detective Ortega showed Thomas Saba the container of pills that Nancy had found on the porch at the Shenandoah duplex, and asked the contractor to compare them mentally to the capsules in the Springbrook apartment. According to Saba, the two groups of pills were identical.

* * *

In addition to the information supplied by the make-ready contractor, Jerri had further jogged Lynn Pease's memory in an interview at the D.A.'s office. Lynn now recalled a time in October or November when she'd dropped in on Nancy at the Shenandoah duplex to find Richard there. Richard and Nancy were in the living room, and it was Richard who responded to Lynn's knock on the door. During Lynn's visit, and in plain sight of the former nanny, Richard gave Nancy a Baggie containing vitamin capsules. He said they were a special formula he'd discovered, and that he'd packed the pills himself in his Springbrook apartment. Nancy's system needed cleansing, Richard said. His estranged wife hadn't been looking well of late.

Jerri still couldn't proceed with the indictment because the medical examiner's report was lacking, but within minutes after she'd watched Richard and Guthrie on the TV news, she was writing furiously. She prepared a motion to disqualify Dan Guthrie as Richard's lawyer, her theory being that Guthrie had made himself a witness in the case. His statement to the press regarding additional suspects, Jerri reasoned, was apart from the attorney-client relationship, and she included in her motion that she intended to call Richard's lawyer before the grand jury to testify. She knew at the time that her motion was, so to speak, in from left field and had little chance of winning approval from the court, but the elaborately staged TV interview had her in an uproar. She would later file the motion and bring the matter before the court in a hearing, and the furor over the D.A.'s attempt to disqualify Richard's lawyer would heap more coals on an already raging fire.

There is a small group of people in various parts of the country who religiously tune in to *Hard Copy* and its clones, *A Current Affair*, et cetera, with more than a passing interest. These people are profiteers, independent television movie producers and quickie paperback writers who know from experience that any story worthy of national *Hard Copy* exposure is a relatively easy sell to networks and New York publishing houses. The reading and viewing public will soon benefit from a slowing down of the practice, as the glut of bad true-crime television movies and even worse true-crime paperbacks lowers Nielsen ratings and diminishes publishers' profits, but at the time the Dan and Richard Hour first aired on *Hard Copy*, true-crime productions were the rage. A case involving both wealth and lewd incest practically guaranteed at least one book contract and TV movie production in the making, so within twenty-four hours of the original *Hard Copy* segment, district attorney and police department phones rang incessantly as profiteers scrambled to be firstest with the mostest. Though she eventually turned out not to have the mostest, a comely young lady named Yvette Ferris was the firstest and definitely the most memorable of the bunch.

Yvette Ferris is, for want of any better description, a cute trick. She is pretty, perky, peppy, and all the other adjectives so abhorred by feminists, and she certainly wasn't wanting for enthusiasm. An acquaintance of Bruce and Mary Ann Will, Richard's downstairs neighbors at the Springbrook condo, Yvette set out early on to "tie up" all the principals in the case. The "tying up" of principals is a rather questionable, albeit common, practice of offering money to persons for the exclusive rights to their knowledge of the case, the assumption being that competitors for movie and book rights, denied access to intricate details, will simply dry up and blow away. Whether Yvette's bank account was equal to her ambition is up for grabs.

Within days after the Lyon case became national news, Yvette, identifying herself as an associate of the California independent producer Carolco Productions, had made cash offers to the police, the D.A., Big Daddy (who got probably his only legitimate laugh of the entire year from the proposal), Bill Jr., Richard, Denise Woods, and anyone else who had seen anything, heard anything, or who happened to live in the neighborhood. A failure to put money where her well-formed mouth happened to be eventually ended Yvette's pursuit of the matter, but for a time she was quite visible. One of her offers for information went to Mary Ann Will.

Sometime in March, shortly after Richard had moved his belongings from the Springbrook apartment to the Shenandoah duplex, Mary Ann looked out her window one day and watched an army-green United Parcel Service truck pull up to the curb. As Mary Ann pushed drapes aside for a clearer view, the UPS man carried a package up a flight of steps to leave it in front of the door to the now vacant upstairs condo. As soon as the truck had rounded the corner and disappeared from view, Mary Ann left her apartment and went up for a look. The UPS label on the package bore Richard's name and Springbrook address, and the sender was General Laboratory Supply in Houston, Texas. The ominous parcel bore every semblance of a real break in the case.

Detective Ortega had already questioned Mary Ann and her husband at length, and had asked that they give the police a call should anything new develop that they thought might be important, so civic duty dictated that Mary Ann phone police headquarters to report the suspicious delivery. Possible profit was her motive for her second call, the one to Yvette Ferris.

The result was a double stakeout. Police set up surveillance via an unmarked car across the street while Yvette made trips by the apartment several times a day to make certain that the package hadn't escaped, both endeavors to no avail. For days on end, through rain, wind and sun, there the parcel lay. If Richard knew or cared about the package he gave no indication; additional plainclothes detectives assigned to shadow the suspect reported that he hadn't gone within miles of the Richardson condo. The policemen charged with watching the package felt as if they'd go bananas from sheer boredom.

Finally, Yvette could bear the suspense no longer. During one of her daily detours by the condo, she parked her car, got out, and looked surreptitiously around. The policemen in the unmarked car sank immediately out of sight behind the dashboard, dribbling coffee on their shirt fronts as they did; the stakeout cops didn't know Richard Lyon from Richard the Lionhearted, and for all they knew this mysterious female was the other woman in the case, Denise Woods, come to make off with the evidence. Slowly, carefully, her gaze shifting left and then right, Yvette crept upstairs to stand outside Richard's old apartment. Then, after a final glance in all directions, the petite and eye-catching young lady snatched up the package and made a running beeline down the steps and across the lawn to her car. After first tossing the parcel onto the front seat, diving behind the wheel, and starting the engine, Yvette then wound her way home with stakeout cops hot on her trail. Once in her kitchen she slit open the UPS envelope and had a look, and barely had time to check the labels on the chemical containers inside the package before her doorbell rang. After a series of none-too-gentle questions, the two burly cops from the unmarked sedan placed Yvette under arrest and took her, package and all, downtown for booking as a material witness.

Other than a somewhat sheepish stint on the witness stand in preliminary hearings, Yvette thereafter personally vanished from the scene. The package itself contained only pesticides, and was never introduced into evidence, so Yvette's chain-of-custody testimony was unnecessary to the trial proceedings. In fact, the young lady relocated to California before the trial was under way. She did keep abreast of the case via long-distance calls to newsmen, however, and continued to state that she had the various principals "tied up," and further stated that once the trial was finished she would be going into production with her movie. She left the L.A. phone number of Carolco Productions with the media folk, and asked that they give her a call should any important developments arise. Long after the verdict was in, curious as to why no camera crews had showed up for filming, one of the newsmen did call Carolco's offices to make an inquiry. The person answering the phone stated that no one named Yvette Ferris was currently employed by Carolco Productions.

The profiteer who eventually showed the mostest in the Lyon case was another California independent, Robert Greenwald Productions. Greenwald pitched and sold the story of Nancy's death to ABC, and eventually transformed the case into a two-hour TV movie (filmed in North Carolina for some reason) with the fine actress Tess Harper starring as Jerri Sims. Greenwald Productions proved to be every bit as strong of wallet as of promise, and bought the rights to Lynn Pease's and Detective Don Ortega's stories. At various times there were rumors of as many as five movie deals in the works (at one time Denise

Woods had not only a local movie producer but an Austin entertainment lawyer peddling her rights; the Dillard family told all callers to submit resumés to their attorney; Richard's story finally became available to anyone willing to foot the cost of his appeal), so among local media types the Greenwald production was known in its preliminary stages as the Ortega-Woods deal (Lynn married in the year prior to Richard's trial and testified under the name of Lynn Pease Woods).

Detective Ortega's comment to local reporters that he "should have held out for more" than the $15,000 fee he received from Greenwald Productions for his time in transcribing the details of his investigation on a tape recorder bears some study. Throughout the investigation and subsequent trial, Ortega received calls from numerous reporters, authors, and movie-making hopefuls, all wanting the details of his work on the Lyon case. Ortega responded to each one that he wouldn't discuss the case until after the verdict was in, and that even then he would talk only to those whom he "liked." The more naive among the profiteers failed to realize that Detective Ortega might have "liked" them more were they willing to cross his palm, but Greenwald Productions had both the savvy and the greenbacks to be counted among the detective's closest friends.

The following may come across as a dose of sour grapes from authors and movie folk on the outside of Detective Ortega's close-knit circle of "pals," and there is doubtless some bitterness involved, but the widespread practice among true-crime profiteers of paying policemen for information has come under criticism from groups other than authors panting for a piece of the policemen's high-priced information. The Supreme Court of the United States, for example. A Florida conviction involving a quite grisly series of roadside murders was recently reversed by the high court because the detectives involved in the investigation were receiving payments from movie folk, and the reasoning of the justices in remanding the case goes to the heart of the intended impartiality of the justice system.

There is a great public outcry of "Hear, hear" with respect to the New York statute known as the "Son of Sam law," wherein convicted criminals are prevented from making money by selling the story of their crimes, but according to our highest court, similar payments to law enforcement personnel may be even more reprehensible. For public employees to profit personally from the sale of knowledge gained as a result of their employment is a crime in itself (though prosecutors who themselves hope for future sales to movie folk are naturally reluctant to pursue indictments against other law enforcement personnel), such payments being known in the common vernacular as bribes. Movie producers and book publishers are quite liability-conscious, having fallen victim to a number of civil lawsuits over the years, and the practice in the true-crime genre has come to be that there is no publication of a book and no making of a movie when the prosecution of the defendant doesn't result in a conviction. In December 1992, a movie crew was in the midst of filming a TV production starring Robert Conrad, based on a triple homicide in Waco, Texas, when one of the defendants in the case had his conviction reversed and, on retrial, was found not guilty. The retrial caused quite a commotion on the set. The script was rewritten on the spot, all names were changed, the author of the book on which the production was based had his name removed from the credits, et cetera, and the movie eventually aired as a piece of fiction. Nearly all movie deals are formulated while the investigation and trial are in progress. So, the Supreme Court reasons, threatened loss of revenue from movie or book deals could easily cause police and prosecutors to be somewhat overzealous in their desire to obtain a conviction.

Actually, the inaccessibility to (or, at least, the equal sharing of) police information for authors and scriptwriters might turn out to be a boon to readers and viewers. Although it is true that listening to a tape recording made by investigating law enforcement personnel is certainly the lazy person's utopia of information-gathering technique, the scope of the story becomes limited to a single viewpoint. Elimination of the practice of paying policemen for information would cause writers to get off their respective fannies and do some heavy research, thus giving readers the benefit of something other than the usual cop-investigation (plod, plod) slant on things.

29

Dan Guthrie had plenty to say when he found out that Richard was still seeing Denise Woods in the face of a murder investigation based on his extramarital relationship. At least until the case was over, Guthrie told Richard, he and Denise would have to cool it. Richard would simply have to explain to her that every public sighting of the two of them together could very possibly drive another nail into his coffin. Richard agreed that in the future he would see Denise only in private, but his method of going undercover with the relationship was, in retrospect, somewhat less than discreet.

Denise moved her contracting operations to Austin, two hundred miles south of Dallas, where she still had contacts from her days as a university student. The reason given for her relocation was that because of the splash of publicity she'd received over recent months, her Dallas business had gone to pot, and that in Austin she could have a fresh start in a locale where her involvement in a murder investigation wasn't generally known. On the surface, Denise's move could have worked out well for Richard's defense, but his frequent trips up and down Interstate 35 to visit his lover didn't go unnoticed by the district attorney's investigators, and at trial Jerri Sims was to portray Denise's move as nothing more than a sham to keep carrying on with Richard out of the limelight.

Having burned his bridges where Architectural Site Services was concerned, Richard needed a job. Allison and Anna still lived with their father, and in addition to supporting his daughters, he had to keep up payments on the Shenandoah duplex. Not surprisingly, a man whose face had been splashed all over the newspapers and on television sets as the prime suspect in a murder investigation—even a man with Harvard credentials— had difficulty in finding work. Eventually Richard had to settle for a job influenced by outside sources, only this time the string-puller wasn't Big Daddy. Concerned over Richard's pending financial straits, Denise Woods made a call, and Richard went to work for her father at Woods Construction. It was understood from the outset that the job was only a stopgap until Richard could clear himself, at which time he'd find work on his own. However, no matter how brief his stint at Woods Construction, his employment with Denise's father was to heap more coals on the fire Jerri Sims was building.

In between the breaking of the story and the onset of the trial, Richard was to make several urgent phone calls to Dan Guthrie and others to give the news that he'd uncovered startling new evidence in the case. The first of these had to do with a phone message recorded on Richard's answering machine. Guthrie, himself a Park Citizen living across the street from the high school, was less than ten minutes from Richard's home, and on this occasion sped to the Shenandoah duplex to hear the recording himself. If legitimate, it could indeed have had a bearing on the case. As is true with most persons aware that they are under investigation, Richard wanted to do everything possible to head off the police before any charges were filed. After a strategy discussion with his client, Guthrie decided first to make a copy, then turn the recording over to Detective Ortega in the hopes that the homicide cop might pursue other avenues and run down other suspects.

Ortega listened to the recording, but wasn't impressed. Guthrie later played the message in open court in front of jurors and spectators, and the man in the recording sounded somewhat like Sydney Greenstreet with a cold. The tone was quite sinister, and guttural to the point that it was difficult to understand the words. The message stated that since the caller had "gotten her," then Richard "was next." The audio evidence came about during Guthrie's cross-examination of the detective, and the expression on Ortega's face as the jury listened made his opinion of the recording quite clear; in fact, it is easy to picture the detective alone in his office, playing the message over and over while he roared with laughter and slapped his thighs in glee.

A second red herring came in to the police department, this one in the form of a letter in a plain business envelope addressed to Ortega. The letter was typed, and purported to be from the hit man who had done Nancy in. According to the letter's author, Bill Jr. had hired the dirty deed done, but since he refused to pay up once the job was over, the letter writer had decided to snitch to the police.

Ortega carefully preserved the envelope, stamp intact, placed the letter and envelope in a sealed evidence carrier, and sent them over to the crime lab for DNA testing. This is a relatively new and highly publicized procedure wherein it's possible to take saliva samples from the stamp or gummed portion of the envelope flap and isolate the sender into specific groups of individuals. Alas, DNA didn't work in this instance because whoever sent the letter had wet both stamp and envelope either with a sponge or rolling moistener. When Guthrie questioned Ortega in court about the strange letter, the detective made it clear in his answer that he believed he knew who had sent the red herring to the police department. The sender, Ortega believed, was Guthrie's own client, who was at the moment seated in the courtroom at the defense table. Inarguably, the entire investigation wore blinders, and the only suspect whom the police were willing to consider was Richard Lyon.

★ ★ ★

It has been long established that the results of a polygraph examination are inadmissible as courtroom evidence, but when the suspect has flunked, police and prosecutors extract a great deal of mileage from these tests by leaking information to the newspapers. By the time Richard went to trial, it was general knowledge that he'd failed a lie-detector test administered by the police. What wasn't known to the press and the public was that Dan Guthrie arranged a second polygraph exam for his client, this one given by a private firm, and that Richard passed the second lie-detector test with flying colors.

Police openly pooh-pooh the results of polygraph tests administered by defense attorneys, claiming that the questions are rigged, and though they know that they can't get the results of tests given by police examiners into evidence, policemen take the results of their own lie detectors as gospel. The public perception of the reason for the inadmissibility of polygraphs is that certain persons are such habitual liars that they can fool the lie detector, but experts on the subject disagree.

According to those who supposedly know their stuff, it is quite easy for a person under stress to bust out on a polygraph and still be telling the truth. When Richard took the police test, he'd just been through Detective Ortega's aggressive grilling session, and no doubt was extremely nervous. From any standpoint, he would have been better off to wait a day or so before submitting to the exam.

None of the foregoing sheds much light on the reason for Richard's failure to pass the police polygraph or his success on Guthrie's; the various lie-detector tests administered to Richard simply provide further food for thought. For all we know, he lied through his teeth at the police station, and the questions on Guthrie's lie-detector test were limited to Richard's name and Social Security number. However, in evaluating the pros and cons of the various polygraph tests employed in the case, a little-publicized fact should also be taken into consideration. In order to clear the air in the face of the finger-pointing done by Richard and his lawyer over television and in the newspapers, Ortega had Bill Jr. come to the station for a police-administered polygraph of his own. To Ortega's surprise, the results of Nancy's brother's test were inconclusive. At trial Ortega had to testify two different times, the first outside the presence of the jury, because the defense had filed a motion that certain testimony the detective was going to give should be excluded. The judge eventually admitted everything Ortega had to say, but during the session with the jury out of the courtroom, Guthrie asked Ortega whether he'd given a lie-detector test to Bill Jr. At that point Jerri Sims objected vehemently. Her objection was sustained, and Ortega successfully dodged the issue.

The medical examiner's ruling of homicide in the Lyon case was in the hands of the police department in early April, eleven weeks after Nancy's death, but Richard still faced no official charges. The Dillards' anxiety increased with each passing day as Big Daddy and Bill Jr. made one telephone inquiry after another, seemingly to no avail. To their way of thinking, the police had simply forgotten the matter. The investigation, however, wasn't nearly as inactive as it may have appeared.

In spite of all the evidence that pointed at Richard, there were enormous snags in the prosecution's case. The information that Richard had ordered arsenic from Houston's General Laboratory Supply had come from Richard himself, an indication to a jury, Jerri Sims feared, that the suspect had nothing to hide. Richard also maintained that the arsenic order was intended to kill fire ants, both at his home and on a job site, and the D.A.'s own investigators had learned that the little red critters were in abundance at both locations. Furthermore, Richard had told authorities that he'd never received the materials from General Lab even though he'd paid in advance, and there was backup for his story here as well. Ellen Rose's records indicated that they'd shipped the order to a Sherry Lane address in Dallas—the headquarters of Architectural Site Services, Richard's employer at the time—but there the paper trail ended. The investigation was further complicated by the fact that the receptionist at ASS who'd receipted for the poison was no longer employed; in fact, she'd been dismissed for embezzlement, and there was no one to refute Richard's story that he'd never received the shipment. Since the police search of the Shenandoah duplex hadn't turned up so much as a smidgen of arsenic, not only was the case against him circumstantial, even the circumstantial evidence was a great deal less than air-tight.

It was another month before law enforcement decided that they simply weren't going to turn up anything else against Richard, and to go ahead with the evidence that they had. Dillard perserverance finally prevailed when, on May 16, 1991, Detective Ortega swore out an affidavit to be affixed to an arrest warrant. In his affidavit Ortega referred to the M.E.'s report, to information supplied by Lynn Pease, to Dr. Bagheri's talk with Nancy in the wee hours of the morning at the hospital, and to Richard's admission of having purchased arsenic from General Laboratory Supply. It still wasn't much, but was sufficient information for a magistrate's determination of probable cause. Detective Ortega obtained his warrant.

Though the magistrate signed the warrant on Thursday, Ortega didn't act until the following morning. Early on Friday, Detectives Ortega and McNear waited around the corner from the Shenandoah duplex as Richard drove by on his way to take his daughters to school. The policemen, driving an unmarked squad car, fell in behind Richard and stayed a block behind as the suspect drove his Alfa Romeo to an exclusive private day school in far North Dallas and, holding Allison's hand and carrying Anna, took the girls inside. When Richard came out he was alone, and as he left the school grounds the detectives were close on his bumper. He'd gone barely a block before Ortega flashed his roof lights. Richard pulled to the curb.

Ortega was brief and businesslike. He showed Richard the warrant and ordered the suspect out of the car; then, as Richard assumed the position against the roof of the Alfa Romeo, Ortega searched the suspect and cuffed his wrists behind him. The detectives then gave Richard his long-overdue Miranda warning, deposited him unceremoniously in the squad car's backseat, and drove the suspect downtown to the Lew Sterrett Justice Center.

In the jail basement, reporters and photographers—alerted, of course, by an earlier call from the police—waited with steno pads and cameras ready. As Ortega and McNear escorted Richard in from the garage, flashbulbs popped.

Richard was booked into jail around ten in the morning; inasmuch as it was Friday, he wouldn't see a judge until Monday morning. Likely, the timing of the arrest was the result of careful planning; arresting suspects on Friday, particularly those who have given the police a hard time, is a common practice, guaranteeing the suspects three nights in jail before they can post bond. Dan Guthrie had feared just such a happening, and had previously asked Ortega whether, if an arrest became imminent, Richard could surrender and post bond without going to jail. Ortega had agreed to the request, but now seemed to have forgotten the deal. So it was that Richard, dazed and blinking in shock, became a prisoner for the first time in his life. He was in for a long, long weekend.

30

By the time Richard finally stood before a judge for a bond determination on Monday morning, he had learned a great deal more about the justice system than he wanted to know. Although the police had shown experienced broken-field running in dodging around his Miranda warnings before charges were filed, now that he was in custody it seemed that every other person he saw wanted to tell him of his right to remain silent and to have a lawyer. Not only had the detectives recited Miranda, he'd heard the warning numerous times in jail processing, and not only that, had been hauled in front of a police magistrate to hear Miranda again. By now Richard could recite Miranda while standing on his head.

After three sleepless nights in a cell so crowded he was lucky to find room to lie on the floor, he'd been rousted at five in the morning, handcuffed, and paraded from Lew Sterrett Justice Center to the Crowley Courts Building on a chain gang. He'd ended up jammed like a sardine into a holding cell behind Criminal District Court No. 4, and after waiting for three hours had been escorted into the courtroom to appear in front of the judge. Dan Guthrie stood alongside Richard, and the fact that his lawyer was shaven and smelled fresh as a daisy didn't do Richard's mood any good. In addition to being so tired he could barely stand, he bore some telltale marks, evidence that dandies from Harvard and street-tough prisoners from South Dallas County don't mix really well.

Richard had a nasty cut underneath his left eye, and the right side of his lip was so swollen that his groomed thin mustache looked like cheap makeup pasted on at a comically crooked angle. He glanced over his shoulder and spotted Ortega, dressed in a flashy gray suit, seated in the courtroom spectators' section. The detective eyed Richard's cuts and bruises, then showed the prisoner a sardonic grin. Humbly, his hope of getting out of jail fading fast, Richard faced front and waited for the judge to speak.

The head man in Dallas County Criminal District No. 4 is a slender light-skinned black man named John C. Creuzot (pronounced, as in Cajun country, *cruise*-oh). Richard didn't know it as yet, but the blind-draw assignment of his case to Criminal District Court No. 4 was the best break that he could possibly have gotten.

In Texas, the state system of electing judges versus the federal system of appointing judges has been the subject of heated debate, but one veteran criminal defense lawyer puts it this way: "What the hell's the difference? Elected judges decide every issue in favor of the prosecution because they're afraid if anybody gets off in their court, their opponents will use it against them at election time. Appointed judges are different. *Their* reason for deciding every issue in favor of the prosecution is that all the prosecutors, cops, FBI agents, whatever, are the judge's fishing buddies. That's the end of the difference, as far as I can see. There's exceptions, but a fair judge in this state is a really rare bird." If our embittered criminal defense attorney is correct in his evaluation, then Judge John C. Creuzot is as rare a bird as one is going to find.

Away from the courtroom, Creuzot rides a hog. That's HOG

as in Harley Davidson, a $12,000 custom-designed Low Rider, and the judge mixes with tattooed and bearded biker groups as well as he does with the refined ladies and gentlemen at political fund-raisers. He definitely looks on defendants in his courtroom as people of flesh and blood.

John Creuzot didn't worry about money as a kid. His family migrated from New Orleans to Houston in the late sixties and, using a family recipe, opened a chain of fast-food restaurants called Frenchy's Creole Fried Chicken. Frenchy's eventually grew to eighteen locations and was listed in *Black Enterprise* magazine as one of the one hundred largest black-owned businesses in America. The family fortune came in handy in putting John through law school at SMU.

Though Creuzot has no experience with being black and poor, he relates closely to indigent minority defendants. He remembers being called a "nigger" as a child in New Orleans, also recalls quite well using separate drinking fountains for "Colored," and paid his dues as a southern black by riding the back of the bus. During courtroom breaks, Judge Creuzot often inquires as to scruffy prisoners' well-being, though once they're convicted, he also hands down heavy sentences to those over whose welfare he's showed concern. A coddler of criminals Creuzot isn't.

The epitome of a maverick, the judge doesn't cotton to the shenanigans of the Dallas County District Attorney's Office and makes no bones about it, and his general distrust of the D.A.'s methods comes from painful experience. As a wet-behind-the-ears young prosecutor fresh out of law school, Creuzot's reputation as a member of the "Hammer Squad" (so named for their relentless "hammering" of defendants who refuse what the D.A. believes to be legitimate plea-bargain deals) earned him a personal assignment from District Attorney John Vance to retry Randall Dale Adams, the drifter wrongfully convicted of murder whose case contributed greatly to Vance's falling-out with members of the press. After Creuzot's investigation convinced him that Dallas County had convicted the wrong man, he went to Vance and begged the D.A. to drop the charges. Vance refused, Creuzot resigned in anger, and the judge and the district attorney are not on speaking terms to this day. Asked if he believes that the Randall Dale Adams case altered Dallas County prosecutors' conduct in the courtroom, Creuzot replies curtly, "Not that I can see."

A Democrat in a stronghold of Republicans, Creuzot owes his judgeship to Ann Richards. Ms. Richards won the governorship of Texas in a nationally publicized campaign over Republican Clayton Williams in 1990. Since she's been in office, three of Dallas County's GOP judges have resigned; two to run for court of appeals benches and a third, Catherine Crier, to become an anchor newswoman on CNN, and eventually to migrate to the networks as a regular on *20/20*. In 1992, Creuzot was to become the only one of Governor Richards' appointees to win reelection over a Republican candidate. In part, he owes his popularity to his presiding over the high-profile trial of Richard Lyon.

So as Richard, beaten down from his weekend in jail, stood before Judge Creuzot at his bond hearing, he had no way of knowing that the judge was a man who lived by one fervent creed. Regardless of the case's outcome, John Creuzot is determined that every defendant before him will receive a fair trial. And in Dallas County, Texas, that is the most any defendant can hope for.

The law dictates in a bond hearing that the state show probable cause for filing of the charges, and since the burden on the state is roughly the same as was Ortega's in applying to the magistrate for an arrest warrant, the showing of probable cause wasn't much of a problem for Jerri Sims. She simply put Ortega on the stand and had the detective testify as to the findings of his investigation thus far, and that was that. The state easily won the question of probable cause. The fight over the amount of Richard's bond, however, turned into a real donnybrook.

Jerri argued that Richard was affluent, that he was able to get on an airplane and be thousands of miles away within hours, and that because of the seriousness of the charges was a high risk to flee (the state, incidentally, always argues that employed defendants are affluent; the truth was that Richard was flat broke and had called on his parents in Connecticut for help in paying Guthrie's legal fees). The state, Jerri said, was asking for bond on

Richard in excess of a million dollars. Not even that much, she argued, was sufficient to guarantee the defendant's presence at trial.

Guthrie, on the other hand, pictured his client as a bereaved widower, a dutiful father, and a pillar of the community. Confidently articulate in the courtroom, his manner and dress the picture of style, the defense lawyer paraded a succession of witnesses to the stand who vouched for Richard's honesty, work ethic, and devotion to his children. The defense's request, Guthrie eloquently stated, was that Richard be released on his own personal recognizance.

Judge Creuzot, as he would throughout the proceedings involving Richard, listened intently to both sides, and once both arguments were finished the judge made a short speech. Though the state definitely had probable cause against the defendant, Creuzot said, their request for bond in excess of a million was outrageous. On the other hand, Creuzot reasoned, the defense's idea that a man charged with intentional and premeditated murder should be walking around, free as the air, on his personal recognizance was every bit as overlenient as the state's request was outrageous. Since neither side had presented a feasible solution, Creuzot ignored both arguments. He set Richard's bond at $50,000 and imposed the additional requirement that the defendant remain at home except for trips to work and for other necessities such as groceries. To insure the defendant's compliance, Creuzot ordered, the county would lock a signal-transmitting device around Richard's ankle, and if he left home at any time without permission an alarm would go to the county pretrial release sector and he would find himself in jail. The conditions of bond, Creuzot said, were adjustable; if Richard was showed to be a good boy, the signal-transmitting device could be removed. Richard hadn't been formally indicted as yet, so Creuzot stated that the bond conditions would continue should the grand jury return a true bill.

In truth, the $50,000 bond was about what Guthrie had anticipated, and the defense lawyer had already arranged with Allan and Rosemary Lyon to post collateral with a local bondsman in just such an amount. The physical posting of bail was a mere formality, and once Richard left the courtroom and returned to jail, he found that his processing for release was already under way. Around three in the afternoon, he emerged on the street, blinking rapidly against the glare from the sun. The proceedings against him had only begun. For the time being, however, he was free.

Guthrie drove Richard to retrieve the Alfa Romeo, and once on the scene where he'd left his car, Richard hung his head. The auto's trunk lock was in tatters; someone had broken into the parked vehicle, stolen the tape deck and whatever else was removable, then smashed into and rummaged through the trunk. His later report to his insurance company doesn't mention the soccer ball. For Richard Lyon, things were not going well.

31

In spite of its listing at the forefront of defendants' constitutional rights, a grand jury proceeding is for the most part a formality, and the outcome of grand jury deliberations is pretty much at the whim of the prosecutor. The district attorney is the only lawyer allowed inside the grand jury room, and the citizens on the panel hear only the evidence the prosecutor wishes to present. The accused has a right to testify at a grand jury hearing, but over the years that right has seldom been exercised. Since the defendant can't have a lawyer present, defense attorneys always advise their clients not to appear, and prosecutors often take cases to the grand jury without the defense's knowledge. Given the foregoing, Richard's indictment was a lead-pipe cinch, but the conflict between Jerri Sims and Dan Guthrie during the grand jury proceedings developed into quite a furor.

Jerri had subpoenaed Guthrie to testify in front of the grand jury, and simultaneously had motioned the court to disqualify Guthrie as Richard's defense attorney. The reason given was that since Guthrie had gone on national television to state that there were three suspects in Nancy's murder other than Richard, Guthrie had information vital to the grand jury inquiry. It's true that Jerri's motion and subpoena met all the legal requirements, but there was likely more than a little spite in her motive for preparing them. The police had already investigated the three "suspects"—Bill Jr., David Bagwell, and Lynn Pease—and had satisfied themselves that all three lacked either motive or opportunity. Guthrie, however, had gone public with an accusation that the police and district attorney had carried on a vendetta against Richard, prompted by pressure from Nancy's family, and in Dallas County, Texas, one does not publicly challenge the district attorney's office and get away with it.

The matter of Guthrie's disqualification all came down to a hearing during the grand jury deliberations, and in this particular proceeding the defense won hands down. It has been long established that anything told an attorney by his client is confidential, and Richard's statements to his lawyer regarding other suspects fit neatly in that category. To force Guthrie's testimony before the grand jury would have been a flagrant violation of the attorney-client privilege. So although the hearing itself was pretty much cut and dried, it was at this proceeding that the conflict between Guthrie and Sims came out in the open. Throughout the brief testimony the two glared and sniped at each other to the point that the judge issued warnings to both parties. Guthrie's personal battle with Sims didn't end with the hearing, either, not by a long shot. For the duration of the case, the air between the two would continue to bristle.

Perhaps the most noteworthy portion of Richard's indictment is to the untrained eye the least significant, a small paragraph seemingly tacked on as an afterthought, stating that the offense of murder was aggravated due to Richard's use of a deadly weapon, to wit, arsenic poison. The Texas aggravated offense statute, originally passed by the legislature with the intent of punishing those committing mayhem with guns and knives, provides that persons convicted of aggravated crimes must serve a quarter of their sentence without regard to good-time credit before they are eligible for parole. It was impossible for Jerri to ask the death penalty for Richard (Texas law, revised in the seventies, provides the death penalty only for specific offenses: murder-for-hire, murder during the commission of a felony such as rape or robbery, and murder of a law enforcement officer or fireman during the performance of their duties), so Jerri had done, from the state's viewpoint, the next best thing. Since the aggravated offense statute came into being, appellate courts have expanded the definition of a deadly weapon to include anything with which one can kill; there is actually a case on the books wherein a man murdered a barroom customer by smashing his head against a wall, and the wall itself became the deadly weapon. The maximum punishment for the murder charge against Richard was life in prison; with the addition to the indictment of the aggravated charge, he was looking at a minimum of fifteen years before parole.

With Richard's indictment now a reality, Judge Creuzot continued the conditions of Richard's bond (as the matter progressed, in fact, the judge was to remove the signal-transmitting anklet restriction, and Richard was to make more trips to Austin to visit Denise Woods) and set the case of the *State of Texas* v. *Richard Allan Abood Lyon* for trial in sixty days. As opposed to most cases, which drag on for months and even years, the Lyon trial would be postponed only once; Richard was to refuse to sign a waiver of his right to speedy trial, thus forcing the state to try him within one hundred eighty days or drop the charges. It was clear that both Dan Guthrie and his client wanted to get the matter over with.

Two significant things happened after Richard's indictment and before his trial, one that gave the state's case a real shot in the arm and another which raised the defense's hopes. The first happening had to do with Stefanie Bates rearranging her cabinets.

Stefanie, a slim brunette, is, like Lynn Pease, a nanny by trade. She shares quarters with a young man named John Tedwell, and in the spring of 1991 the two were in the market for an apartment. The vacant condo at 3616 Springbrook Lane in Richardson perfectly suited their needs, and it wasn't until they'd already moved in and set up housekeeping that they learned from Mary

Ann Will, their downstairs neighbor, that the apartment had a history. At first, the fact that they were living in the same condo where Richard Lyon had supposedly plotted his wife's murder was a topic of conversation for Stefanie and John, and nothing more.

Life being the whirlwind that it is, Stefanie didn't have time to put her cabinets in apple-pie order until early June, three months after she'd moved in. On the day when she firmed her resolve to make things shipshape, she started in the kitchen. She first removed everything from the overhead cabinets, lined the bottoms of the cabinets with bright new shelf paper, then stacked plates, saucers, cups, and glasses in orderly fashion. Her job in the kitchen finished, she now headed for the bathroom.

There she stood with hands on hips for a moment, sizing up the chore, then went briskly to work. First she emptied the medicine cabinet, rearranged toothpaste, combs, brushes, headache and cold remedies to suit her, then turned her attention to the cabinet below the built-in vanity. Down on her haunches, Stefanie peered inside the shelf. She paused and blinked.

At the far back of the lower vanity cabinet shelf was a small prescription bottle with a plastic cap. The label was turned away from Stefanie, and inside the bottle were tan gelatin capsules. At first she thought that the bottle was her roommate John's, that possibly he'd bought some medicine without mentioning it to her. Frowning in curiosity, Stefanie reached in to pick the bottle up and turn it around.

The prescription was for the general-purpose antibiotic Keflex, and had come from the drug department at Eckerd's on Mockingbird Lane, near SMU. The recipient of the medicine, who was instructed on the label to take one every four hours, was Nancy Lyon.

Stefanie very nearly dropped the bottle. Only that morning there'd been another story in the paper having to do with Richard's upcoming trial. Her fingers trembling nervously, Stefanie called downstairs and told Mary Ann Will what she'd found. Mary Ann bounded up the steps to Stefanie's, and on seeing the bottle and its contents, she didn't hesitate. She put in a call to the police department at once. Before the day was out, the bottle, encased in a plastic evidence envelope, was on its way to the crime lab. An analysis of the capsules' contents showed each to contain Keflex save one; that suspicious pill, near the bottom of the prescription bottle, was packed with sodium nitroferrocyanide.

There was a problem with the pretrial incident which stood to bolster the defense's position, the same problem, in fact, which was inherent with nearly all of the defense's evidence: the source was Richard himself. He spent a great deal of time in playing detective prior to his trial, and though his discoveries might well have been untainted as newborn babes, Jerri Sims was to have a field day in making the defense's case appear manufactured by the accused.

Shortly before relocating her contracting business to Austin, Denise Woods got a call from Richard one day. He seemed so excited that she dropped what she was doing and sped to the Shenandoah duplex, and arrived to find a cardboard box on the kitchen table with Richard frantically going through the box's contents. In the box were pages and pages of notes taken in Nancy's handwriting, notes which, according to Richard, were reflections made during Nancy's incest counseling. The contents of the notes would become a major factor at Richard's trial, but it was another item found inside the box that had his undivided attention when Denise arrived.

The item was an invoice from Chemical Engineering. Its owner, Charles Couch, is the man who responded to a request in the fall of 1990 from a woman who lived near SMU, by devising a formula for fire ant poison. The invoice stated that on September 6, 1990, Chemical Engineering had sold chemicals including arsenic trioxide to a customer identified as D.P. Foundation, whose address was shown as "in care of Nancy Lyon." D.P. Foundation was one of the many charities to which Nancy had donated her time, and the invoice bore what appeared to be her signature. Underneath that was the number of her driver's license. As Denise read over the sales ticket, she gave Richard's arm a hopeful squeeze.

If legitimate, the invoice was critical to Richard's defense. If the defense theory that either David Bagwell, Bill Jr., or Lynn Pease had done Nancy in failed to hold water, then her purchase of arsenic lent credence to the idea that she might have committed suicide. As Richard showed Denise the invoice, his eyes shone with excitement.

In retrospect, there were serious questions regarding Richard's discovery that never occurred to Denise in the heat of the moment. According to him, he'd located the box while moving some of Nancy's things, but his previous story had been that he'd gone over the duplex with a fine-tooth comb within days of Nancy's death. If he had, how could a box the size of the one now on the table have gone unnoticed? Another question: Why had he made his revelation to Denise instead of Dan Guthrie, his lawyer? Of course, Richard may have been so excited at his discovery that he wasn't thinking clearly, but there could be a more sinister reason for contacting Denise. Richard may have needed a witness.

32

During the lull between his indictment and the storm which was his trial, Richard had things on his mind other than the murder charges. Now that their suspicions were out in the open, the Dillards had no reason to continue their charade of sympathy for Richard. The hostility between Nancy's family and their former in-law was about to become a public matter because in addition to his hatred for Richard over Nancy's death, Big Daddy was worried sick about his young granddaughters. If Richard would poison his wife for profit, Big Daddy reasoned, why would he stop short of killing his children as well? Allison and Anna were, after all, the beneficiaries on Nancy's $500,000 life insurance policy, and Richard stood to inherit the money should anything happen to the little girls.

The solution that Big Daddy's army of lawyers suggested was a custody suit, an attempt in civil court to take the children forcibly away from their father. The court wouldn't likely consider Big Daddy and Sue as acceptable guardians for Allison and Anna due to the grandparents' age, the lawyers said, and suggested that the named plaintiff be one of Nancy's living siblings. So far so good, but the Dillards' choice of plaintiffs in the Dallas County action headed, "In the matter of Allison and Anna Lyon, minor children," seems critically flawed to an outsider looking in.

Nancy's older sister, Susan Dillard Hendrickson, was married to a practicing Wichita Falls orthodontist, and Susan had all the credentials that family judges look for in placing children in foster homes: a nice residence, a stable home life, a husband capable of adequate support. For reasons known only to the Dillard clan, however, the family chose not to use Susan in the lawsuit. The plaintiff instead turned out to be Bill Jr. and his wife, Mary Helen, and the thought of facing his hated former brother-in-law in civil court would have Richard licking his chops.

"It mystifies me," an experienced family law specialist says, reclining his high-backed swivel chair and clasping his hands behind his head, "why they ever filed that suit to begin with. At the very least, the timing was bad. Christ, they were beat going in." Visible behind him through his office window, downtown Dallas stretches far into the distance; the glistening ball atop Reunion Tower is outlined in sooty haze.

"They feared for the kids," the interviewer says. "It's what they've claimed all along."

The veteran lawyer scratches his nose and brushes thin gray hair from his forehead. "Right, but look at the circumstances. To begin with, getting a judge to terminate somebody's parental rights is damn near impossible, and I've been doing this twenty-eight years. I had a case, let's see, seventy-eight or -nine. The guy was in the pen down in Huntsville, for rape, mind you, and he'd beaten some of these women damn near to death. His wife, ex-wife, had remarried and her new husband wanted to adopt the kids. I put her on the stand at the hearing. She testified how the guy had beat her up, beat the children, and that she was scared to death that if he ever got out he might kill all of them. And guess what happened?"

"From your tone," the interviewer says, "I guess you lost."

The elderly lawyer laughs out loud. "Lost? *Lost?* Hell, man, the judge gave us the hook before I could put my second witness on. That's when I made up my mind, no more custody suits, not when you're talking about taking somebody's parental rights away. This Richard Lyon, he hadn't been convicted of anything at the time, no way was anybody going to take those kids. All those Dillards accomplished was getting their dirty laundry aired."

The interviewer regards his crossed legs. "The hearing didn't go well for them."

"That's what I understand. That stripper, didn't they have her down there?"

"She's not a stripper, not any longer," the interviewer says. "But yes, I think I get your point."

"Sure," the lawyer says, turning to his credenza to pour water from a chrome carafe into a styrofoam cup. He sips. "Now, I know Dillard Jr. has taken the cure, and for all I hear around he's a changed man. But what have you really got? You've got a man, a drug and alcohol addict who's on record for having been up to Sierra Tucson, what, a couple of years ago? He's been keeping a stripper, at least there was evidence to that, and buying the girl dope to boot, and to top it all off the other side shows he used to get in bed with his sister. And this is the guy that's trying to take custody of another man's kids? And the other man hasn't even been convicted of anything? Christ, why they went for that hearing to begin with. It mystifies me." The lawyer raises shaggy gray brows. "That hearing, that's really what made a media circus out of the whole affair, wasn't it?"

"It didn't help," the interviewer says. "There'd been hints, the *Hard Copy* piece and whatnot, but that hearing was the first time anyone testified to the skeletons in the family closet."

"It looks to me," the lawyer says, "that if they were bound and determined to do it, they'd have used the older sister, not the brother. Hell, everybody in town knows it was the old man's doing to begin with, Dillard Sr. What difference does it make to him which of his living children has custody of the grandkids, he can see the little girls anytime he wants. It's almost like they *wanted* everybody reading their family secrets in the newspaper."

"Don't ask me," the interviewer says. "I'm sure they had reasons that we can only speculate about." He clears his throat.

268 / *A. W. Gray*

"While we're on that subject, though, I've got another question for you."

The lawyer cocks his head to one side. "Shoot."

"Well, if you feel that they never had a chance to get the children to begin with, and that seems to be the consensus of everybody I've talked to, why did the Dillards' lawyers go ahead with the thing?"

The custody hearing was indeed a bad day in court for the Dillard family. It was an embarrassing day as well, particularly for Bill Jr. The string of witnesses whom Richard's lawyer paraded in and out seemed to know every transgression that the elder Dillard son had ever committed, and before the day was over Bill Jr. regretted every alcohol-induced conversation he'd had with his brother-in-law.

The media was present in force for the hearing, and as the sordid tale of Nancy's adolescent relationship with her brother unfolded, reporters scribbled madly away. The Dillards were crushed. Not only had they lost Nancy, it seemed now that every mistake a member of the family had made in a lifetime was about to become public knowledge. Furthermore, at least on the date of the custody hearing, Richard seemed invincible. It appeared to the Dillard clan that if he could get away with smearing the family in public, he might even get away with murder. Hatred for Richard, already a sore spot among the Dillards, now became a malignancy.

In addition to the barbecuing of Bill Jr., the hearing also brought a second murder suspect into the public eye. Richard's casting of suspicion on Lynn Pease had previously been a nebulous sort of thing, but on the day of the custody hearing her possible motive for killing Nancy came to the forefront. Lynn herself took the stand, admitted under oath that she'd resented Nancy's handling of the two Lyon children, that her dismissal as Allison and Anna's nanny had driven her to distraction, and finally stated that she and her new psychologist husband were planning an addition to their home in which the two little girls could live. When Lynn's testimony was finished, note-taking media people spoke to one another in whispers.

Once the evidence was in for the day, the court quickly ruled in Richard's favor. He was Allison and Anna's father, and as far as the judge was concerned, he would remain so. His confidence building, the risk of losing his daughters gone for the time being, Richard went home and gave a party.

Rosemary Lyon, who'd moved down from Connecticut to be with her son until after his trial, charcoaled steaks in the backyard of the duplex, and Richard invited several of the neighbors in. There was beer and wine for all, and after dinner he entertained his guests by strumming his guitar and singing ballads. As the evening drew to a close, he sat in a folding chair and held Allison on one knee and Anna on the other until long after everyone had gone home. His trial was scheduled for the week following Thanksgiving. By Christmas, Richard thought, a jury would have declared him an innocent man.

Evan Fogelman is a literary agent, which in New York City would make him one of the masses, but which in Dallas sets him apart from the crowd. Not that he's the only literary agent in Dallas. There are a few others, to be sure, flashy types who hang around cocktail parties and make literary agent noises, but Fogelman seems the only one with clients who actually publish anything. In a city far removed from the Big Apple, a flesh-and-blood literary agent is a novelty.

Fogelman, a constantly smiling and energetic young man with horn-rim glasses and a deep devotion to his business, specializes in authors who write historical romance novels. Like all agents, however, Evan is interested in anything with the potential of making a buck. Which brings us to his role in our story.

In his constant search for talent, Fogelman makes numerous speeches to unpublished writers' groups. It was at just such a gathering, held on the campus at the University of Texas at Dallas in the fall of 1991, that Fogelman encountered a would-be profiteer in the Lyon case who, on the surface at least, showed potential.

Fogelman, drink in hand, was in his usual writers' group posture of responding to—or fending off, as the case may be—rapid-fire questions from a surrounding crowd of men and women with best-seller millions on their minds, when a man who'd jock-eyed for post position in the mob nudged his elbow. "Tell me," the man practically shouted in Fogelman's ear, "are you in the market for true-crime books?"

"Yeah, I . . ." Fogelman said. "Sure, there's a market for true crime. Depends on the case, and depends on how much the author knows about it. And whether the author can write, though these days that's not nearly as important as it used to be."

The elbow-nudger held his ground against would-be writers who shoved him from behind. "What about the Lyon case? Poison murder trial, you familiar with that one?"

Fogelman snapped his head around for a good look at the man. "What, are you kidding? Who hasn't heard about it?"

"That's the subject of my book," the man said.

"You and every Tom, Dick, and Harry," Fogelman said. "There's certainly a market for it, but you've got to have an angle. To sell a publisher on true crime you need inside information. An exclusive pipeline to the police, or maybe even the defendant."

"I've got an exclusive," the man said. "When can we talk?"

Fogelman whipped a business card out of his breast pocket and handed it to the man. "We should visit," he said. "This week's tough, but call me Monday."

The guy put Fogelman's card away, and then handed the agent a business card of his own. "Don't worry, I'll be in touch," the man said, then made his way through the crowd and headed for the exit.

Fogelman read the card over, then snapped to attention and craned his neck for another look at the man. "Well, I'll just be damned," he said to no one in particular. "That guy who just left. He's Richard Lyon. Gee, isn't he the suspect?"

Balmy fall moved into its annual pre-winter chill. Halloween came and went, and Dallas cheered loudly through November as the Cowboys marched with certainty toward their first playoff berth in eight long years.

Rosemary Lyon fixed the Thanksgiving turkey at the Shenandoah duplex. Allan had come in from Connecticut to be with his wife, son, and grandchildren for the holidays, and to remain in Dallas throughout Richard's trial. Once Allison and Anna had gone outside to play after dinner, Richard and his mom and dad retired to the living room to relax, sip cognac, and make a few plans. Texas had not been a good influence on Richard at all, they decided, and once the trial was over he would take the little girls and move back to the Mansfield-Willimantic area. Back in his old home stomping grounds, Richard could put the tragedies of the past year out of his mind and get on with his life. A conviction was a possibility the Lyon family simply refused to consider.

33

The Frank Crowley Courts Building, magnificent edifice that it is, isn't steeped in tradition because it isn't very old. The red brick courthouse where Ruby went to trial and where, fifty years ago, Benny Binnion and his cohorts sauntered in to pay their fines and slip a few dollars into the sheriff's campaign fund, is a mile to the west of the Crowley Building on the western edge of downtown. That's where Dallas history lies. Before the first Monday in December 1991 the grand and gaudy Crowley Building was nothing but a curiosity for old-time Dallas courthouse buffs. The events of the pre-Christmas fortnight to follow, however, gave all local trial addicts a satisfying fix, and then some.

Towering over acres of rancid Trinity River bottomland on the opposite side of elevated Stemmons Freeway from Reunion Arena, the Crowley Courts Building draws double takes from passersby and is, some say, the epitome of government excess. A three-story glass-enclosed arch rises above its front entry, and its lobby, also three full floors in height, holds a network of suspended escalators for access to the second and third levels. Visitors approaching from the north exit the freeway at Continental Avenue, pass alongside the minimum-security jail for wayward gamblers and homeless drunks—which in a not-too-distant and glorious past was the ultra-suave Dallas Cabana Hotel, and claimed the celebrated actress Doris Day as its principal stockholder—then hang a little dipsy-doodle right-and-left onto Industrial Boulevard. From there it's a two-block jaunt to the wide paved drive that runs along the northern side of the Crowley Building, and which leads to the covered six-level parking garage.

In-the-know reporters and lawyers keep up with judges' vacation schedules; with fourteen felony and six misdemeanor courts located on the premises, a number of jurists are always absent, and the savvy news hound or attorney can scoot into the missing judge's reserved parking space near the building's southern entry. The inexperienced courthouse visitor is stuck with the leftovers, a winding climb up a series of ramps to paid public parking, a brief jaunt through the garage with footsteps echoing from bare cement walls, and an elevator ride to the second-level crossover to the Crowley Building. On rain-drenched days the crosswalk is hell, and during the trek over to the courthouse the visitor is acutely aware of the Lew Sterrett Justice Center looming ominously behind the Crowley Building.

The justice center, an uptown name for the main branch of the Dallas County Jail—and known by certain less reverent monikers to its more imaginative residents—is the main reason for the Crowley Building's existence to begin with. Massive from its inception, and growing by leaps and bounds, Lew Sterrett is the be-all and end-all of updated incarceration. There are no steel bars in the justice center; instead, one wall of each cell is inch-thick bullet-proof plastic through which guards can keep a watchful eye. Each floor of the jail contains a central control room where deputies sit before panels of levers and switches that cause lights to brighten and dim, and electronic doors to open and close. Lew Sterrett owes its own existence to a series of federal court orders in the seventies and eighties regarding prison overcrowding. With access to the penitentiary denied until Department of Corrections population levels lowered to a mandated ninety-five percent through inmate release, the existing Dallas jails were bulging at the seams with prisoners awaiting transfer; thus the demand for jail space begat the Lew Sterrett Justice Center, and its location in turn begat the new criminal court facility. In December 1991, construction crews added the finishing touches to still another jail addition; with a final shuddering glance at the justice center, the visitor moves past grand stone pillars and through the revolving door into the Crowley Building.

Once in the lobby, the visitor has a choice; he may either mount the escalator or proceed to the back of the building for an elevator ride. Since the escalators extend only to the third level, the trip to the sixth floor requires elevator assistance in any event, so most opt for the second choice. Elevators are crowded and ripe with courthouse gossip; reporters in transit bend finely tuned ears.

On this rainy December Monday, the south wing of the sixth floor features all the courthouse excitement; prisoners awaiting hearings on other near-deserted courtroom levels could probably escape and never be missed. The eleven other felony courts in the building are in business, to be sure, but their plain-vanilla robbery, rape, and murder cases are only sideshows to the sixth-floor spectacle. In the days and weeks to follow, clerks and bailiffs from other areas of the building will creep from their own courtrooms to the sixth floor for updates on the featured proceedings, and then return quickly to work before their absence is detected; often these truants will bump into their own courtroom's judges, there to sneak a peek at the action as well. The visitor exits the elevator and proceeds through double glass doors into the southern wing. The hallway is a babbling madhouse of humanity, with all the hoopla of a three-ring circus. Literally.

That Dallas County's three most publicized trials of the year took place at the same time, in the same wing, and on the same floor of the Crowley Courts Building was likely careful planning with the media in mind. Some reporters covered all three events at once, hopping back and forth between courtrooms like impulsive TV channel changers. The featured courts were and are on the west side of the corridor, adjacent to one another, and it required no stretch of the imagination to picture a ringmaster, top hat, tails and all, standing in the hallway and directing attention to the various acts in progress. Not only were the trials sensational, they had something in store for just about everyone.

Racial tension fans flocked through the ornate door nearest the lobby exit, where superchief prosecutor Mike Gillette brought his felony leg-breaking case against Commissioner John Wiley Price into the spotlight. Dallas County would pour thousands upon thousands of taxpayer dollars into still another futile attempt to convict the embattled commissioner as Price, black business leaders firmly on his side, would hang the jury and, since the commissioner's own office was right there in the Crowley Building, would use breaks in the trial to go on about his business. It would be Dallas County's final hurrah in the Price battle; failing to convict John Wiley for anything other than the fabled sign-painting and windshield wiper–breaking misdemeanor charges, Dallas County would drop the shaky rape prosecution and finally admit defeat.

And in the center courtroom—or center ring, if one prefers—bloody gore enthusiasts could drink their fill. With *The Silence of the Lambs* still showing in scattered theaters, Dallas County had had its own bona fide serial killer on the loose. *"Butchered whores,* ladies and gentlemen," the ringmaster might shout, "complete—or *incomplete,* heh, heh, just a little play on words—with missing eyeballs. Step right up." The suspect in the prostitute-mutilation trial was a former college halfback, part-time landlord, and full-time con artist named Charles Albright who, although having confessed to check forgery, forging transcripts in order to gain a teaching position, and having sex with a fourteen-year-old girl when he was fifty-one, had nothing in his past to indicate that he was also a madman. As an added attraction the trial would feature expert testimony from a member of the FBI's Violent Criminal Apprehension Team, the same group on which the Jodie Foster/Anthony Hopkins movie is based. Though only called in as a consultant, the VICAT man would give interviews during trial that would lead many to believe that it was the VICAT team who cracked the case to begin with, and the interviews would ruffle local police department feathers. Albright would be convicted on hair sample evidence, sentenced to life in prison, and continue to protest his innocence to this very day.

The Lyon trial ("Far left, folks, the courtroom nearest the corridor windows," the ringmaster could bellow) had a little bit of everything for almost everybody. Agatha Christie readers would enjoy the poison angle, and soap opera viewers could savor the infidelity theme. And don't forget the *Dallas* and *Dynasty* nuts, who could ogle the marquee society types who would come and go, both as witnesses and spectators. And finally, fashion connoisseurs could drool in silence as Park Cities ladies paraded their Neiman-Marcus and Saks Fifth Avenue labels in.

And so, as the Crowley Building opened for business on the first December Monday of the year, television news crews set up shop on the sixth floor and pointed cameras in three different directions. A slobbering public, starved for stories of sensational real-life crime, was about to dine to the point of gluttony.

The Richard and Dan Show (or the Ortega/Woods movie rehearsal if you prefer) played without a key performer for its first few days because Jerri Sims was completing a trial elsewhere. Her stand-in for the time was another D.A. superchief, George West, a smiling black man who seemed to hold a grudge against no one other than Richard. During breaks he chatted amicably with Dan Guthrie, causing one spectator to comment on how well the prosecution and defense seemed to get along. When Jerri Sims showed up to prosecute, the cordialities would cease for good.

On opening day at nine sharp, Judge John Creuzot faced a packed house. Dan Guthrie sat at the defense table dressed in a charcoal gray suit and, uncharacteristically for a trial lawyer, a hand-painted Nicole Miller designer tie. Guthrie would wear a series of the ties during the trial, and his crazy-quilt neckwear would draw remarks from the gallery and ribbing from Judge Creuzot. Guthrie's legal assistant, Leila Thomas, a striking brunette with chiseled features and a model's figure, also sat at the defense table. With Leila on the defense side, Jerri conducting the prosecution, and chic Park Cities ladies in the spectator pews, this trial would never lack for beautiful women. Leila would be at her post by Richard's elbow every day, taking notes and making trips to corridor pay phones to keep Guthrie abreast of his office calls. The defense trio, Leila in front and Richard and Guthrie bringing up the rear, would become a familiar sight in courtroom hallways during the weeks to come.

Richard's suit was a conservative navy blue. His appearance had changed drastically since his arrest, and spectators who'd only seen his picture in the paper weren't sure if Richard was the lawyer and Guthrie the defendant, or vice versa. Richard had gained weight, largely due to his mother's cooking at the Shenandoah duplex, and he'd shaved off his thin mustache. The added poundage and smooth-featured look made Richard seem a trifle laid back and almost lazy. His handsome Lebanese face holds dark eyes with heavy lids, and there were times during the trial when he would seem about to go to sleep. His generally assured and bored demeanor would not help him.

There was hardly a vacant seat in the spectators' section. Since Big Daddy, Bill Jr., Susan and her husband, Billy, were all on the prosecution's witness list and couldn't sit in on testimony, grande dame Sue held forth as the Dillard family's lone courtroom representative. Strong, slim, and erect, her lovely graying hair shining like dusted licorice, she would sit surrounded by friends every day in the second row. Dillard supporters and friends would jam the rest of the pews, with Allan and Rosemary Lyon the only outsiders. Rosemary, petite, pretty, and even darker of complexion than her son, showed slight worry lines at the corners of her eyes; Allan, a stocky man with nearly white thinning hair, appeared sad and confused at what was happening to Richard. Every day the Lyons would be in place directly behind the defense table, and occasionally would catch Richard's eye and smile support in his direction.

Almost without exception, the balance of the spectators were Park Citizens, well-dressed men and ladies, all Caucasian, all sitting silent as wealthy executioners. It was clear from the beginning where Highland Park sympathy lay, and equally apparent from the outset that if Richard had any friends they'd neglected to attend. One slender lady, a brunette with a dazzling smile, had brought her knitting along; throughout the trial, testimony would be punctuated by the click of plastic needles. Somehow the lady managed to refrain from shouting, "Guillotine." Her restraint doubtless required some effort.

In Judge Creuzot's court the first two rows, left-hand side, are reserved for media, and writers both real and imagined would attend the trial in abundance. The only steadily employed writers were newspaper folk, one each from the *Dallas Morning News* and *Times-Herald*, and one from *Park Cities People*, a dignified lady who would have seemed more at ease in covering the opening of a play. The rest of the media section hangers-on were doing books on the case or articles for magazines: *Texas Monthly*, *GQ*, *Ladies' Home Journal*. During the trial, writers would come and go.

As courtroom business opened for the day, the assembled cast waited patiently through a series of plea bargains and arraignments, and would learn as the trial progressed that they were in store for more of the same every morning. The daily procedure was roughly identical, with Judge Creuzot calmly assuming his seat on the bench promptly at nine as bailiffs escorted a series of prisoners in from the holding cells. Be a judge lazy or energetic, a prosecution pawn or a staunch fighter for fairness, every jurist is above all a politician. At election time the number one campaign issue between opponents is the speed with which the incumbent has moved his docket along; therefore, as opposed to popular belief, disposal of cases is the court's number one goal. Move 'em in and move 'em out; make a deal, accept the plea, and on to the next one.

On the opening day of the Lyon trial, however, the cast was in for a surprise. The string of pleas consumed just about an hour, after which Creuzot smiled, welcomed one and all, and then promptly cleared the courtroom except for the media people. Spectators' seats were needed for jury selection. Miffed, grumbling among themselves, Park Cities lords and ladies trooped out into the corridor while common-folk jurors streamed in to take their places in the visitors' pews. As Dallas' disappointed chosen elite left the courtroom, Creuzot threw his bailiff a guarded wink. It wouldn't be the last time that the judge would pull a few Park Cities legs.

Of all courtroom processes, jury selection is probably the most overrated. The methods used by attorneys in attempting to select the juror most likely to vote in the lawyer's favor vary, from employment of psychology and body-language experts down to something as mundane as a coin flip, and, most say, all selection strategies show equal results. Jury makeup is simply the luck of the draw.

"It's all bullshit," one veteran defense attorney says, "and, believe me, I've tried 'em all. Psychics, soothsayers, you name it, and anybody that says they can tell what a juror's going to do by what he does for a living or how he crosses his legs or scratches his ass is lying to you. They should cut through all the hokey and pick the first twelve people in the courtroom, it'd save everybody a helluva lot of time."

Actually, courtroom procedure established by law cuts severely into a lawyer's options. In Texas voir dire, each side has twelve strikes, peremptory challanges whereby either attorney may dismiss a juror without cause. Peremptory strikes are easy to predict, and make it simple for the defense to eliminate all judges' and prosecutors' wives, and the state to kick out everyone with a relative in the penitentiary. Beyond that, jury selection is pretty well catch-as-catch-can. In a high-profile case such as Richard's trial, everyone who admits to knowing the defendant or any of the lawyers, or who acknowledges having a preconceived opinion of the case, will go. Those who confess to having read about the case in the newspapers, but maintain that what they've read will not affect their decision in deliberations, will stay. Enough said.

While the selection of Richard's jury was a rather cut-and-dried affair, Judge Creuzot's handling of the panel was anything but. Within the first few weeks of his governor-appointed tenure on the bench, Creuzot noted something he believes gives him a leg up on future political opponents. Prior to assignment to the various courts, prospective jurors report to a central panel room for preliminary instructions, and it falls on one of the judges to meet with these selected citizens to explain the jurors' duties and responsibilities. Since jury room duty begins a full hour before court convenes, most judges regard the jury room assignment as the ultimate pain in the ass—not to mention the loss of sleep involved in having to report to the courthouse an hour early—but Creuzot saw the assignment as an opportunity. Prospective jurors' names come from the registered voters' list, and the judge who presides over preliminary jurors' instruction will be in the jurors' memories at election time. So Creuzot volunteered, and found that other judges would gladly let him take their places. Since the panelists in Creuzot's court for the Lyon trial were the same ones whom he'd instructed in the central room only hours earlier, the judge had a special interest in every juror who stood to be counted.

Of particular interest to Creuzot were those who served with somewhat less than boundless enthusiasm. Jurors are not, after all, volunteers, and many report for duty with manufactured reasons for which to be excused. The judge listened patiently to descriptions of the various ailments, spouse fatalities, and homes on fire that citizens erroneously believe will excuse them from jury duty, then calmly explained to each protester that they were the chosen, and that was that.

Creuzot took more time with the connivers, experienced panelists who'd been there before, and who understood going in that nothing short of an affliction with Alzheimer's—and then only in the disease's latter stages—would excuse them from duty. These folks' trick is to play with the number system, a procedure by which panelists select an identification number on entry into the central jury room. There are fifty jurors, in numerical order, sent to each court, one through fifty here, fifty through a hundred there, and those not selected for final duty once they're assigned to a court can then go home. Veteran duty dodgers know this system, and also understand that, due to the number of preemptive strikes accorded to each side, it is less likely that the latter numerical portion will be chosen. Therefore the informed malingerer will, on first entering the central room, chose one of the numbers from forty to fifty, ninety to a hundred, and so forth, thus insuring that no matter to what court he's assigned he'll have one of the latter numbers in that particular court.

Alas, the best-laid plans, etc., and Juror Number 42 in the Lyon case, due to the unusual number of dismissals for cause, found himself on the hot seat and likely to be chosen. This gentleman, a well-dressed, I-don't-have-time-for-you business type, then made a fatal mistake. He suddenly developed an emergency, an excuse not to serve, even though Judge Creuzot had plainly asked for excuses when the panel had first entered the courtroom, and the time for giving such excuses had long passed by. Creuzot wasn't amused. He called our well-dressed friend to the front of the courtroom, gave him a good old-fashioned tongue-lashing in front of media and panel members, and instructed the gentleman to have a seat and wait his turn. The malingerer won out in the end, however; during his voir dire he suddenly developed a strong conviction that Richard didn't do it, and the prosecution excused the man for cause and sent him on his way.

Such small nuances aside, Creuzot assembled twelve jurors and two alternates in a day and a half. On the main panel were five women, four blacks, zero Hispanics. Three jurors were retired, the balance held jobs. None lived in the Park Cities; Richard was to be judged by a group of ordinary Joes and Janes. The stage thus set, Creuzot dismissed the balance of the panel and permitted the lords and ladies to return. Jurors, writers, and spectators alike would be sitting for quite a spell.

34

George West, Jerri Sims' stand-in for jury selection and preliminary proceedings, wasn't able to hang around for the trial itself. On the evening before the opening arguments, a teenage locker room attendant at L.B. Houston Municipal Golf Course in far North Dallas robbed the pro shop and murdered three employees in the process, and West drew the prosecution assignment on that case. An avid golfer himself, West had played the course many times and was personally acquainted with the deceased golf course workers, as were many courthouse employees and some of the writers covering the Lyon trial. The morning after the murders was a sad time for all. Park Citizens in the courtroom, having spent what golfing lives they may have enjoyed at the country clubs, didn't know the public course workers and saw the killings as just another article in the newspaper. The ladies and gentlemen from the wealthy sector were much more interested in the initial courtroom appearance of Jerri Sims.

It would be difficult not to notice her under any circumstances, and her role as one of the principal players in the unfolding drama would keep most gazes in her direction during the balance of the trial. She made her debut in *Texas* v. *Lyon* wearing a dress of divided color, half black, half orange, the colors split by a line running dead center down her spine and on from there in the direction of the floor. Wave after wave of soft hair the shade of gourmet cornsilk cascaded over her shoulders to a point a good eighteen inches below her waist. As Jerri went down the aisle and through the gate in the direction of the prosecution side, one chic Park Cities lady remarked to another, in an audible stage whisper, "My kingdom for a pair of scissors. God." Titters rippled through the spectators' section.

Striking as is her appearance, Jerri's trial demeanor is elegantly reserved. She questions witnesses in a businesslike alto, her words precise as if chosen like ripe fruit. It is a peculiarity of Texas courts that lawyers question witnesses from seats at their respective tables, and may only rise after asking the court's permission to approach the witness, and then only to show the witness an admitted piece of evidence. In the Lone Star State there is none of the menacing, close-encounter witness harassment and rail pounding prevalent on *L.A. Law* and the like, and Jerri Sims plays to her audience like a virtuoso, her questions brief and to the point, her innuendos unmistakable. In the Lyon trial, she would leave the strutting up to the defense side.

As would be typical of her game plan, Jerri waived her opening statement to the jury, and her silence spoke volumes. *We're going to prove that this guy murdered his wife, folks. Why belabor the issue?* Like a containment football defense, Jerri would give ground and wait for the other side to cough up the ball.

Guthrie, resplendent in a navy blue suit and still another Nicole Miller tie, did make a brief opening statement but gave nothing away that hadn't already been hashed and rehashed in the newspapers for days on end. His statement consisted of a single sentence: "We will show that, number one, there are multiple suspects in the case other than the defendant and, two, this might not have been a murder at all. Thank you." On the surface at least, the defense strategy hadn't changed from the outset: Either Bill Jr., David Bagwell, or Lynn Pease murdered Nancy, or, in the alternative, Nancy committed suicide by ingesting the poi-

son on her own. His point made, Guthrie sat down. Jerri then
led with a straight hard right. She put Big Daddy on the stand.

Big Daddy keeps a low profile in the business community—
though he's well known by those whose livelihood depends on
acquaintances with men of influence—but the newspaper and
television stories relating to the case had thrust him into the public eye. As Jerri called William Wooldridge Dillard, Sr., to be the
first prosecution witness, there was a loud rustling in the courtroom as all heads turned as one to the rear. Big Daddy didn't
disappoint. He entered and strode down the aisle at a brisk clip,
pausing only long enough to give his wife, seated on the aisle, an
affectionate pat on the shoulder. Sue responded with a sweet-sad
smile.

For those having only read newspaper accounts of the case,
Big Daddy's physical appearance was a surprise. The ballyhoo
and hoopla practically dictated a larger-than-life character, perhaps wearing a ten-gallon hat, string tie, and diamond-studded
stickpin in the shape of an oil well or dollar sign, but a Southfork
type Big Daddy isn't. As he went through the gate wearing a
conservative gray business suit and dark red tie, then stood before the court reporter for his swearing-in, Big Daddy's gaze
rested briefly on Richard, then swept contemptuously away. The
patriarch of the Dillard clan swore to tell the truth in a strong
voice, mounted to the witness stand, and waited for questions
like a fighter between rounds. For the most part, his testimony
would be anticlimactic to his entry.

Asking questions in a clear but soft tone that those near the
back had to strain in order to hear, Jerri systematically led
the witness through a brief life story, touching momentarily on
the births and childhoods of each of his children, then asked a
series of questions that, at least to those already familiar with the
story, didn't seem particularly relevant. Yes, Big Daddy had gone
to the hospital on the morning of January 9 because he'd learned
that Nancy was there. Sometime during the day Mary Helen had
told him of Nancy's suspicions (Big Daddy's testimony at this
point was pure hearsay; Guthrie didn't object because he knew
of Mary Helen Dillard's presence at the courthouse, and knew

that Jerri could put Bill Jr.'s wife on the stand if need be), and Big Daddy had relayed the story to Dr. Bagheri. Big Daddy had also interfered when, on Richard's instructions, the hospital staff had tried to disconnect Nancy's life support, and he'd been one of the family members present when, after meeting with doctors, the life support was turned off with the Dillards' consent. Big Daddy related the entire story deadpan, answering Jerri's questions clearly but with no outward display of emotion.

The tale of Nancy's death complete, Jerri took the witness down a different path. Big Daddy now gave his personal viewpoint of Nancy's marriage to Richard, told of his feeling that at some point Richard had simply tired of Nancy, and related what he knew about Richard's affair with Denise Woods (whom Big Daddy never called by name, and merely referred to as "that flashy blonde"). When Big Daddy said that he thought Richard spent far too much money, glances were exchanged throughout the courtroom, both between parents who had given similar advice to their own kids, and between the kids who had been the recipients of same. As far as his giving of unsolicited financial advice, Big Daddy seemed no different than any other father-in-law.

Interesting though his testimony had been to this point, Jerri's motive for putting Nancy's father on the stand wasn't clear. It was apparent that Big Daddy thought Richard had murdered Nancy, but so what? Big Daddy knew absolutely nothing that pointed to Richard as the killer other than the tales of the wine and pills and the Coke in the movie, all of which Jerri could have gotten into evidence through other witnesses, and eventually did. Those questioning Jerri's strategy didn't have long to wait, however. With a calm movement of manicured hands, a faint rustling of papers as she went through her file, Jerri prepared to deliver her punch line.

She stood holding two photographs, offered both to Guthrie for the defense's inspection—Richard's gaze dropped as he glanced at the pictures over his attorney's shoulder—then handed them to the court reporter. The reporter, a pleasant light-skinned black woman, applied gummed evidence labels to each picture. Jerri, pictures in hand, then faced the judge. "Your honor, we offer what have been marked state's exhibits one and two."

Creuzot accepted the pictures over the top of the bench, glanced at them, looked toward Guthrie. "Any objection?"

"None, Your Honor." Guthrie's tone said that this was all procedure; an objection to admission of evidence such as the photos is pointless.

"So admitted," Creuzot said.

Jerri then handed the photos over for passing through the jury box; some jurors' faces remained impassive while others looked closely at the first picture, then quickly averted their gazes from the second. Jury inspection complete, Jerri said, "Your Honor, may I approach the witness?"

Another formality. "You may," Creuzot said.

Big Daddy had watched the admitting of evidence impassively. As Jerri walked near and laid one of the photos on the rail in front of the witness, Big Daddy bent forward, still without expression.

Jerri now assumed a sympathetic tone. "Mr. Dillard, I show you what has been marked state's exhibit number one, and ask if you can identify it."

"It's a picture of Nancy."

"And is there anyone else in the picture?"

"My . . . granddaughters. Allison and Anna." Big Daddy's voice broke slightly.

"And is this picture representative of the way Nancy appeared in life?" Jerri said.

"It's a good likeness."

"During the time that she was in the hospital, did Nancy's appearance change any?"

Big Daddy removed his glasses. "She became swollen. Bloated."

Jerri's tone of respect now became gentle and caring. "Sir, I'll now show you state's exhibit number two. Can you identify it, please?"

Big Daddy was able to glance quickly at the second photo. Tearfully he said, "It's Nancy again."

"Mr. Dillard, is this Nancy as she appeared in death?"

Big Daddy now broke down completely. "Yes," he cried. "Yes, that's Nancy." Tears ran down his cheeks. He took a handkerchief from his pocket and gently blew his nose.

Jerri paused. She looked straight at Richard, then at Guthrie. "Pass the witness," Jerri said. She then sat down, and a full thirty seconds elapsed while a silent courtroom watched a broken elderly man grieve for his child and strive to regain his composure. It was the only outward emotional display from one of the Dillard clan during the entire ordeal.

There was a lengthy recess before Guthrie's cross-examination while Creuzot considered a motion. This motion, filed by Dillard attorneys, asked that the court throw out the defense's subpoena for Big Daddy's financial statement. Just what Guthrie had intended to show using this statement was never clear; Creuzot eventually granted the motion and allowed Big Daddy's personal dealings to remain secret.

During the recess, writers milled about and inspected the television camera at the rear of the courtroom, which had previously been the subject of still another motion; early on in the trial, Creuzot spent as much time on the various legal papers filed by parties outside the case as he did on the arguments of the state and the defense. The motion to televise—in this instance filed by Belo Corporation on behalf of its subsidiary, Channel 8—is becoming almost standard procedure in high-profile criminal cases. The question of the presence of television cameras in the courtroom has been a weighty one, First Amendment versus Fifth, the right of the press to tell and the public's right to know versus the defendant's right to a fair and impartial trial. In most cases the press wins out and the TV cameras come rolling in. Defendants' rights proponents argue vehemently against the practice, but, at least to those attending the Lyon trial, the whole furor seemed much ado about nothing.

The camera, mounted on a tall tripod to the left far rear of the spectator section, was never in the way and made no noise whatsoever. Many attending the proceedings were never aware of the camera's presence, and on seeing themselves on the 10:00 P.M. news wondered where in the world the pictures had come from.

The TV setup, in fact, became a boon to writers and spectators alike as, when all courtroom seats were taken, the crowd around the monitor in the hallway became half again as large as the gathering in the spectators' section. The jury was never sequestered—and exactly how much heed jurors give a judge's instruction not to watch the case on television or read about it in the newspapers is up for grabs to begin with—but since the television camera recorded nothing that the jurors hadn't already seen in person, it couldn't possibly have affected the verdict. Consensus of trial attenders' opinion: Let the cameras in; the practice might keep more spectators out and give us a better seat. Judge Creuzot announced his ruling on Big Daddy's financial statement. The trial resumed.

Guthrie's cross-examination methods were every bit as pointed as Jerri's handling of witnesses was subtle. The defense wasted no time; Guthrie revealed the main thing he wanted from Big Daddy in the defense's very first question. "Mr. Dillard," Guthrie said, sitting intently forward, "when were you first aware that there was incest between Nancy and her brother, Bill Dillard, Jr.?"

There was a deathly silence, a pause resembling a collective gasp. The incest issue had already been widely reported after the Lyon vs. Dillard child-custody hearing, and there were few present who didn't know that Nancy's relationship with her brother would come up, but the abruptness of Guthrie's question was shattering. All courtroom attention riveted on William Dillard, Sr. How would he hold up to this?

The elder Dillard's manner was a surprise. Shaken and in tears at the end of Jerri's direct examination, Big Daddy now regarded Guthrie as he would a pesky door-to-door insurance salesman. "Nineteen-seventy," he said. "Thereabouts." It was apparent that the prosecution had spent a great deal of time in preparing Big Daddy to deal with this line of questioning—Yes, Virginia, Perry Mason aside, all witnesses on both sides are rehearsed at length—and as Guthrie's lengthy cross wore on, many would seriously question Big Daddy's demeanor. Some, in fact, would wonder if his display of grief on seeing the photo of Nancy in death hadn't been rehearsed as well. The entire scenario seemed a bit too prearranged. Asked about his children's incest, Big Daddy hardly batted an eye.

His blow delivered, Guthrie now settled back in his seat. "And how did that come about, sir?"

Big Daddy seemed only slightly irritated. "Their mother caught them. The kids were just playing doctor."

Guthrie paused to let that answer sink in, then said, "Playing doctor? How old were they?"

Here Big Daddy's answer was much too quick; he didn't even pause to think. "Eleven and thirteen."

"And at eleven and thirteen, they were just playing doctor." Guthrie's question was more of a statement.

"That's what I said," Big Daddy snapped. Jurors looked incredulously at one another.

"Immediately after Mrs. Dillard caught them . . . playing doctor, wasn't Bill Jr. sent away?"

"He went to school up in Dublin, New Hampshire, but not because of that."

"Because of the incest?" Guthrie said.

"Right. He was dyslexic."

"Dyslexic." Guthrie rolled the word; it was clear that the defense attorney didn't believe dyslexia had anything to do with Bill Jr.'s going away. "Mr. Dillard, was Bill Jr. ever arrested when in college?"

Big Daddy waved a hand as if batting mosquitoes. "A prank or something."

"A prank. Wasn't he stealing football equipment? Selling it out the back door when he was student manager?"

"Something like that."

"And the following year? Was he arrested for drugs?"

Big Daddy nodded, stone-faced. "He was."

"And was that a prank?"

Jerri objected and Creuzot sustained, all too late to keep the jury from getting the point. Guthrie seemed deep in thought, then said, "Over the past few years, Mr. Dillard, how would you describe Bill Jr.'s financial condition?"

"He's been broke four or five years." From the prosecution

standpoint, it was pointless to hedge here. The various suits filed against Bill Jr. were a matter of public record.

"And during that time, have you loaned him money?"

"I've loaned all my children money at one time or another."

"One loan in particular, sir," Guthrie said. "Did Nancy have to cosign for Bill Jr. to get some eighty thousand dollars?"

Here Big Daddy glanced at Jerri; the defense had a great deal more information than the Dillards had realized. "I believe she did," Big Daddy finally said.

"And, if you know, why was it necessary for her to sign?"

"Collateral for the loan. There were some trust funds involved."

"Trust funds, funds you've established for your children?"

Big Daddy angrily uncrossed and recrossed his legs. "That's right."

"How much money is in trust for your children, Mr. Dillard?"

"I'm not sure. Couple of hundred thousand each, I suppose."

"And in the event of Nancy's death," Guthrie said, "what happens to her portion of that money?"

"It goes," Big Daddy said, "to the other children."

"That's Susan, Nancy's sister, and Bill Jr.?"

"Those are my children, sir. My . . . living children." Big Daddy now glared pointedly at Richard.

"So in the long run," Guthrie said, "Bill Jr. profits from Nancy's death."

Jerri objected. Her grounds for objecting here are not clear, but it's apparent that she had to do something—anything—to divert this disastrous line of questioning. Once again Creuzot sustained. Guthrie tossed a knowing look in the direction of the jury box, then prepared to go on; the defense was making points, and Guthrie was only beginning. Before the defense could throw another punch, however, Judge Creuzot interrupted. It was late. Creuzot asked Guthrie how much longer his cross would take, and Guthrie replied that he had several hours planned. Creuzot then recessed the trial for the day. As the jury filed out, there was a general feeling that Big Daddy had, temporarily at any rate, been saved by the bell.

35

The burning desire of the press to inform being somewhat tempered by its knowledge of what the public wants to know, the following morning's headlines were hardly surprising: TESTIMONY REVEALS INCEST. Both dailies reported Nancy's adolescent mistakes with Bill Jr. at length; one reporter, having called Bill Jr.'s home for an interview, failed to contact Nancy's brother but did receive a return call from one of the family friends, relaying Bill Jr.'s statement that there had been only touching between the two, never intercourse. Having broadcast the really important details of the trial, both papers reported the testimony relating to Nancy's death from arsenic poisoning in single paragraphs at the end of their respective stories. The public's thirst for knowledge was quenched once more.

That morning, with Big Daddy still on the witness stand and the prospect for more lurid details imminent, the Lyon trial completely upstaged the courtroom dramas down the hall. As Guthrie prepared to continue his cross-examination, his audience included two young ladies who folded their copies of *The*

Silence of the Lambs into their purses, and four well-dressed black businessmen who occupied seats on the back row. On this day John Wiley Price could battle the county on his own.

Before Guthrie was ten minutes into his questioning, however, defectors from the other trials fidgeted and glanced toward the exits, their feelings clear. *What's all this crap? Get on with the sexual stuff.* Instead of diving immediately into the incest issue, Guthrie opened with a series of fifty-dollar canceled checks. What boredom.

The checks were a means to an end, but that wasn't apparent at first. Guthrie had gone through the Lyons' joint account, and now showed Big Daddy a series of drafts that Nancy had written her father for various inconsequential items, had Big Daddy identify the checks and Nancy's signature thereon. So harmless did the checks appear, when Guthrie returned to his folder for some common pieces of notebook paper, spectators yawned. Jerri Sims wasn't bored, though. She looked at the new evidence with a sort of resignation. She knew exactly what was coming, and so did Big Daddy.

Having gone through the procedure of having the papers marked as evidence, submitting them through Judge Creuzot, and passing them through the jury box, Guthrie approached the witness and laid the papers on the rail. "Mr. Dillard," Guthrie said, "I show you these pieces of evidence and ask that you identify them."

Big Daddy held the pages at arm's length and examined them through the lower portion of his bifocals. "Notes of some kind."

"And having identified those checks to be in Nancy's handwriting," Guthrie said, "could you please tell us if you can identify the writing on those pieces of paper."

"It looks to be Nancy's." Big Daddy's voice was tired.

"And are these notes which Nancy took during incest counseling?"

"I wouldn't know that," Big Daddy snapped.

"Mr. Dillard, do you know that your daughter was in fact in counseling for incest?"

"Yes."

"And you do acknowledge that that writing appears to be hers?"

"Yes."

"Thank you." Guthrie leaned forward to read over Big Daddy's shoulder. "If you would, sir"—pointing at one of the pages—"please read the jury, beginning here, the rest of this page."

Big Daddy shifted his position. He didn't want to do this. "Beginning here?" he said.

Guthrie nodded. "Yes, sir."

Big Daddy cleared his throat and, hesitantly, began to read. "Trying hard to have the June Cleaver family . . . wanted to be better behaved . . . angry, frustrated, anxious . . . lack of time for one on one . . . working hard, giving, demanding, controlling . . . when I don't have power, I feel inadequate." Big Daddy looked up as if to say, Is that enough?

"Please go on, sir," Guthrie said.

The elder Dillard tensed in his chair. He glanced at Jerri, then at Judge Creuzot, both of them watching intently. As if he saw no way out, Big Daddy finally continued. ". . . fear of Bill and what his desires are . . . sex . . . sick sex . . . incest issues with me? . . . my girls?"

There were long seconds of pin-drop silence. From the rear of the courtroom came a nervous cough. Finally Guthrie took the pages from Big Daddy's now trembling fingers. "Thank you, sir," Guthrie said.

Having accomplished his goal of establishing the incest and pointing the finger in Bill Jr.'s direction, Guthrie now directed attention to David Bagwell. He returned Big Daddy to the hospital scene. The elder Dillard grudgingly acknowledged Bagwell's presence at the hospital, and also verified that David's brother John had been doing work at Presbyterian during Nancy's final hours. Guthrie then dropped the Bagwell issue; he would extract more information relating to Bagwell from other witnesses. Having scored hits in all directions thus far, Guthrie then changed the course of his cross-examination to a discussion of Richard, and here the defense strategy is puzzling.

Guthrie introduced a string of recommendation letters that Big Daddy had written in Richard's behalf in the past. Some were job references, some were glowing accounts of Richard's achievements for the consideration of the membership committees of various civic organizations, all were addressed to well-known business leaders. Under Guthrie's direction, Big Daddy read each letter aloud. Evidently the defense strategy was to show that Richard was civic-minded, industrious, and a leader in the community, and that, at some point at least, Big Daddy had considered his son-in-law virtually a jewel. But there was a problem in all this. The letters were overlong, and dropped many names, and this jury of everyday folk with jobs weren't interested in who Richard and Big Daddy had counted among their circle of friends or how much money any of the principals possessed. After an hour or more of hearing Big Daddy read letters to Dallas' equivalent of the Carnegies and Rockefellers, the jury was clearly fidgeting. Additionally, it was during this session that Guthrie, inadvertently to be sure, permitted Big Daddy to somewhat turn the tables.

The elder Dillard, as he prepared to read the umpteenth in the series of recommendation letters, seemed to falter. He closed his eyes and cleared his throat.

Guthrie's face showed concern. "Are you uncomfortable, sir?"

"Well, I have been talking for several hours," Big Daddy said.

"Would you like a drink of water?"

"Yes, that would help. Please."

Guthrie approached the defense table, on which sat a chrome carafe and several empty glasses. As if on cue, Richard bent quickly forward, righted one glass, uncapped the bottle and poured, and handed his lawyer a full glass of water. Guthrie carried the drink to the witness stand and handed it to Big Daddy.

Big Daddy hammed this one up quite well. He looked at the glass in his hand, stared at Richard, then squinted closely at the water in the glass. "I don't know if I should drink this or not," Big Daddy said. Then, as the courtroom vibrated with laughter, the elder Dillard took a huge gulp and swallowed hard.

The foregoing byplay aside, and excluding the string of less than stimulating recommendation letters, Guthrie scored points during the elder Dillard's cross-examination. As Big Daddy finally stepped down after a day and a half's testimony, in fact, the defense had rammed the ball over the goal line several times. The prosecution at that point had tallied, at the very most, a field goal.

36

"I've already showed you the duty nurse's record, Doctor. I'm asking if Nancy Lyon was in restraints at the time you entered her room." Dan Guthrie, calm and collected, his confidence growing by leaps and bounds. Day Five.

Dr. Ali Bagheri seemed confused. "I don't recall," he said. Bagheri's coal black hair was immaculately groomed, his mustache clipped in a measured line. A huge and quite undoctorlike gold medallion hung from a chain around his neck. During Jerri's direct examination, Bagheri had testified about the wine and pills and the Coke in the movie, all of which he'd said Nancy told him in her room. Guthrie was in the process of attacking the doctor's testimony with both barrels.

"Well, you'll agree, won't you," Guthrie said, "that the duty nurse recorded the placing of the patient in restraints because Nancy was struggling to get up, and the time of the nurse's note was one hour before you visited. Will you agree to that?"

"It's on the hospital record," Bagheri said. "I'd have to say it was so."

"I see." Guthrie made eye contact with one of the jurors, as if he was about to tell one strictly between him and the jury. "When you spoke to Nancy," Guthrie said, "and when she told you these stories to which you've testified, did you remove her breathing tube?"

Bagheri shifted nervously in his chair and didn't reply.

"The record states," Guthrie went on, "that she had a breathing tube, which she constantly tried to remove—another reason for the restraints—and that she was on oxygen. So I'm asking, when you talked to her, did you first remove her breathing tube?" Some of the jurors were sitting forward; Guthrie now had their undivided attention.

"She did tell me those things," Bagheri said, rather huffily.

"That wasn't my question."

"It's possible to talk with a breathing tube," Bagheri said.

"What about an oxygen mask? Did you remove that?"

"She told me those things," Bagheri doggedly repeated.

Jerri, zeroing in as usual on the main issue, offered few objections. Whether or not Nancy had told Bagheri the stories no longer mattered; whether or not to believe the doctor was the jury's choice. What mattered was that Bagheri's testimony was an exception to the hearsay rule, that the stories were now before the jury, and that Jerri had more witnesses who could now repeat Nancy's tales on the stand as backup to what Bagheri had to say.

As Guthrie continued to hammer at the witness, a stranger sat among the writers on the second row of the spectator section. The newcomer was a slim and attractive lady of around thirty, and she was vigorously taking notes. Precise notes. She wrote down every question that Guthrie asked, also recorded Bagheri's answer, and had gone through the same meticulous procedure during Jerri's direct examination. Seated among writers who scribbled reminders to themselves on napkin edges—and sometimes had to turn their houses upside down to find the notes they'd taken—this lady stood out.

One writer leaned over and whispered to the stranger, "Are you with a magazine?"

She went on with her note taking and didn't answer.

The local scribe attempted a second question. "Are you a lawyer?"

She snapped her head around and hissed, "Why do you ask?"

"What you're putting down. You know the difference between direct and cross-examination, and the average yo-yo in court doesn't know that much."

She favored the man with a look that would melt solid steel, scooched away from him on the bench, and continued to write. She now covered her work with her free hand.

As he had throughout the trial, Guthrie continued to make serious inroads into the prosecution's case. Before he was finished with the doctor, Guthrie had elicited the information that the hospital personnel had administered Compazine to Nancy in the emergency room, and that Nancy's bedside records showed that she'd been in restraints, breathing tube and oxygen mask in place, when she'd had her alleged conversation with Dr. Bagheri. The dashing defense lawyer had also trotted out reams of hospital records for the doctor's identification, and had gone over every treatment given to Nancy before she died. On most of these treatment prescriptions Bagheri stood firmly behind the Nuremberg Defense; he was only a resident, consultant doctors had ordered the treatments, and the hospital merely had been carrying out orders.

When a tired-looking Dr. Bagheri finally stepped down, Judge Creuzot called for a recess. As Park Citizens and writers stood, stretched, and moseyed for the exit, the note-taking young lady did an excellent imitation of a broken field run, dodging in and out among spectators as she hustled out the back door and headed directly for the witness waiting room. She reappeared immediately after the break, assumed her seat among the newspaper folk and authors, and began her note-taking anew.

The next witness, coincidentally, was also a Presbyterian Hospital employee, Genevieve Eisman, a registered emergency room nurse who was on duty the night that Richard brought Nancy in. There was no break after Nurse Eisman's testimony—which consisted merely of her observations during Nancy's admittance—but our mystery lady once again rose, pad in hand, and left the courtroom, returning just before another Presbyterian employee,

Kim Grayson, gave chain-of-custody evidence regarding her acceptance of the wine and pills from Lynn Pease in the hospital lobby. All through Nurse Grayson's stint as a witness, the lady continued to write like mad. Nurse Grayson finished her testimony. The mystery lady bustled out. Jerri Sims called her next prosecution witness, Misty Don Thornton, another Presbyterian nurse, and the mystery lady returned to her seat. There she sat, notepad on her lap, ballpoint ready for action. Dan Guthrie rose grandly from the defense table and faced the court.

"Your Honor," Guthrie said, "information has come to us that someone has been going in the witness room and briefing the prosecution witnesses on previous testimony."

Now the mystery lady made tracks. She excuse-me'd her way into the aisle and hustled toward the exit as if the building suddenly had caught fire.

Guthrie turned and pointed. "I think it's that lady there." The lady disappeared into the hallway with a swish of swinging doors.

"Bailiff." Creuzot indicated the exit. "Go bring that woman back in here."

The bailiff, a burly young sheriff's deputy in his twenties, took off up the aisle in pursuit of the mystery lady. He left the courtroom, then returned with the slim young woman in tow. Her cheeks were the color of ripe plums.

Creuzot beckoned. "Come down here, please, ma'am."

As the mystery lady went hesitantly through the gate and walked toward the bench, Jerri Sims stood to one side of the prosecution table. Rather sheepishly she said, "She's helping me, Judge." Jerri is fortunate that she never chopped down her father's cherry tree; like George Washington, she'd be unable to lie about it.

Creuzot, sensing a possible mistrial, had the bailiff usher the jury out. He then gathered both sides, Guthrie and Jerri, before the bench, and placed the mystery lady squarely in between them. The judge demanded in no uncertain terms to know what was going on.

The mystery lady, it turned out, was a lawyer. Creuzot, noting that there seemed no shortage of lawyers already involved in the case, inquired as to the young woman's function. The lady re-

plied that she represented Presbyterian Hospital (more specifically, she represented the hospital's liability insurance carrier, but
for the court's purposes at that moment, the two clients were one
and the same), and that since none of the hospital personnel had
previously testified in court, the hospital wanted to be certain
that its people minded their p's and q's on the witness stand.
The judge wanted to know what was on the lady's notepad. The
incriminating evidence dangling in plain sight near her hip, the
lady had no choice other than to show the judge. Judge Creuzot
regarded defense attorney Guthrie with inquisitive, upraised eyebrows.

Clearly, the call here was up to Guthrie. The court's granting
of a mistrial on the defense's motion at that point was by no
means automatic; had Guthrie made such a motion, Creuzot
would have questioned each hospital witness individually to find
out what their lawyer had or had not said to each of them prior
to their taking the stand, then would have made a ruling based
on the witnesses' knowledge of previous testimony. Should
Guthrie have made a mistrial motion, however, the odds seemed
clearly in his favor.

Guthrie declined to move for mistrial and, twenty-twenty
hindsight be damned, one cannot fault his strategy. At that point
the defense felt that it had the prosecution on the ropes, and no
one who'd been present at the trial up to then would likely disagree. Creuzot dismissed our mystery lady with a stern warning,
returned the jury to the courtroom, and bade the trial go on.

Propriety of the mystery lady's actions aside, the reasons for
her presence at trial bear scrutiny. The hospital, having confessed to giving Nancy the wrong drug in the emergency room,
to not checking for poison as a matter of course, and to not or-
dering so much as a toxology screen on Nancy's blood until a
day and a half after she'd entered the hospital, had its neck thrust
out elastically. Dr. Bagheri, the only witness available to the prosecution whose testimony skirted the hearsay rule—and whose
testimony, once again, was quite possibly as accurate as on-the-
spot photography—was the only physician treating Nancy who
was a paid employee of the hospital, the others being outside
consultants in private practice. There are likewise no ear-

witnesses to what the mystery lady said to the various hospital people; rather than making sure that the witnesses had their stories straight, she may have been protecting the insurance carrier's interest in making certain that Dr. Bagheri and the nurses involved were enrolled in the hospital's group health care plan. However, since Richard as Nancy's surviving spouse would be the proper party to bring any malpractice suit against the hospital, it was clearly to the hospital's best interests that Richard be convicted. Thus from all outward appearances, it would seem likely that Presbyterian Hospital was, heavily, into C.Y.A.

Just when it appeared that the game was turning into a rout, Jerri Sims went on a little scoring spree of her own. It is true that most of her points during the streak were emotional ones, but often, where a jury is concerned, emotional points are the most important.

Mary Henrich told of representing Nancy as divorce counsel, and repeated her versions of the wine and pill and Coke-in-the-movie stories—all of which now became admissible as corroboration to what Dr. Bagheri had said—but these tales were now old hat. Everyone in the courtroom was convinced that Nancy had indeed related the stories, if not to the doctor, then to others, and the only question left was whether or not Nancy herself had been truthful. Something Ms. Henrich said from the witness stand, in fact, might make one wonder whether Nancy had been fibbing.

According to Ms. Henrich, Nancy had refused to bring the suspect items to her own lawyer's office, stating that she didn't want anyone knowing she was suspicious of Richard, and for a woman concerned that someone was trying to poison her, this seemed strange behavior indeed. And for the same woman to allow the suspect to move in with her later . . . well, the overall picture was enough to give pause. Any damage done to the prosecution by Nancy's unusual reaction to the items on her doorstep, however, Ms. Henrich made up for in her reading of a letter.

The letter, copy to my lawyer, et cetera, was one Nancy had sent to Richard. In it she told of the emotional pain that his affair had caused his wife and children, and further told how his comings and goings during the year when he lived in the Springbrook duplex had torn Nancy apart inside. In the final paragraph, Nancy gave Richard his freedom. *Insisted* on Richard's leaving, in fact, and said that it was the only choice she could make in order to keep her sanity and secure the little girls' futures.

No one could possibly have read that letter more effectively than did Mary Henrich. She was obviously deeply involved with the case emotionally, and during the more heartrending portions of the letter, she had to stop several times to compose herself and wipe away her tears. By the time she had finished, several of the jurors were crying, and there were sniffles here and there in the spectator section. Judge Creuzot himself had to clear his throat a couple of times before offering Guthrie a chance to cross-examine.

Guthrie seemed overcome with emotion in his own right, but his failure to offer much in the way of cross-examination had nothing to do with the defense lawyer's being somewhat weepy-eyed. As an attorney, Mary Henrich would also be a skilled and experienced witness. Unlike unwary civilians thrust on the stand, she would understand that, while on direct examination witnesses are limited to yes and no answers, under cross-examination one may wander in answering questions as much as one likes, and may say pretty much what one wishes to say. The prospect of cross-examining an attorney being akin to grabbing a rattler by the tail, Guthrie asked a couple of perfunctory questions and let Ms. Henrich go. She had damaged his case and he knew it.

The wine and pills left on Nancy's doorstep having been discussed at length in front of the jury, Jerri got the items themselves into evidence through Lynn Pease. Lynn (now married, nearing her first anniversary, and answering on the witness stand to the name of Lynn Pease Woods) identified the large plastic container and fifth of white wine as the same ones that Nancy had given her to hide in the trunk of her car, and the same ones she and Bill Jr. had brought to the hospital. In retrospect, the inclusion of Lynn in the gathering party that had left the hospital to retrieve the suspect items turned out to be a fortunate move for the prosecution; Lynn's ID of the wine and pills kept Bill Jr. off the stand. At the time of Nancy's death no one could predict that Richard would eventually point the finger at his brother-in-law, and the fact that Bill Jr. never had to suffer a lengthy cross-examination from Dan Guthrie was a boon to Jerri's case as a whole.

Although Lynn further described finding Nancy in bed, too sick to move, and went into great detail regarding Nancy's change of insurance beneficiaries, her physical presence did as much for Jerri's case as did her testimony. Lynn is a not-unattractive young woman with an innocent, roundish face, and there is a slight but apparent hitch in her gait due to her suffering from multiple sclerosis. During her direct examination, Lynn mentioned that she suffered from M.S. four different times. She spoke in a clear voice with a heavy Maine accent, and her descriptions of her relationship to the Lyon children—her walks with Allison and Anna, the children's love of her old car, the Zoomobile—absolutely charmed the pants off of everyone in the courtroom. The message to the jury was apparent: This, ladies and gentlemen, is one of the suspects that the defendant has claimed may have murdered his wife. By the time Lynn was finished, no one present believed that this enchanting creature could be guilty of so much as an unpaid parking ticket.

Just as with all witnesses, there is one portion of Lynn's testimony worth a double take. She was the first to mention the fire ant problem at the Lyon duplex, and—coached or on her own, as the case may be—was also the only one to downplay the insect situation. According to Lynn, if there was a problem with the ants at all, it was a small one, and the children were never in danger from the little red critters. Her statement here is in direct contrast to the remembrances of several other witnesses, including the Lyons' tenant in the duplex, who all recalled that the backyard was near overrun with the dangerous varmints. Lynn's testimony about the ants didn't get far with either jurors or spectators; as anyone who has lived in Texas knows, there is no such thing as a "small" fire ant problem.

At the tail end of Lynn's testimony, Jerri scored her first extra-base hit of the trial. When Guthrie, acting as if walking on eggs, had failed in his attempt to shake Lynn's story during cross-examination, and had passed the witness, Jerri stood. "I have re-direct, Your Honor." With each witness, re-direct and re-cross are optional, and normally are waived.

Creuzot told Jerri to proceed.

"Lynn," Jerri said gently, "during your time as the Lyons' nanny, did you come to regard them as your own family?"

Lynn smiled brightly and wrung her hands. "Oh, yes."

"And did you have a favorite between Mr. and Mrs. Lyon?"

"*Weh*-ell." Lynn's smile broadened. "I knew which one liked me the most."

"Oh?" Jerri said. "And who was that?"

"Nancy talked down to me some," Lynn said.

"Then your favorite was Richard?"

"Oh, yes. I was crazy about them all, but I loved Richard dearly. I thought he was the finest man I'd ever worked for." She looked straight at the defendant, her eyes glistening with adoration. At that moment any doubt among jurors or spectators that Lynn had told the truth, the whole truth, and nothing but the truth went flying out of the courtroom.

With the wine and pills now sitting innocently among the evidence exhibits, Jerri brought on the county forensics boys. For the next two days a series of scholarly types—one, complete with German accent, brought back memories of World War II A-bomb research—paraded to the stand to fondle the wine, shake the container of pills, and give clinical evidence regarding Nancy's autopsy, all the while glaring knowingly in the direction of the jury box. During this portion of the trial the audience thinned considerably. One teenage boy accompanied a chemist's description of the suspect capsules with a series of loud snores, thus earning a dressing-down from Judge Creuzot, and some of the well-dressed Park Citizens developed sudden interest in the racial tension and whore slashings down the corridor.

For those who remained awake during the Albert Einstein show, however, there were several points of note. While the wine and pills revealed not the barest trace of arsenic, a lone capsule in the container was packed with a toxic substance called barium carbonate. Though no one ever connected Richard to the gifts-on-the-porch incident—and the defense pointed vigorously, first in Bill Jr.'s and then in David Bagwell's direction—it was clear that whoever had left the items for Nancy had poison in mind. Here, score one for the prosecution.

Guthrie's intrusion amid the scientific testimony, however, showed an even more significant fact on the defense's side. Hair and fingernail samples from Nancy, it seemed, showed five times the level of arsenic in her hands as in her head, though the forensics people acknowledged that the levels should have been roughly the same. As Guthrie stalked among the county folk during cross-examination, only one explanation for the difference seemed possible: Nancy herself had handled the poison. It was the first evidence in the trial suggesting the possibility of suicide.

As though fearing the loss of customers through defection to the adjacent courtrooms, the prosecution picked up fan interest a bit as Detective Ortega played to a half-filled house. His testimony was somewhat droll and quite professional, and totally concerned his interview with Richard at police headquarters. Referring continuously to the suspect by both first and last names, as in, "Richard Lyon said" this, or "Richard Lyon said" that, Ortega detailed the process by which he'd discovered that Richard had indeed ordered arsenic trioxide from General Laboratory Supply. Though Guthrie was successful throughout the trial in thwarting all attempts to show that his client had ever received the shipment, the mere fact that Richard ordered the stuff at all planted ample suspicion in the jury's mind. Ortega, in fact, did more damage to Richard than any other prosecution witness, his testimony bolstering the theory that had Richard never talked to the cops, he likely never would have been under indictment to begin with.

Guthrie made few inroads on cross other than to elicit Ortega's admission that he'd never considered any suspect other than Richard. If Richard was indeed guilty of the crime, however, that the police hadn't searched every nook and cranny for other suspects seemed, overall, insignificant. When Ortega stepped down, the general courtroom feeling was that the detective had done his job, and done it well.

The police and the forensics people now out of the way, Jerri made an announcement guaranteed to bring them running from competing courtrooms down the hall, and indeed from even the streets and boulevards in all corners of the city. She was putting Denise Woods on.

37

Though Denise's testimony didn't begin until mid-afternoon, she arrived at the Crowley Building shortly after lunch and upstaged the proceedings in the courtroom by occupying a bench outside in the corridor. Her lawyer was with her—Denise was appearing under protest, as a result of Jerri Sims' subpoena—as was her sister, a stunning blonde in her own right, shorter than her sibling, with showpiece layered hair trimmed to reveal delicate ears; as Sis bent her head to brush her skirt, diamonds twinkled on perfect lobes.

Rumor at the courthouse being the prairie fire that it is, Denise hadn't been seated on the bench for over five minutes before someone had alerted all the writers of her presence, the result being that the testimony preceding hers received somewhat less than perfunctory coverage. Authors and reporters alike gathered around the hallway TV monitor, some fifty feet down the corridor from where she was seated, and pretended to watch the trial on the screen while shooting glances in her direction. Every writer had a question in mind for Denise. Up to the moment when she took the stand, none had gotten up the nerve to approach her. She was dressed in a conservative blue business suit and wore rose-tinted glasses. Her hair was brushed down straight in a serious manner. She seemed demure and somewhat frightened. Her demeanor would soon change.

There was a recess just prior to Denise's taking the stand, and as word of her pending testimony spread, what had been a half-filled courtroom suddenly became a jam-packed madhouse. It was brother against brother and husband against wife as the public fought for seating space and exercised its right to know. Once every pew was filled to overflowing, those excluded from the courtroom proper then jockeyed for standing space before the TV monitor. When the bailiff came into the hallway to escort Denise inside, humanity parted like the Red Sea to permit her access to the courtroom.

Once inside, she moved hesitantly down the aisle. She went through the gate and toward the stand in proper finishing-school strides, raised her hand for swearing-in, then sat in the witness chair and crossed her legs. She locked gazes with Richard and smiled at him. He briefly returned her smile, then concentrated on his own folded hands.

Now it was just Denise and Jerri. The most important women in Richard Lyon's life at the moment faced each other from twenty steps apart: the city-raised contractor's daughter and the trim and athletic Future Farmers of America sweetheart, claws bared and ready for combat. Denise favored Jerri with a look of stone. Jerri slightly tossed her head; the awesome blond hair swished challengingly from side to side. The column of air between the strong-willed young women sizzled with pent-up lightning.

"Please state your full name for the record," Jerri said.

"Debi Denise Woods. As you already know."

"That's right," Jerri said. "I do."

From there the relationship went straight downhill.

Firmly, unyieldingly, with Denise fighting her every step of the way, Jerri led the witness through her early meetings with Richard, their first sexual encounters, their secret affair before Richard's separation, their more open romance when he lived at the Springbrook duplex. Those panting for lurid bedroom details— and there were a number of those persons in the courtroom— were to be disappointed; Jerri Sims was there to convict and not to arouse. Her questions were pointed and precise, Denise's answers as brief as possible, her resentment clear.

They approached the weeks preceding Nancy's death. "Did Richard seem upset during that time?" Jerri said.

"He was upset during the entire separation."

"But was he more so in December?"

"I didn't see him that much then. After the divorce hearing, where I had to testify, I didn't see him that much at all," Denise said.

"What about the week before Christmas? Did you see him then?"

A slight shift in Denise's gaze. "Yes."

"And when was that?"

"He came by my apartment when I was having a party. We spent the night together then." Calm now, steady-eyed, not a hint of hesitation.

"He left his wife and children at home?" Jerri said.

"I wouldn't know that," Denise snapped. "You're putting words in my mouth."

"He didn't tell you where his wife was?"

"I assumed it wasn't my business," Denise said.

Jerri paused. Her whole purpose in having Denise as a prosecution witness hinged on the next few questions. Ask them incorrectly, and Denise would slip away.

"After that," Jerri said, "did you see him again that week?"

Denise blinked. "Once."

"And was that on the day after Christmas?"

"Yes."

"In the afternoon?"

"It was."

"And where was that meeting?" Jerri said.

"At my apartment. He came by."

"Did he give you something then? A present?"

"A coat."

"A thousand-dollar leather coat?" Jerri said.

"I didn't ask him for a receipt. Come on."

"But it was a leather coat."

Denise rolled her eyes. "Yes." Exasperated.

"Did he tell you that he was leaving town that evening?"

"He did." Short, irritated words snipped off as if cut with scissors.

"Where was he going, Miss Woods?"

"To New York. With Nancy."

"Just to New York?"

Denise rested her elbow on her armrest and massaged her forehead with a thumb and forefinger. "That's where he told me he was going."

"Did you later learn that wasn't true?"

"Yes, I did."

"You later learned that they also went to Connecticut, to visit Richard's parents?"

"That's right," Denise said.

"Miss Woods, what was the reason Richard told you he was taking Nancy to New York?"

Denise squirmed. "He was only . . ."

"Please answer. More to the point, did he tell you he was taking Nancy to the hospital at Mount Sinai?"

Denise looked at Richard, then quickly away. "He did."

"Why did he tell you he was taking her there?"

"Because . . . she was sick."

"Because she was sick. Miss Woods, didn't Richard Lyon tell you that Nancy in fact had a fatal disease? That she might die?"

"That's not . . ." Denise looked desperately around the courtroom. "It's the only time," she said. "The only time he ever lied to me."

"But on that occasion," Jerri said, "you found that what he said was a lie."

"I did."

Jerri searched her file in a blanket of heavy silence. She seemed in thought. "Pass the witness," she said.

At the defense table, Richard looked to his mother in the audience. At that moment the defendant seemed ready to cry.

★ ★ ★

As an adverse witness to the prosecution, Denise naturally did everything she could to help the defense during cross-examination, and Guthrie pumped the well for all he was worth. Richard, she said, was the gentlest man she'd ever known, was sensitive and caring, and certainly wasn't capable of committing murder. He'd cared deeply about his wife and family, Denise said, and the prospect of getting divorced had torn him apart. It was Nancy's frigidity, Denise thought, after the Sierra Tucson incident when the incest had come out into the open, which had driven the couple apart, and Denise had merely come along when Richard needed someone. She spoke these words in a straightforward and convincing manner, and no one in the courtroom doubted her sincerity, but the damage done to the defense's position by Richard's outright lie about the New York trip was irreversible.

Realistically, Denise regretted telling about Richard's falsehood, but under the circumstances she had no choice. She'd already spilled the beans at the police station, and had she changed her story on the witness stand she would have risked a perjury charge. As she left the courtroom she didn't look at Richard, and he seemed busy with some papers before him on the table. It is important that, while Denise had done harm to Richard's cause, she'd helped herself no end. Up until the time she took the witness stand, there had been innuendos, both at trial and in the newspapers, that the police believed Denise might have helped Richard kill his wife; after she'd delivered her testimony, however, it was apparent that she knew nothing whatsoever about the murder. Whatever the public's opinion of her affair with a married man might be, Denise was, simply, an innocent woman in love.

Having done all the damage that she could, Jerri folded her tent and rested her case, and Guthrie made a motion for an instructed verdict of acquittal. This motion is standard in all criminal trials, and the court's denial is standard as well. In this instance, however, Creuzot pondered the defense's request for many long minutes. The judge had serious matters to consider.

The burden on the state in their case-in-chief is to bring sufficient evidence so that it's possible for the jury to convict on what the state has presented alone. Thus if a man is charged with armed robbery of a supermarket, and the state presents evidence only that the grocery store was robbed without showing anything on which the jury could conclude that the defendant was the robber, the court is required to instruct acquittal. This never happens, of course, because if the state didn't have witnesses to identify the robber, they wouldn't have brought the case to trial to begin with. In the case of Richard Lyon, though, the judge's consideration was on a much higher level.

The charges against Richard were admittedly circumstantial. No one had placed arsenic in his hands, no one had seen him leave any wine or pills on Nancy's doorstep—no one, in fact, had witnessed Richard doing anything other than purchase arsenic (with no evidence that he'd ever received the order), cheat on his wife, and lie to his lover. The question Judge Creuzot had to ponder, then, was whether Richard's actions, statements, and behavior before and after Nancy's death were sufficient for the jury to legally return a conviction. In the end, Creuzot denied Guthrie's motion, but the judge could have made the call either way and escaped criticism. Jerri's witnesses and admitted evidence had been barely enough.

The instructed verdict issue decided, Creuzot recessed for the day and told Guthrie to have his defense ready by early in the morning. It was the sixteenth of December. In relation to the trial's beginning, it was over halfway to Christmas.

38

There was a death during the Lyon trial, and a period of mourning among the writers. After seventy years of spirited competition, the *Dallas Times-Herald* gave up the ghost and surrendered its mantle to the *Morning News*. The *News* bought a mere shell: desks, typewriters, printing presses. The spirit of the *Herald* was not for sale; Dallas, a city of two voices, simply woke up that morning with only one. The earnest young man who'd reported the Lyon trial for the *Herald* merely, *poof*, was no more.

Pete Slover does his thing for the *News*, and seemed even more lost than the rest of the writers. "It's like a team with nobody to play," he said. "It's always been a challenge, me trying to scoop the other guy, find out something he doesn't know. Now I've got nobody on the other side to keep me on my toes. Takes a lot of the fun out of it, you know?"

Writers bowed heads, suffered long moments of silence, then turned attention to Dan Guthrie's defense of his client. It was as if concentration on the unfolding courtroom drama would keep minds off of a dear departed friend and hold back the unfallen tears.

Grandstand quarterbacks abound in the practice of criminal law, and those who go along with Guthrie's strategy and those who would have done it differently are about equally divided. Half would have rested the case without putting on a single witness, and argued before the jury that the state's evidence, lacking positive proof that Richard had ever possessed any arsenic to begin with, and further failing to show that he had sufficient motive, in itself produced reasonable doubt. In retrospect, the failure to offer any defense at all would have been preferable to the disasters ahead, but ability to predict the future is not a prerequisite to the securing of a law license. Richard's entire defense hinged on his credibility. Guthrie placed his best foot grandly forward, and put his client on.

Richard rose from his seat at the defense table wearing a three-piece, I'm-from-Harvard pinstripe suit, stood erect, right hand raised, for his swearing-in, and mounted to the witness stand like a director at a board meeting. His olive complexion was clear, his manner confident. Jurors sat at rigid attention.

"I'll ask you first," Guthrie boomed, "did you poison your wife, Nancy Dillard Lyon?"

"No, I did not." The words were perfect; the tone, however, was nasal, flat, emotionless, and tempered with what Texans call the impersonal damyankee way of saying things. Richard, alas, was in a far different culture from his roots. He was definitely a Connecticut Yankee in good-ole-boyland, and so he would remain.

The stage thus set, Guthrie began with a series of photos. Pictures of buildings. Multimillion-dollar skyscrapers whose construction Richard had supervised, the message apparently being that a man involved in such high finance had too much on his mind to plot the murder of his wife. A jury of weekly paycheck recipients squirmed and fidgeted. For those who had seen the Richard and Dan Show on television, the live act wasn't nearly as mesmerizing.

Guthrie then led his client through his Harvard years, his

meeting of Nancy during the warm fall of '79, their growing romance, their close relationship as both sought their respective master's degrees. Richard touched on the couple's marriage, their move to Dallas, their purchase of the two M-Street duplexes, their eventual migration into the Park Cities. He spoke of his and Nancy's separate careers. Not surprisingly, he downplayed Big Daddy's role. To hear Richard tell it, the couple had done it on their own. The jury had already heard the same story from Big Daddy's standpoint, and the rerun didn't seem to catch their attention. With the jury steadfastly on nap alert, Richard droned through the financial details of the deal on the Shenandoah duplex as if his mortgage and second lien bore heavily on Nancy's death. Just as the courtroom seemed ready to doze, however, Dan Guthrie changed directions with a grinding clash of gears.

"In the spring of '89," Guthrie said, "did you and Nancy attend a Dillard family meeting at Sierra Tucson, in Arizona?"

Throughout the room, heads shot to attention. The audience was to receive another dose of the incest deal. Hallelujah.

"Yes, I did. We drove out, Nancy and I, and took the baby."

"What was the occasion of the meeting?" Guthrie said.

"Bill Jr., my brother-in-law, was there in alcohol rehab. It was family week."

"Where the family receives counseling on how to deal with alcoholic recovery? Codependency?"

"Yes."

"Richard, did you and Nancy meet with a counselor?"

"We did," Richard said, deadpan.

"What did you learn during that session that you hadn't known before?"

Jerri Sims sat motionless at the prosecution table, back straight, hair billowing out over her chair back and almost touching the floor, offering no objection. Give them enough rope . . .

"I learned that my wife and brother-in-law had engaged in incest when they were teenagers," Richard said. "Nancy took it up with the counselor."

"Richard." Guthrie here assumed a tone of male-bonding

sympathy. "During your entire marriage, had you ever been aware of the incest?"

"Never."

"Nancy had never told you about it?"

"Not once. I couldn't believe my ears."

"And Richard, if you remember," Guthrie said, "what was your reaction?"

Richard paused. He licked his lips. "The idea disgusted me," he finally said.

Throughout the courtroom and in the jury box, women stiffened. They understood. Richard, on learning of his wife's problem, hadn't been understanding. He hadn't been caring, he hadn't been gentle. He had been disgusted. When the women left the courtroom and returned home that evening, there were some husbands who were going to be in for it.

Guthrie led Richard through the family meeting where Big Daddy's reaction to the incest was somewhat less than one would have expected—and where Richard continued to be disgusted by it all—then went through the arguments with Nancy on the way home, through her alleged frigidity once she started counseling, through the beginnings of the affair with Denise Woods. From Richard's lips, jurors and spectators learned of the events of that fall, of Richard's secret trysts with Denise both in Dallas and points east and west, his continued worry over Nancy's coldness to him, his agreement to accept sex-addiction treatment at Sierra Tucson and ultimate defection from same. They learned of his leaving home after New Year's, and his setting up residence in the Springbrook condo.

"Richard," Guthrie said, "during January of 1990, did you have occasion to buy chemicals in Houston, from General Laboratory Supply?"

"Yes, I did."

"And what were those chemicals for?"

"Mercury, for a battery I was building. Barium carbonate, to use as fire ant poison. Sodium nitroferrocyanide, to use as an agent to color the poison red."

Guthrie now spoke to Judge Creuzot. "Your Honor, may I approach the witness?"

Permission granted, Guthrie showed Jerri a piece of paper—which she handed back with barely a glance—then had the page marked for evidence, gave it to the judge, and had the page admitted. He asked Richard to identify the piece of paper.

"It's a diagram of my design to combat the fire ants." A picture came to mind, Richard in a steel helmet and army fatigues, M-16 rifle held ready while ants the size of Shetland ponies thundered over the rim of his foxhole.

There was a wooden three-legged easel set up near the witness box, holding a giant sketch pad. Guthrie had already used the sketch pad numerous times during the trial to illustrate medicines (when cross-examining Dr. Bagheri), points in time, etc., and he now flipped over a page on the pad to reveal a professional-looking diagram. It consisted of a picture of a sidewalk, so marked, a colony of scurrying ants entrenched beneath the walk (marked, interestingly enough, "ants"), and a huge drawing in the lower right-hand corner that resembled an updated version of Buck Rogers' ray gun. There were handwritten notations in many places on the diagram.

"For the record," Guthrie said, "this merely is a blowup of the diagram we've just had marked as evidence. For the jury's convenience."

Creuzot leaned over the bench, squinted at the smaller diagram that lay before Richard, then peered at the sketch pad. "Looks the same to me," the judge said. "Miss Sims?"

Jerri waved a hand. "No objection, Your Honor," she said, but her expression and body language said, God, when will this be over with?

"And, Your Honor," Guthrie said, "so that the jury may see, I ask the court's permission for the witness to join me in front of the jury box."

Creuzot did a double take and looked at the jurors. None of the panel members seemed particularly frightened at the prospect of having a murder suspect stand arm's-length away. Creuzot shrugged. "Okay with me." Jerri Sims sat back in her chair and folded her arms.

Richard climbed down, and he and Guthrie carried the easel, sketch pad and all, over to set up shop in front of the jury. As the two men stood on either side of the easel, Guthrie glanced toward the prosecution table. Jerri was bent urgently sideways in apparent danger of developing a crick in her neck in her effort to see the drawing. Guthrie slanted the easel at an angle so that the sketch pad was visible to both jury and prosecutor. Jerri relaxed.

"Now, Richard," Guthrie said, "will you please identify the various items on this drawing for the jury?"

"This," Richard said, using a pointer he'd lifted from the easel's ledge, "is the sidewalk in the backyard of my Shenandoah Avenue duplex, and this"—moving the pointer—"shows where the fire ants had burrowed under the sidewalk to build their nest."

In the writers' section, two men winked at each other. Earlier one had remarked, "I didn't think they allowed fire ants in Highland Park. I thought the bastards all came over to my house."

"Richard, would you please read this notation to the jury?" Guthrie indicated handwriting in the upper left-hand corner of the drawing.

Richard fished in his pocket, produced wire-framed reading glasses, and put them on. " 'Maybe the sprayer could be connected to the drill,' " he read.

"And who made that notation?"

"It's Nancy's. We worked on this together."

Suddenly, Jerri sat erect. "Objection. Hearsay."

"Your Honor," Guthrie said, "we will show through expert testimony that the handwriting on the drawing is indeed Nancy Lyon's."

"We'll stipulate as to the contents of the note, Judge," Jerri said. "With relation to who wrote it, our objection stands."

"I'm going to . . ." Creuzot paused. "Mr. Guthrie, I'll overrule the state's objection with the understanding that they may raise it later on, if you fail to show the proof. Overruled, Miss Sims."

"Thank you, Your Honor," Guthrie said. Having gotten his point across, he now indicated the ray gun–like figure in the lower right-hand corner. "And what," Guthrie said, "is this?"

Spectators and jurors alike sat forward. Christ, maybe they were about to see the murder weapon.

"It's my electric drill," Richard said.

Spectators and jurors sank back in disappointment.

"Thank you. Let's return to the stand." Guthrie, aided by Richard, moved the easel back to its position facing the audience. Richard ascended the one step and resumed his seat behind the witness railing. Guthrie sauntered in the direction of the defense table.

As the defense attorney approached, Leila Thomas bent over and picked up something from under the table. The beautiful legal assistant stood with a common battery-operated Black & Decker electric drill and handed it to Guthrie. The drill had an unusual bit attachment, a steel rod with its end flattened into a wicked-looking rectangular point. Guthrie pulled the trigger. The point of the rod spun immediately into a blur, accompanied by a loud *BZZZZZZZZZZT*. Jurors and spectators now exchanged astonished glances. Christ, the thing was loaded.

Guthrie offered the drill to Jerri, who waved it away with her shoulder heaving in silent laughter, then went through the evidence admissions procedure. Creuzot held the drill between both hands, shot the bit attachment a puzzled look, admitted the evidence, and returned the drill to the defense lawyer.

As the entire throng in the courtroom jumped as if touched with live wires, Guthrie approached the witness, constantly pulling the trigger so that his initial question sounded something like this: "Richard"—*BZZZZZZZT*—"I show you"—*BZZZZZT*—"this admitted evidence"—*BZZZZZT*—"and ask if you can identify it"—*BZZZZZZZT*. He released the trigger, and the sudden silence was deafening.

"It's my drill."

"The same drill"—Guthrie pointed—"depicted in the drawing."

"Yes."

"Please tell the jury," Guthrie said. "Precisely, what was your plan to get rid of the fire ants?"

"Normal poisons wouldn't work, because the workers removed the queen to safety so quickly." Richard sat forward and eyed his drawing as he spoke. "To get these ants you have to zap them in a hurry. I was going to use the drill to smash through the sidewalk and poison the bed before they knew what hit them."

"And that was the purpose of the barium carbonate and the sodium nitroferrocyanide which you bought from General Laboratory Supply?"

"Well, the barium carbonate was the poison," Richard said. "The sodium nitroferrocyanide was a coloring agent, so that the poison would be red and we could show the girls not to touch the red stuff."

"To protect your daughters."

"Yes."

"And did your plan work?" Guthrie said.

"Not initially. The poison, in order to be effective, had to be in liquid form. The barium carbonate was insoluble. It wouldn't dissolve."

Outwardly comical—not to mention eardrum shattering—as the demonstration had been, the jurors were sitting up and taking notice. Richard certainly seemed to know what he was talking about.

"Did you later find the solution to the problem?" Guthrie said.

"Nancy did," Richard said.

Jerri stiffened as if to object, then relaxed. Any action on Nancy's part that Richard had personally observed wasn't hearsay.

"While the two of you were separated?"

"All during the separation we continued to work together on problems that came up around the duplex. Nancy came up with a formula that included arsenic trioxide."

Guthrie moved to the defense table, returned holding a piece of paper, had the paper admitted, and asked Richard to identify it.

"It's an invoice," Richard said. "I found it in some of Nancy's things after she'd died."

"An invoice," Guthrie said, "from Chemical Engineering in Dallas?"

"Yes."

"And does the signature in the receipt column look like Nancy's?"

"Yes. I'd know her handwriting anywhere," Richard said.

Guthrie then had Richard read the items on the invoice, which included, of course, arsenic trioxide. The quizzical grins that had showed around the courtroom when Guthrie had produced the drill were no longer there. The defendant was making sense. It was also at that moment when those present first began to sense a midstream change of direction in Richard's defense. All the pretrial hoopla and TV drama, all the finger-pointing at Bill Jr. and David Bagwell, all of this was about to drift out of the courtroom in a puff of smoke. The defense now directed its entire game plan toward the theory that Nancy had committed suicide.

The suicide theory came into sharper focus during Jerri's brief but aggressive cross-examination. "Mr. Lyon, is it your thought that Bill Jr. murdered Nancy, or that the killer was David Bagwell?" When she so desires, her soft and cultured tone can drip with sarcasm.

"Neither," Richard said.

Even Jerri seemed taken aback. "Could you explain that?"

"We thought so at first," Richard said, "but we've located other factors."

"In your . . . investigation?" Jerri stopped short of using the words *smoke screen,* but her inference was clear.

"Yes. In our research."

Jerri dropped this line of questioning like a hot potato. Richard had clearly surprised her, and, good lawyer that she is, she wasn't about to ask another question to which she didn't already know the answer. Richard's stint on the witness stand had damaged the prosecution considerably, and Jerri now tried to recoup what ground she could by, for want of a better description, slinging a little mud. "Mr. Lyon," Jerri said, "you testified earlier that during your separation from Nancy, and after her death, you regarded Denise Woods as only a friend. Is that right?"

"*Mostly* as a friend and confidant," Richard corrected. He had said this during Guthrie's direct examination; whether Richard was in fact not as enamored of Denise as she was with him, or whether he was merely downplaying their fervent relationship, isn't known.

"And," Jerri said, "was it friendship which caused you to give Denise a watch priced at forty-five hundred dollars?"

"I gave it to her . . . as a friend."

"And a necklace and a coat, each one priced at one thousand dollars?"

"Yes. As a—"

"Thank you, Mr. Lyon," Jerri said testily. "I pass this witness." For the only time during the trial, she had blown her cool, her final remarks to Richard coming across as desperate and, yes, just a bit on the catty side.

And, finally, Richard stepped down. He'd told his story and had met the prosecution's major points head-on. The feeling in the courtroom was that Jerri had failed to lay a glove on him.

The suicide theory having bumped all other defenses from the arena, Guthrie now put on his own version of the Albert Einstein show. His array of expert witnesses was every bit as impressive as the state's, if not more so. He had, in fact, borrowed the forensics staff from down-south San Antonio, the seat of Bexar (pronounced *Bayer*, as in aspirin) County. For prosecution-oriented people from foreign counties to testify as experts for the defense in Texas is not unusual, and rumor has it that the side income derived from the practice equals the forensics people's public salaries. The leaping from one side of the fence to the other seems to pose no integrity problem; at least no one has ever raised the issue. The victory in the battle of the experts generally hinges on the side with the most degrees and awards, and which scientists happen to be the most scholarly in appearance. Fresh-faced recent grads are limited to backstage roles.

Dr. James C. Garriott's position as head of Bexar County forensics does the impact of his testimony no harm at all, and the fact that he was formerly in the same capacity with Dallas County, and supervised the very people who'd testified as experts for the state in the Lyon trial, gave him a serious leg up in the jury's eyes. Further, as a steady-eyed Dr. Garriott told one and all that he'd investigated over twenty poison deaths (the Dallas

County experts, under rigid cross from Guthrie, had rather sheepishly admitted that they'd never seen an arsenic poisoning in their lives prior to Nancy's), the entire courtroom sat up and took rigid notice.

The doctor's credentials took up more of the court's time than did his testimony. The defense had furnished him Nancy's hair and fingernail samples, and the fact that the level of arsenic in the nail clippings was five times that in the hair roots led the doctor to only one conclusion: Nancy had directly touched the poison with her hands. Had *directly* handled the arsenic and not merely held a glass or cup filled with lethal contents. Barring the possibility that someone had held a gun on Nancy and forced her to eat the poison, the inference was clear as a bell.

Guthrie had promised proof when Jerri objected to Richard's identification of Nancy's notation on the fire ant diagram, and the defense lawyer was true to his word. The Bexar County handwriting man stated unequivocally that every piece of scripted evidence submitted by the defense had indeed been written by Nancy Lyon. Since no one had challenged the authorship of the incest counseling notes or the suddenly pertinent Chemical Engineering invoice up to that point, the handwriting evidence seemed perfunctory. Later, the origin of the writings attributed to Nancy would become a very big deal.

For his psychology expert, Guthrie stole some of Dallas County's own thunder. James Grigson, Ph.D., known better locally under the colorful nickname of "Doctor Death," is personally responsible for sending hundreds to sit on the hot seat or, in more recent humane years, to lie on the gurney and receive their lethal injections. In fact, Grigson's appearance caused several veteran courtroom observers to check their programs to be certain that the right team was on the playing field; Grigson on the witness stand normally meant that the state was fixin' to fry another one. An eloquent speaker, Grigson informed the jury that he'd carefully examined Nancy's writings in light of his knowledge of adult incest survivors, and that this was a troubled woman who, at the slightest provocation, could become bent on self-destruction. With Grigson, Jerri wasted little breath in cross-examination; the years had proven that challenging Dr. Death was a fatal mistake.

As Guthrie brought on one expert after another, there was a distinct feeling of overkill, as every witness seemed to dally on the stand far longer than necessary. There was a reason for this filibustering. Out on the streets of Dallas there was a search in progress for the witness whom Guthrie believed would once and for all clear his client. Even as he waxed eloquent in the courtroom, Dan Guthrie was stalling for time.

39

Jim Bearden is a youthful man with thinning sandy hair and a thick, broad-shouldered body suited for beer joint crowd control. That he sees the world through a slightly jaundiced eye is hardly surprising. He's made a career out of criminal investigations, both on the law enforcement side and, more recently, in his highly successful private detective business, and he assumes that most of the people he interviews are lying to him.

"One in a hundred," Bearden says, "are on the level. Their side lies, our side lies. Everybody lies. Out of the hundred, Richard Lyon was the one. That guy didn't poison his wife. If anybody did, and I doubt that, it damn sure wasn't him."

Guthrie had retained Bearden's services for Richard's defense from day one. After months of following homicide detectives' tracks, and also digging up evidence apart from the police investigation, the detective had reached a conclusion. Bearden thought that although making a lot of noise regarding other suspects had created pretrial doubt, there wasn't enough evidence linking either David Bagwell, Lynn Pease, or Bill Dillard, Jr., to

Nancy's death to create reasonable doubt of Richard's guilt in a jury's mind. The other-suspect ship simply wasn't going to sail.

Long before Richard had come up with the invoice from Chemical Engineering, Bearden had suspected that Nancy, either accidentally or on purpose, had poisoned herself. Dan Guthrie considered the implications of the invoice—that Nancy had purchased arsenic on her own, completely apart from the suspicious shipments from Houston's General Laboratory Supply—critical to Richard's defense, and Bearden agreed with the lawyer, but unless there was testimony to verify that the invoice was legitimate, it was just Richard's word against the state. Finding backup for his word was Bearden's assignment, and giving Bearden time to locate corroborating evidence was Guthrie's reason for conducting a series of witness filibusters in the courtroom.

Early on, months before trial, in fact, Bearden had interviewed Charles Couch, the owner of Chemical Engineering Company. At that time Couch had been cooperative, and Bearden had thought him just the witness they were looking for. He'd included Couch's name on his list of defense witnesses as a matter of course.

As the trial date approached, however, Couch had suddenly become reluctant to testify; in fact, Bearden had been trying for weeks just to talk to the man. Couch didn't return telephone calls, and when Bearden dropped by Chemical Engineering's office the owner was never around. Just what Couch's reason for the abrupt one-eighty was, Bearden didn't know, but the detective's criminal investigation experience told him that either (a) the police had talked to Couch and scared him out of testifying or (b) Couch had personal problems that had caused him to hide from everyone, Bearden included. Since Bearden had learned that Couch was in financial trouble—including a $27,000 judgment in favor of Dixie Chemical of Houston for an unpaid bill—the detective assumed that it was the latter situation that had made the witness unavailable.

Time had now run out. If Bearden couldn't come up with Couch as a witness, he'd have to try the next best thing. As Guthrie racked his brain for additional questions to keep his experts on the witness stand, Bearden armed himself with two sub-poenas: one for Couch individually and one for Chemical Engineering Company records of sales. Legal papers in hand, the detective drove out to the industrial district to Chemical Engineering's offices.

The area known as Trinity Industrial District sprawls to the northwest from downtown Dallas along Irving Boulevard, and consists of row upon row of warehouses, loading docks, and one-story glass-front office buildings. Bearden had been to Chemical Engineering so often he likely could have found his way with his eyes closed, and he pulled into the head-in parking in a curtain of icy rain just a few minutes before noon. He jammed the sub-poenas into his inside breast pocket and, minus raincoat or umbrella, made a mad dash over the curb and through the swinging glass door.

Chemical Engineering was a counter-front operation, a waist-high wooden partition separating a tiny lobby from the desks, tables, chairs, and copy machines in the work area. Bearden leaned on the counter and called out for assistance. An alert, rawboned fortyish man came from the rear of the office and approached the counter.

Bearden identified himself and stated his business. "I'm looking for Charles Couch," the burly detective said.

"So are a lot of people," the man said. "Charles isn't here."

"Okay, then, who around here can get me sales records on Chemical Engineering?"

"That would be either Charles or David Green," the man said disinterestedly. "Who isn't here, either."

Bearden fished in his pocket and produced the records subpoena. "When will one of them *be* here?"

"David's about to leave town. Charles . . ." The man snickered. "Well, Charles is sort of catch as catch can."

"I've got a subpoena here," Bearden said, extending the folded legal paper, "for Chemical Engineering records, which I'll now hand you. I need the records. Now."

The man, whose name is John Reamer, took the document, carefully read it over, then regarded Bearden through unfriendly slitted eyes. "This would be nice," Reamer said, "only I don't work for Chemical Engineering. I've got my own business here, and I don't know from nothing about Chemical Engineering. Like I said. You need to talk to Charles. Or David. Who aren't here. See you, huh?" He dropped the subpoena on the counter, turned his back, and retreated to the rear of the office.

Bearden snatched up the subpoena and crumpled it in his fist. The detective was furious and by now more than a little desperate. Ignoring the driving rain, he ducked his head, sprinted to his car, and made a beeline downtown to the sheriff's office. Bearden returned less than an hour later, only this time he was accompanied by a hard-eyed, very businesslike, gun-toting deputy. Bearden pounded the counter and once again called for service.

Reamer came from the back, this time accompanied by a shorter, stockier individual. Both men wore work shirts and jeans. "I already told you," Reamer said, "Charles isn't—" He cut himself off and now stared at the badge thrust in front of his nose by the deputy sheriff. "Here," he finally said.

"You—" Bearden pointed first at one man, then the other. "—and you, are both under arrest. We're going down to the courthouse, and you can tell the judge all about it."

Reamer raised a hand. "Now, wait a minute."

"I've got no minutes to wait," Bearden said. The deputy sheriff stood by, hands on hips.

Reamer laughed nervously. "Look, Charles is out of town, and David's leaving town. I told you, I know nothing about Chemical Engineering's business."

"Well, can we catch David," Bearden said, "before he gets away?"

The men exchanged glances, and then shrugs. "I guess we'd better try," Reamer finally said.

Just before two in the afternoon David Green, a tall, handsome, and intelligent thirty-year-old, stood in line at DFW Airport with his briefcase in hand and his boarding pass in his front shirt pocket. Unlike many businessmen, David doesn't travel in a suit and tie; his customers are men who feel more comfortable in boots and jeans. Green had on a clean plaid shirt and smooth, unwrinkled jeans, and he smiled patiently as the flight attendant ahead took her time in examining each traveler's boarding pass. Visible through the huge glass window, a fanjet stood ready at the end of the accordion walkway. Raindrops spattered the plane's wings and fuselage.

There was a commotion among the crowd behind Green, and he turned to look. His eyes widened in surprise. Elbowing their way through the waiting passengers in the boarding area were two men from Green's own office, a uniformed cop with a hol-stered pistol at his hip, and a man with thinning sandy hair built like a strong-side tackle, wearing slacks and a plaid sports coat.

The thick sandy-haired man approached and handed Green a folded legal-sized sheet of paper. "Mr. Green," the man said, "I'm Jim Bearden. I'm afraid we're going to have to cancel your travel plans."

Green frowned, looked past Bearden and the deputy at his two excited and frightened co-workers. "Who the hell's minding the office?" Green said.

"I'm afraid you're closed until further notice," Bearden said.

All of which created the situation during the Lyon trial around three-thirty in the afternoon, the jury out for recess, Judge Creuzot still on the bench attending to other cases, Jerri Sims going over notes at the prosecution table, Dan Guthrie on the defense side discussing strategy with Leila Thomas and Richard Lyon. The rear courtroom door burst open and a strange proces-sion entered, Jim Bearden in the lead, three nervous-looking jeans-wearing guys following timidly behind, a uniformed deputy bringing up the rear and keeping an eye on the jeans-wearing guys.

Bearden came through the gate with the youngest of the three strangers in tow, while the deputy placed the two other men on the front row of the spectator section and sat beside them. Bearden approached the defense table and said to Guthrie, "This is David Green, one of the Chemical Engineering guys. These people needed some encouragement."

Within the space of less than a minute, Guthrie stood in front of the bench with David Green alongside. Jerri Sims watched from the prosecution table with raised eyebrows.

Creuzot, though all business, was obviously getting a kick out of the entire affair. With a somewhat sardonic grin on his face, he said, "Mr. Green, you understand the meaning of this?" The judge indicated the subpoena, which lay unfolded before him.

"I understand this is costing us a lot of business," Green said. "Shutting down our office and bringing our whole crew down here."

"That's unfortunate," Creuzot said. "But Mr. Lyon over there has something more important than that going on. He's on trial for murder." The judge nodded toward Richard, who sat attentively at the defense table.

"I've already told him," Green said, pointing at Guthrie, "that we don't know a thing about Charles Couch's records."

"Wait a minute," Creuzot said, examining the subpoena. "Are you with Chemical Engineering?"

"Well," Green said. "Yes, but—"

"No buts." Creuzot raised a hand. "Tell you what, Mr. Green. I'm going to let youall go home, which means you won't have to spend the night in jail. But tomorrow morning, by nine o'clock, you or somebody's going to have to bring these records down here. I don't want to have to send the sheriff after you again. You think you can produce those records for us?"

Green looked over his shoulder at his cohorts sitting disconsolately beside the deputy in the spectators' section. He faced the judge. "I suppose we'd better, huh?" David Green said.

Chemical Engineering's response to the subpoena actually came a bit in advance of the judge's nine o'clock deadline. It was eight-thirty on the dot the following morning when a huge bear of a man shambled into court and headed down the aisle. Guthrie was in his usual seat at the defense table, papers spread before him. Leila sat two spaces down from her boss, her elegant neck bent as she made notes on a yellow legal pad. Richard hadn't arrived in court as yet.

The newcomer was well over six feet tall, with sloping shoulders and hamlike hands. He wore a sports shirt and slacks, and carried a bulging leather satchel. He had blondish hair parted on the left and wore glasses. He came through the gate, stood near the defense table, and said in a deep resonant voice, "Which one's Guthrie?"

The defense lawyer looked up. "I'm Guthrie."

"Well, I'm Charles Couch," the newcomer said. "You've been looking for me?"

Thus began one of the most unusual courtroom appearances in the annals of American law.

Charles Couch faced a packed house, a television camera mounted at the rear of the courtroom, a judge whose head was inquisitively cocked to one side, an apprehensive Richard Lyon, an attentive Leila Thomas, a suavely dressed Dan Guthrie, and a skeptical Jerri Sims. Couch seemed bored by the attention. He stated his full name at Guthrie's request, then leaned back and waited for more.

"What's your occupation, Mr. Couch?" Guthrie said.

"Owner. Chemical Engineering."

"And in what business is Chemical Engineering engaged?"

"Industrial cleaning compounds. I've got a carpet-recycling business, too, but that's under another name." Couch placed his elbows on his armrests and touched his fingertips together.

"Do you also deal in insecticides?" Guthrie said.

"No way."

Guthrie frowned. Jerri sat up a little straighter.

"Do you ever have anything to do with poisons at all?" Guthrie said.

"Not if I can help it," Couch said.

Guthrie scratched his forehead, obviously in trouble. "Mr. Couch, are you appearing here today under subpoena?"

"I suppose so. If you call arresting my men and interfering with my business a subpoena—"

"Mr. Couch," Guthrie said.

"—then I guess you're right. I got called in from out of town to straighten this out."

Judge Creuzot interrupted. "Mr. Couch, just answer the questions. I'm so instructing you."

Couch shifted his position in the chair. He was obviously irritated.

"I'll ask you now," Guthrie said, "if sometime during the summer of 1990 you ever had anything to do with any poisons."

"It was in August," Couch said, "if you're talking about the ant deal."

Guthrie now relaxed somewhat. Jerri slumped in disappointment.

"I got a call from a woman," Couch said.

"And what was her name?" Guthrie now seemed in complete control.

Couch shrugged. "Don't ask me."

"I beg your pardon?"

"I said, I don't know her name."

Guthrie was walking a tightrope with this witness. Other than Bearden's brief interview several months earlier, no one with the defense had spoken to Couch. Guthrie thought he knew the answers to his questions, but Couch was giving the lawyer plenty of doubt. "You don't know her name, but you remember the call," Guthrie said.

"I remember the time because the Cowboys were in training camp," Couch said.

Thus enlightened, Guthrie said, "And what did this woman want?"

"She said she lived over by SMU, and that she had fire ants in her yard."

"Mr. Couch," Guthrie said, "are you listed in the Yellow Pages under Pesticides? Insect control?"

"Nope. I'm known far and wide in the industry, though."

"As what?" Guthrie couldn't keep the puzzlement out of his tone. At the prosecution table, Jerri laid down her pen and folded her arms.

"I'm known," Couch said, "as someone who does a lot of research on things. I get calls all the time."

"Out of the blue? Are you a chemist?" Guthrie said.

"I've been to four colleges. Don't have a degree, but I do a lot of research."

"And you don't know who referred this woman to you?"

"Someone who'd heard of me, I guess," Couch said.

"If you could tell us," Guthrie said, "what did this woman want?"

"She asked me for a formula for fire ant poison. Fire ants are tough. Roaches and whatnot, they have a soft underbody that's easy to penetrate, but fire ants are hardshells. You need something really strong."

Guthrie looked at Richard. He shrugged. Guthrie now said to the witness, "And as a result of the call, did you then do anything?"

"I told her I'd look up some things at the SMU library and let her know. I do research out there all the time, so it wasn't any problem."

"Mmm-hmm. Well, did you?"

"Yes," Couch said. "I'm familiar with SMU because they recruited my son heavily for football. Those coaches never made any sense to me."

Jerri covered her mouth as if repressing a grin.

Guthrie ignored the football talk. "So you did the research. Did you come up with anything?"

"Yes sir," Couch said. "A formula."

"And did the," Guthrie said, almost hopefully, "formula include arsenic trioxide as one of its ingredients?"

"Sure did," Couch said. "Like I said, you need something strong."

"It included arsenic." Guthrie was practically smiling. "Your Honor, may I approach the witness?"

"Go ahead," Judge Creuzot said.

Guthrie went to the front, searched among the exhibits, picked up a piece of paper, showed it to Jerri. As if everyone in the courtroom didn't already know, Guthrie was holding the Chemical Engineering invoice.

"Mr. Couch," Guthrie said, approaching the box, "I show you this piece of admitted evidence, and ask if you can identify it." He laid the invoice on the rail before the witness, stood aside, and folded his arms over his coat lapels.

Couch picked the invoice up, tilted his head back to look through the bottom half of his bifocals, held the invoice at arm's length. He turned the page upside-down, then right-side up. He looked at the back side of the page. He dropped the invoice on the railing before him. "Never saw it before in my life," Couch said.

Guthrie's jaw dropped. At the defense table, Richard buried his head between his crossed forearms. Jerri Sims didn't move a muscle, but likely wanted to jump up in the air and clap her hands.

Guthrie said quickly, "But you did make up the formula."

"That's right," Couch said. "But I never sold her anything. She came by my office and picked up the formula."

"You mean," Guthrie said, "you did all that work and didn't make any money?"

"Not a cent," Couch said. "Do it all the time. I don't mind helping people."

"And you're sure that isn't your invoice," Guthrie said weakly.

"Not only is it not mine," Couch said, "it's not even on my company form. That invoice, sir, is a total counterfeit."

Jerri Sims, standing near the witness box, was doing her best not to show a look of triumph. "Tell the jury, please, Mr. Couch. How can you be sure that the invoice isn't yours?" Two minutes earlier, Guthrie had given up the ghost and turned the witness over for Jerri to finish the slaughter.

Couch glanced at the evidence, which still lay before him on the rail. "Well, it's typed, for one thing," Couch said. Judge Creuzot leaned sideways and craned his neck to peer at the invoice over the witness' shoulder.

"You don't type your invoices, Mr. Couch?" Jerri said.

"Nah. Don't even own a typewriter. I handwrite everything."

Jerri picked the invoice up, held it between herself and the witness. "Would you please read what's written down there?" It was the first indication that she knew more about the invoice than she'd been letting on.

Couch leaned forward and squinted. " 'Contact Keith or Charles for pickup at 617–2913 and' . . . there's another phone number down here," Couch said.

"And what is that?"

" '438–1363,' " Couch read.

"And," Jerri said, "do those phone numbers mean anything to you?"

Couch folded his arms. "Sure do."

"And what are they?"

"It'll take some explaining," Couch said.

"Take your time, sir." Jerri folded her own arms and walked back a few paces so as not to obstruct the jury's view of the witness.

"When the lady came by," Couch said, "I was at my desk on the phone. I didn't see her myself, but one of my men came back and said she was up front, by the counter, and wanted her fire ant poison formula. There was a scratch pad at my elbow, so I dashed the ingredients off, tore the top sheet from the pad, and gave it to my man. He carried it back to the front.

"Anyway," Couch said, pointing, "these phone numbers are ones I'd jotted down myself while I was on the phone, talking to one of my suppliers."

"And those names down there, Keith or Charles," Jerri said. "Those aren't people who work for you?"

"Nah. They work for my supplier, and I was supposed to call them up when my order was ready. I'd jotted the numbers down, and inadvertently left them on the pad I tore off to give to the lady."

"So you're saying," Jerri said, "that whoever prepared that invoice did it using the notations you'd made on the scratch pad."

Guthrie rose quickly. "Objection. Calls for a conclusion."

Creuzot sustained, but everyone in the courtroom had already reached the same conclusion that Jerri was calling for the witness to make.

"What about your letterhead? The one on the invoice," Jerri said.

"That's easy," Couch said, looking at Richard for the first time. "This is a blowup of the same letterhead engraved on the scratch pad I was using."

"Thank you, Mr. Couch," Jerri said after a pause. "No further—*oh*, one more thing. This woman. You didn't see her?"

"No, ma'am," Couch said. "From my desk I can't see up to the counter."

"So you can't give a description?"

Couch answered quickly. "My man said that she was a blonde."

Jerri paused for a long moment in order to give the jury time to picture Denise Woods impersonating Nancy and picking up the formula. Denise had exonerated herself when she'd testified, but now the cloud of doubt returned.

"Thank you, Mr. Couch," Jerri said, returning to her seat. "Pass the witness."

Guthrie declined to ask more questions, and Couch climbed down the step to walk away. He'd been on the witness stand for less than a half hour and had given the briefest testimony of the entire trial. As he disappeared through the exit, an acrid odor lingered. It was the smell of cooked goose. Richard's.

Much was to be made later on of some expert testimony that drove the final nails into Richard's coffin—and the last bit of handwriting evidence produced by the state was devastating, to be sure—but it was Couch who torpedoed a huge hole in the defense ship's side from which the boat couldn't possibly recover. Expert witnesses are, after all, paid advocates, and for every such expert who shouts " 'Tis" for one side, there will be an equally impressive individual on the other team who will holler, " 'Tain't," just as forcefully. Couch, though, was an individual with no apparent stake in the outcome, and, furthermore, he was *Guthrie's own witness*! After Charles Couch testified that Richard's invoice was a fake, the jury simply wasn't going to believe anything that the defense had to say.

The grim reaper of an expert whom the state produced was named Hartford Kittle, and he testified during the state's rebuttal. Rebuttal is the third phase of testimony, after the prosecution's case-in-chief and the defense portion, and is optional. Re-rebuttal is also an option for the defense, but after Kittle had taken the stand, Guthrie seemed to have had enough. The handsome defense lawyer, in fact, likely began to think of arguments for mitigation of Richard's punishment from the moment that Charles Couch stepped down.

Hartford Kittle was the Vaunted Expert from the East, flown in all the way from Washington to take dead aim on Richard and score the final bull's-eye. Kittle is an earnest-looking man whose appearance belies his age; that he was old enough to have retired from the FBI surprised most who heard his testimony. He'd been a questioned-document examiner for the feds for nigh onto three decades. Once Jerri had established his credentials, she wasted little time in cutting directly to the chase.

"Mr. Kittle," Jerri said, "have you had occasion to examine documents furnished you purporting to be in the handwriting of Nancy Dillard Lyon?"

"I have." Professional witnesses are easy to spot; Kittle spoke directly to the jury and ignored the audience at large.

"And what did those documents consist of?"

"Notes, mostly, apparently taken in classes of some sort."

"In counseling?" Jerri said.

"I wasn't furnished that information." The inference was clear: Hartford Kittle doesn't concern himself with who was supposed to have written what where; he merely calls 'em as he sees 'em.

"Thank you. What other documents did you examine?"

"An invoice from a company, Chemical Engineering, purportedly receipted by Mrs. Lyon."

"And what did you use for comparison, Mr. Kittle?" Jerri said evenly.

"Exemplars furnished by Mrs. Lyon's family. Letters she'd written over the years."

"Was that all?"

"No." Kittle's demeanor was serious and confident.

"And with what else did you compare the documents?"

"Known writings," Kittle said, "also furnished by Mrs. Lyon's family. Known writings of Mrs. Lyon's husband, Richard Lyon." At this point, anyone in the courtroom who didn't know what was coming had spent the previous weeks in a coma.

"And were you able," Jerri said, "to reach any conclusions?"

"I was."

"And what were those conclusions, Mr. Kittle?"

Kittle now took dead aim on the jury, swiveling around so that the spectators' section viewed only his profile. "Well, as respects the invoice, the results were inconclusive."

"Could you restate that in layman's terms?" Jerri said.

"I meant," Kittle said, now favoring the jury with an apologetic smile, "that I was unable to determine whether Mrs. Lyon signed the invoice or if it was her husband."

"And is such a finding unusual?"

"Quite. I've never seen two handwritings as similar as those of Mr. and Mrs. Lyon." Which wasn't an accident, the jury already knew, since Richard and Nancy had tried in college to make their handwriting identical.

"I see," Jerri said. "Were you able to reach any conclusion regarding Nancy's notes taken during her incest counseling?"

"I beg your pardon?" Kittle said. This exchange was somewhat thespian; he had already stated that he didn't know the origin of the notes, but Jerri wanted to be certain that the jury knew of which notes her expert was speaking.

"Excuse me, Mr. Kittle," Jerri said. "The notes of Mrs. Lyon which were furnished you."

"Yes, I reached some conclusions on those."

"And what were your conclusions?"

"For the most part," Kittle said, "the notes were written by Mrs. Nancy Lyon."

"For the most part?" Jerri didn't bat an eye; this exchange between the prosecution and its expert was obviously well rehearsed.

"There was a portion at the end," Kittle said, now swiveling to look toward Richard at the defense table, "which was written by Richard Lyon."

"You're certain of that?" Jerri said.

"It is my unqualified opinion."

"And if you would," Jerri said, "please read the jury the portion of the notes which, in your opinion, were written by Richard."

She had earlier laid the already admitted evidence on the rail in front of her handwriting expert, and Kittle now picked up the piece of paper to read, " 'Fear of Bill and what his desires are . . . sex . . . sick sex . . . incest issues with me? . . . my girls?' " The words were, of course, familiar. It was the same portion of Nancy's notes that Guthrie had had Big Daddy read during the most emotional part of the trial.

"If you would, Mr. Kittle," Jerri said, "please explain what characteristics of the writings led you to believe that the handwriting is Richard's."

"Certainly." Kittle was in his own ballpark now, speaking with the confidence of a man intimately familiar with his subject matter. "The *s*'s, for the most part. Mrs. Lyon consistently writes a printed letter *s*, while Mr. Lyon alternates his *s*'s, sometimes printing them and sometimes writing them in cursive."

"And is there any other characteristic of the writing which leads you to believe it is Richard's?"

"There is."

"And what is that?" Jerri said.

"With the capital *S*'s," Kittle said, "though both Mr. and Mrs. Lyon consistently printed them, Mr. Lyon's capital *S* ends with a curl at the bottom, which is missing in all of Mrs. Lyon's known writings. Also, Mr. Lyon's lower-case *f*'s are noticeably different."

Jerri paused briefly for the testimony to sink in, then said, "And are you certain, Mr. Kittle?"

"Yes."

"Absolutely?" Jerri said.

"Absolutely," Hartford Kittle said.

Closing arguments seemed more of a wrap-up than anything else, but to Guthrie's credit he did his best. He was quite brief and concentrated only on the possibility of suicide. That Nancy might have killed herself was the only avenue left to him, and even that route seemed one of desperation. At this point there simply was no reasonable doubt. The jury listened to Guthrie's closing statement with looks of stone.

Though obviously already victorious, Jerri couldn't resist a few additional punches at a staggering defense. Richard's motive, she said, was profit, plain and simple. When Nancy wouldn't accept the financial settlement proposed by Richard's mediator during divorce proceedings, Jerri said, and when Nancy began to fight for what was rightfully hers, Richard had decided to murder her.

Jerri did provide an instant of comic relief during her close. Standing in a defiant posture midway between the jury box and the defense table, she once again showed the jury the incest-counseling notes and indicated the "sick sex" portion that Kittle had identified as being in Richard's handwriting. Holding the notes in one hand and pointing at Richard with the other, Jerri said, "If Richard Lyon didn't write this, folks, I'll shave my head when this trial's over." Titters rolled through the audience, and the same Park Cities lady who'd made the "kingdom for a pair of scissors" remark on the opening day of the trial now looked at her companion, raised a hand, and made a cutting motion with her index and middle fingers.

Excluded from the courtroom during testimony due to their status as witnesses, the Dillard clan assembled in full force for closing arguments. Big Daddy occupied the aisle seat, second row, with Sue graciously beside him and the heirs strung out to Sue's right: Bill Jr., Mary Helen, Billy Hendrickson and Susan. When Jerri had finished, the Dillards patted shoulders and squeezed one another's arms. Allan and Rosemary Lyon sat down front in lonely silence.

And, finally, Judge Creuzot instructed the jury and sent them off for deliberations. To those present it seemed months since the trial had begun, but in fact it had been a mere twenty-two days. Down the hall, Charles Albright had long since been declared a prostitute butcherer and John Wiley Price had laughed in the D.A.'s face yet one more time. The corridor seemed deserted. In forty-eight hours it would be Christmas Eve.

Two writers, strangers only weeks ago but now fast friends, left the courtroom together. One said, "Wonder how long the verdict will take."

"I'll miss it," the other writer said, "because I'm headed for home. Tell you what. I've got one stop to make, so the trip will take me a couple of hours. Bet you the jury's in before I get to the house. Lay you odds, huh?"

★ ★ ★

Deliberations, including time out for the jury's county-furnished lunch, required one hour and thirty-eight minutes, most of which was taken up by the eating of the sandwiches. The one ballot required less than a quarter of an hour.

Defense and prosecution assumed their places, and the courtroom filled for one last time. Judge Creuzot called for the verdict, glanced at the piece of paper without emotion, and returned the verdict via bailiff to the foreman. The foreman pronounced Richard Lyon guilty without batting an eye. At his seat in between Dan Guthrie and Leila Thomas, Richard dropped his head. He was the only person in the courtroom who seemed surprised.

Doubt lingers. Serious doubt among some, mere conversation grist for others, but doubt nonetheless.

The life sentence that Judge Creuzot handed Richard during the third week in January 1992 was automatic in light of the enormity of the crime, but Big Daddy treated Richard's sentencing as if the judge's choice was a toss-up between probation and six months' Peace Corps duty. Calling in markers from all corners of the nation, Big Daddy had letters delivered to the courthouse from upstate New York, Georgia, California, and points in between. There were over a hundred requests in all from Dillard supporters, and each letter begged the judge to hand Richard the maximum. Many of the letters, such as the one from Tramell Crow himself, reeked of political clout, but it's doubtful that the upcoming elections influenced Creuzot's decision one iota. A man convicted of poisoning his spouse is looking at extended time.

Allan and Rosemary Lyon did what they could, but their efforts produced little of consequence. There were the standard requests for leniency from family, friends, and school acquaintances from the Mansfield-Willimantic area, but Connecticut residents could shed no light on a death that occurred so far from their homes. Denise Woods wrote, once again expressing her belief that Richard was innocent, and so did a few other Dallas residents, but requests for leniency amid the pile of damnations from Dillard supporters were like so much chaff in the wind.

Jerri sat silently at the sentencing proper and let the defense put on the show. Guthrie preempted the hearing with a motion for a new trial, presenting evidence located among Richard's files which purported to show that Nancy's handwriting had occasionally borne the same characteristics which Hartford Kittle had attributed to Richard alone. The defense also produced a juror willing to testify that had she seen the new evidence beforehand, she never would have voted for conviction. Such motions are never granted. The system lends almost zero credence to recanting jurors. Furthermore, the "new" evidence had been in the defense's possession all during the trial, and thus was not eligible to be called new. It is a kink in the American idea of justice that once a conviction is had, innocence has no bearing on appeals, and that only errors made at trial can come under scrutiny. Creuzot denied the motion with barely a moment's hesitation.

Those who stood up to speak in Richard's behalf numbered four: Richard's parents, who both entered tearful pleas, a contractor whom Richard had personally paid for work rather than have the man totally stiffed during the last days of Hughes Industries, and Denise Woods' father, who was obviously there more for his little girl than he was for Richard. Dads are like that. Not one Park Citizen with whom Richard had worked, played, or labored beside at charity functions made an appearance. Park Cities, it would seem, is rife with fair-weather friends.

Richard himself emerged from his county jail cell, where Creuzot had placed him on the day of his conviction, and read a prepared statement to the judge. He said for the thousandth time that he didn't poison Nancy, that he was a man with no interest in profit, and that his main goals in life were to paint his paintings and strum his guitar. Richard was obviously overcome with emotion; his statement, in fact, came across to those present as just a bit on the corny side. Under the circumstances, the James Cagney, oh-you-dirty-rat posture would likely have served Richard just as well. If portraits and music are indeed Richard's preference, Creuzot insured that he will have ample time for pursuit of such endeavors.

The custody fight for Allison and Anna continues; in a hearing conducted in Dallas County as recently as March 1993, a judge once again refused to terminate Richard's parental rights. The girls continue to live with Bill Jr. and Mary Helen, with Big Daddy and Sue serving as baby-sitters every time the opportunity arises. Only time will tell the effect of the trauma on Allison and Anna's lives. Prayers may help. They often do.

Richard filed a self-researched lawsuit against Presbyterian Hospital from his jail cell in early 1993, but those familiar with procedure in the civil courtroom consider Richard's suit hopeless, regardless of the hospital's role in Nancy's death. Presbyterian's lawyers merely answered the suit and then fell silent. Depositions are the next step, and under Texas law no one is required to appear to be deposed who is more than a hundred miles from the deposition site. Richard's location on Wynne Unit, a prison near Huntsville, is outside the hundred-mile perimeter from Dallas, so unless he can persuade the doctors and nurses involved to waive the distance limitation and meet in the prison visiting room to give their depositions, the suit will likely die on the vine.

The Richard and Dan Show has gone the way of Martin & Lewis, Simon & Garfunkel, and other such acts. Guthrie's firing as Richard's lawyer was quite predictable under the circumstances; most convicted men lay blame on their attorneys. To handle his appeal, Richard has chosen Mike DeGuerin of Houston, whose brother Dick was the prominent legal figure in the 1993 ATF siege at the Branch Davidian complex in Waco, and who is ranked among the top appellate lawyers in the state. In the legal profession, alas, "top" also translates as "expensive." Allan and Rosemary Lyon have totally depleted their finances in an attempt to free their son, and were only able to come up with about half of DeGuerin's fee. As of today, Richard's appeal brief remains unfiled. Parents go the limit for their kids, as Allan and Rosemary have certainly shown.

The believers in Richard's innocence are many, though not as numerous as those who believe him guilty, but there is one thing on which both sides agree. It was Charles Couch's testimony that totally destroyed Richard's credibility, and without Couch to say that the Chemical Engineering invoice was fraudulent, the evidence on both sides appeared nearly equal. Richard's supporters point unwaveringly at Couch's testimony as a falsehood, and their reasons for saying so bear close study.

Rita Green is a well-kept mid-fifties, slim and efficient. For many years she has been a probate judge's assistant, the current elected occupant of the bench that Rita serves being an equally energetic and youthful woman named Nikki DeShazo. Judge DeShazo and Rita Green make a lively pair. Rita examines estate inventories and annual accountings, and keeping on her good side is as important to Dallas County probate lawyers as is having stroke with the judge. Rita works in her own niche just outside the judge's office and keeps busy most of the time; conversations with her are constantly interrupted by business calls. For the five years previous to the Lyon trial, Rita Green was Mrs. Charles Couch.

"He lived in Plainview, out in West Texas, when I met him," Rita says, "and made business trips to Dallas just about every week. He claimed to own apartments and houses in Plainview, and goodness knows, he spent money like a rich man. I'd known Charles for four or five months before I knew he was married."

"He never told you?" the interviewer said.

"He said his wife had died," Rita says. "All that time he took me on trips with him, even on weekends. Once we went to New Orleans on Thursday and stayed through until Tuesday. Things were pretty serious between us, so a friend of mine called out to Plainview and checked up, or I might never have known."

"And when you found out . . . ?"

"I ditched him in a hurry. It's the way I am. Married men just aren't open season."

"But he didn't stay ditched, right?" the interviewer says.

"You're right there. I didn't see him for a year, and by that time he was really divorced. And, boy, had he ever lost his money—might have been his wife's money all along, for all I know. By the time I saw him again, Charles was living alone in a one-bedroom apartment here in Dallas. We started dating again and six months later I married him. Live and learn, I suppose. He moved into my house with me, and five years and many thousands of dollars later, here I am."

"Rita, you said earlier," the interviewer says, "that you believe Charles really did sell arsenic to Nancy Lyon. Why?"

"I've got no proof of it," Rita says matter-of-factly, "but that's what I think. Charles makes up things. Like, the whole time I knew him he kept saying that he had two hundred hours of college. I came to find out that he went to Oklahoma Christian College for one year, flunked out, and that was the extent of his college."

"That doesn't prove," the interviewer says, "that he sold any poison. I mean, Charles had a business, and the total price on that invoice was, what, a couple of hundred bucks?"

"Which Charles desperately needed at the time," Rita says. "To keep up with the hairdresser he was fooling around with. I put up the money, eight thousand dollars, for Charles to buy Chemical Engineering to begin with, and if he'd taken any money out of the business the bookkeeper would have caught it. You know David Green?"

"The guy they snatched off the airplane and hauled into court?"

"Right. He's my son. One of the reasons I gave Charles the money to buy that business was, he promised David a job. Now David's running the business, and we don't know for sure what Charles is doing."

An elderly lawyer comes in to file an accounting in a guardianship case. Rita perfunctorily checks the papers for content, thanks the lawyer, and he leaves. Rita faces the interviewer. "You've seen that invoice, the one Charles said in court was a phony?"

The interviewer pats his own briefcase. "There's a copy right in here."

"All those asterisks before and after the Prepaid notation? Those are typical of Charles' work on a computer. It's exactly the way he writes things. Didn't you wonder how Nancy Lyon got to Charles to begin with? If I was looking for a fire ant poison, I certainly wouldn't call a man in the industrial soap business."

"Charles said at the trial," the interviewer says, "that he was well known in the industry as someone who would research a question until he found the answer."

"Bull," Rita says. "The only thing Charles is known for anywhere is not telling the truth. He'd go to all these bars and sit around drinking, and any subject one of the customers wanted to talk about, let me tell you Charles Couch was an expert on it. If someone mentioned that they had fire ants in their yard, then Charles would suddenly be a world-renowned insect expert. He said in that trial that he didn't even own a typewriter, didn't he?"

"That's right, he did."

"My daughter," Rita says, "worked for Charles, and her job was typing up letters and invoices for him. On his typewriter. One day, unbeknownst to me, Charles told my daughter that he needed five thousand dollars to keep the business afloat, just for a week or so until some contracts came in. She didn't really have it, but she and her husband cleaned out their savings and loaned Charles the money. And you know what? Ten days after that, Charles fired her. He said he couldn't afford to pay her any more."

"Sounds like Charles isn't one of your favorite people, Rita," the interviewer says.

"Hmm. He borrowed money from my own daughter to finance his drinking and running around. That was during the time he was seeing the hairdresser."

"How'd you find out about that?"

"Because it's a small world. One of my friends who lives in Richardson happened to be one of her customers, and she was talking about this wealthy man she was dating. The wealthy man turned out to be Charles."

"Think, Rita. Do you have any information that could connect Charles to Nancy Lyon, anything at all that might indicate that he knew her?"

"No proof. I never knew where Charles was from one day to the next, though. You know Arthur's?"

"Sure. It's a swanky bar right on the edge of Park Cities."

"He made that his stomping ground. Hung around in there and talked to all those Highland Park people like he was just one of the crowd. If you wanted a connection between Charles and Mrs. Lyon, I'd start from there."

"And the bottom line is," the interviewer says, "that you don't think Charles was being truthful when he testified that he never sold any poison to Nancy Lyon."

"I'd bet my life on it," Rita says.

David Green and John Reamer, who worked with Charles Couch at Chemical Engineering state collectively, "We think it was Charles' invoice. We told the judge that, but it doesn't look like anybody was listening. It sure looked to us like one of his invoices."

"And the day he was out of town," the interviewer says, "and they served that subpoena on youall and hauled you into court. You didn't know what was happening?"

"First of all," they say almost in unison, "we don't think he was out of town. We think he was hanging around someplace and hiding out from that subpoena. Early on, when the detectives started coming around asking about that invoice, Charles tried to accuse *us* of selling the woman the poison out the back door."

"The day the lady came in, Charles said on the witness stand she picked up a formula. He was on the phone and never saw her. Did any of you guys get a look at her?"

"Not only did we not see her, none of us waited on any woman. And at no time was anyone else here other than the three of us and Charles. If it had happened the way he said, one of us would remember. Something else, too. She couldn't have come in here without Charles seeing her, either."

"Oh?" the interviewer says. "How's that?"

"Charles' desk"—pointing to the rear of the office—"was right back there. Do you see anything between where he sat and this counter?"

"Well, no," the interviewer says.

"The point exactly. There was nothing to obstruct his view, and if she'd been here at all he would have seen her."

"Can you think of a reason," the interviewer says, "that Nancy Lyon or anyone else would come to Charles Couch to develop a fire ant poison?"

"Sure. They'd been listening to Charles."

The interviewer frowns. "How's that?"

"We got calls here all the time from people asking for 'Doctor Couch.' *Doctor* Couch, and the guy never even graduated from college. He'd run into people around all these bars where he was hanging out, and he'd tell them anything that would make himself sound like some kind of big deal."

"He said on the witness stand," the interviewer says, "that he was well known in the industry as a researcher."

This remark produces snickers. "He's well known in the industry, okay."

"What about now?" the interviewer says. "Charles has nothing to do with Chemical Engineering any longer?"

"Not any more. If we can ever get these bills paid off, the business is ours."

"Do you know how to get in touch with him?"

"We've got a phone number. You'll get an answering machine. The odds on him returning your call are about fifty-fifty. Even less than that, probably."

"I've talked to several people," Charles Couch says. "One lady making a movie, she asked if I had a preference of which actor played me."

"She gave you a choice?" the interviewer says.

"Sure did."

"Was the lady's name Yvette Ferris?"

"Yeah. Yeah, that's her."

"I see," the interviewer says. "Mr. Couch, do you know why someone would contact you, a man in the industrial-soap and recycled-carpet businesses, about a formula for a fire ant poison?"

"She said she looked us up in the Yellow Pages," Couch says. "We were listed under Chemicals."

"My notes must be wrong," the interviewer says. "I thought you said in court you were well known as a researcher. And on that subject, do you have a background, education or whatnot, in pesticides?"

"Education is relative," Couch says. "I have a hundred and eighty college hours, but I never got a degree because I've studied in so many different fields. They told me if I'd take thirty more hours, they'd give me a doctorate."

"You mean, a university told you that?"

"That's right."

"Which university?"

"Several."

The interviewer is writing so fast that his fingers ache. "What colleges have you attended, Mr. Couch?"

"Texas Tech . . . University of Texas and the University of Chicago . . . Harvard School of Business . . ."

"Did you know Richard or Nancy Lyon up there?" the interviewer says.

"Up where?"

"At Harvard. That's where they both went to school."

"Can't say that I did," Couch says.

"One thing troubles me," the interviewer says. "The Harvard School of Business is a graduate school. I'm surprised they'd let you in if you don't have an undergraduate degree."

"A lot of these colleges didn't want to at first," Couch says. "But then I'd just endow a professorship, and then they'd let me take whatever course I wanted to."

"Endow a . . . ?"

"You have to know how to talk to these people," Couch says.

"I see. Let me ask you something else. Before you got involved in the Lyon case—"

"Now, I wasn't *involved*."

"Sure. But before the bit came up about that invoice, did you happen to know any of the Dillards?"

"Not personally. When I was head of operations at Love Field, they kept a plane out there, though."

Jesus Christ, the interviewer thinks. "You were head of operations at Love Field?"

"It was a part-time job," Couch says.

"Before you testified, did you talk to the police or district attorney?"

"They had me up in their office the night before."

"I see. Mr. Couch, can you think of any reason that someone might say they thought you weren't telling the truth when you testified in the Lyon trial?"

"Just that ex-wife of mine. She's a drug addict."

"Rita Green is a drug addict?"

"That's right," Couch says.

"I see," the interviewer says. He rolls his eyes in disbelief.

"Sure, the guy was lying," Jim Bearden says. "Not five minutes before he went on the witness stand he told me he *did* sell her the poison. You think Guthrie would have put him on if we'd known what he was going to say? You work like hell on one of these cases, then you get a guy like Couch that gets up there and turns you around."

"I've got to admit," the interviewer says, "it looked strange, youall putting on a witness that would've said that."

"Do you think," Bearden says, "that Richard would have spent all that time, that *we* would've spent all that time hounding the guy to testify if we hadn't thought the invoice was legitimate? I'll tell you something else, too. Ortega, that police detective, he thought the invoice was for real, too."

"He did?" the interviewer says.

"We furnished the state everything we had," Bearden says. "And they talked to the guy. If they'd known he was going to say he never sold the poison and the invoice was a fake, don't you think Couch would have been a state's witness to begin with?"

"Sounds reasonable to me," the interviewer says.

"Sounds reasonable to me, too," Bearden says.

EPILOGUE

Richard continues to vehemently protest his innocence from his prison cell, and his cries in the wilderness have attracted quite a following. From the time of Nancy's death until the present, his story about the day of her final poisoning has never changed: Richard was out of town and doesn't have the slightest idea where the arsenic came from. His outside intermediaries have contacted police and prosecutors alike, digging for information that they hope will someday clear his name.

Since his conviction, Richard has come up with a number of theories concerning Nancy's death, some of which are mere rehashes of things known prior to his trial, and some of which are entirely new material. It's possible that the pressures of living in prison have caused Richard to fabricate some things, either to bolster his truthful claims of innocence or to cover his actual guilt, but at least one piece of information he provides is quite mindbending. No study of the Lyon case is complete without a telling of the "Leave Her to Heaven" tale.

★ ★ ★

The story involves *Madame Bovary* as well, but since "Leave Her to Heaven" is a more melodic title, that's what I call the entire scenario. *Madame Bovary*, of course, is a classic French novel that ends with a systematic description of the main character's slow death by arsenic poisoning. *Leave Her to Heaven* is a novel written in 1944 by Ben Ames Williams and made into a movie thriller a year or so after that. The book was out of print for three decades and then revived in 1981, and made its way to the small screen as a made-for-television production in 1988, under the title, *Too Good to Be True*. I never read the book or saw either motion picture, but since the TV movie starred Loni Anderson it had to be a corker. (Leonard Maltin's *Movie and Video Guide* lists the television production as a "substandard remake," but what does Leonard know?) The plot involves a woman who poisons herself and frames her husband and his lover for her own murder. Sound familiar?

I met with Richard's intermediary at an International House of Pancakes, and to keep from having to spell *intermediary* over and over, I'll henceforth refer to this person as Bob. Bob told me he had the key to unlock the mystery of Nancy's death. He immediately produced Big Daddy's Highland Park Public Library card, which I'll admit got my attention. The library card was among things Richard had stored in Dan Guthrie's office and was never able to retrieve during his incarceration. According to Bob, Nancy never had her own library card and used Big Daddy's to check out what books she wanted to read.

Bob said that Richard had learned from Dr. James Grigson, the psychiatrist who testified for Richard at his trial, that in order to know a person's state of mind, one needed to check on that person's reading habits. Richard, Bob said, had spent a lot of time before his trial in finding out what Nancy had been reading. He had taken Big Daddy's card to the library, identified himself as one of the Dillard clan, and asked the librarian to list for him the books Nancy had drawn out in the months prior to her death. The librarian used her computer, Bob said, and library records showed that Nancy had checked out both *Madame Bovary* and the novel of *Leave Her to Heaven*. According to Bob, Richard then checked out both books and read them.

My God, I thought, this information is precedent, and is almost conclusive proof that Nancy was contemplating suicide. Armed with the number of Big Daddy's library card, I went to the Highland Park Public Library the very next day, identified myself to the librarian, and also handed her a written request under the Texas Open Records Act for all books checked out on Big Daddy's library card for the previous two years. After the librarian finished sizing me up, she quickly set me straight.

There is, it seems, an attorney general's opinion specifically excluding library information from the Open Records Act. Furthermore, she said, the library computer doesn't have the ability to call up such records even if the librarian had been of a mind to give them to me. Which she wasn't. I did talk her into looking up *Leave Her to Heaven*, which she informed me wasn't a book in stock at the Highland Park Public Library, and that furthermore she could locate no record that the library had ever carried the book. Red-faced, I left.

Incidentally, I later learned that Richard had told the same story to Dan Guthrie prior to the trial, but that Guthrie couldn't use the information because he'd run into the same blank wall as I had in trying to produce evidence that Nancy had read either *Madame Bovary* or *Leave Her to Heaven* in the months prior to her death. Denise Woods also called a friend of Richard's named Bruce Berger after Richard went to prison, and had Berger try to find *Leave Her to Heaven*, all to no avail. If Richard had other sources by which the story can be verified, he hasn't provided them. If Nancy really did read the books, of course, the implications are both self-explanatory and earth-shattering.

The story of the death of Nancy Dillard Lyon is true, and everything told in this book I either personally witnessed or have confidence in my sources. Dialogue—other than the interviews described—is reconstructed; in other words, I know the conversation took place and I know what was said, based on my research, but since I wasn't there I am naturally unable to quote word for word. Interview dialogue is taken from notes made during the interviews themselves.

Some of the events described are told out of the sequence in which they actually occurred, sometimes because my sources couldn't remember exactly what happened before what, but often because I felt the story would be clearer if related events were told as if they'd occurred one after the other. I have consolidated much of the trial testimony for clarity's sake; as happens in all trials, much testimony took the form of a rambling discourse. This trial took place over several weeks, and some of the witnesses were on the stand for days. Witnesses whose testimony merely repeats something I've told earlier in the book, I've totally deleted. So, though much of the trial dialogue has been shortened, I have gotten across the highlights of what the witnesses had to say. Those wanting the unabridged version are welcome to plunk down the twenty thousand dollars required to buy a transcript, but let me warn you. I've read portions of the transcript, and it's boring as hell.

I've changed some names, for various reasons. Barbara Moore, the exotic dancer turned college student, for example, is an assumed name even though her real name is public record. She has a new life now and is entitled to her privacy, and those suffering from sufficient curiosity to feel they have to know who she is can go look up the trial record and get a copy of the witness list. Whatever turns you on.

Dame Hazel Vincent, the old-time Highland Park eccentric, is an assumed name for another reason. Middle-agers who were the Park Cities kids of the era (I'm one of them, by the way) all remember Dame Vincent and know her name, but why embarrass her living descendants by printing it? The story stands on its own and is a jewel.

Just about everyone who was willing to talk about Richard, Nancy, or any of the Dillard family asked that their names not be used, and I obliged. Most notable was the fellow who knew Richard way back when, identified herein as a Garland contractor. This gentleman told me in no uncertain terms, "Well, okay, I'll tell you some stuff if you'll quit bugging me. I guarantee you, though, if I see my name in your book I'm going to whip your ass." I changed his name with barely a second's hesitation.

Those familiar with the case will immediately recognize Debi Denise Woods as a pseudonym, and many will be shocked. This young lady was featured prominently in newspapers and three national magazines, and it is public record that she testified at trial and was the other woman in Richard's life. I changed her name at her request. She granted me interviews and provided valuable information without which this book likely could not have been completed in its current form; I gave my word that I would not use her name and have kept it, and sincerely hope that whatever speck of anonymity I have provided is beneficial to her.

I offer sincere thanks to the following, and if I've left anyone out, please believe it's an oversight. Individually:

Pete Slover of the *Dallas Morning News,* father of the most beautiful baby girl born to man since my own daughter's birth some fifteen summers ago.

Bud Gillette of Channel 4, who gave me tremendous insight in a fifteen-minute conversation one evening at the Ozona Grill & Bar.

Michael Hill of Channel 8, for providing choice monitor space when the courtroom was jammed, and who probably still wonders to this day whatever happened to the book that "Mr. Green" was writing.

Carlton and Pat Stowers, Carlton for listening to my complaints and providing an old hand's advice in the true-crime field; Pat for the best chocolate brownie ever conceived.

Beautiful and brilliant psychologist Kathy Finch, for her insight and marvelous research on incest in general and sociopaths in particular.

Skip Hollandsworth, the last word both on Dallas' Black Widow and the Charles Albright cases, for giving of his time and sharing his research.

Janet Fiske of the *Hartford Advocate,* for her research into Richard's rural Connecticut and college backgrounds.

Dominick Abel, the agent who fished my prison-cell letter out of the stack eight years ago, and who continues to nurse me along.

And collectively:

J. W. Davis, Carol Poor, Nancy Khazabian, Jerri Sims, Dan Guthrie, Leila Thomas, John Creuzot, Rita Green, David Green, John Reamer, Charles Couch, Richard Lyon, Andy Hanson, Reed Prospere, Evan Fogelman, Stan Wetsel, Jim Bearden.

And, with apologies to none, last and most important, my beloved wife of seventeen years, Martha Crosland Gray, who chided me gently when I wanted to quit, provided late-night vittles, small talk in the wee hours of the morning, a boot to the rear when the golf course beckoned, and loving arms when all else failed.

Fort Worth, Texas
May 16, 1993
3:00 A.M.

About the Author

A. W. Gray is the author of six critically ac-
claimed novels: *Killings, Prime Suspect, The
Man Offside, In Defense of Judges, Size,* and
Bino, all published by Dutton. A life-long
Texan, he lives with his wife and family in Fort
Worth.